T0113214

THE KING WHO LOST AMERICA

Books by the author

THE KING WHO LOST AMERICA

FRANCO

THE SPANISH CENTURIES

THE MAKING OF THE KING: 1066

THE DRUMS OF KUMASI

THE KING
WHO LOST
AMERICA

A Portrait
of the Life and Times
of George III

ALAN LLOYD

1971
Doubleday & Company, Inc.
Garden City, New York

Grateful acknowledgment is made for the use of the following copyrighted material:

Selection from *George III, Letters to Lord Bute* by Romney Sedgwick. Reprinted by permission of St. Martin's Press, New York, the Macmillan Company of Canada and Macmillan London and Basingstoke.

Selection from *The Correspondence of George III* by Sir John Fortescue. Reprinted by permission of Curtis Brown Ltd., London.

BVG·01
146484122

To the memory of my memorable aunts

Jennie and Mary.

CONTENTS

Part III—DECLINE OF A DESPOT

THE KING WHO LOST AMERICA

Part I

A ROYAL IDEAL

CHAPTER 1

London Pageant

In the sunny September of 1761, London, which could provide a surprising variety of diversions, from the *bal masqué* to an itinerant entertainer who specialized in eating cats, prepared for the greatest show on earth—a coronation. Across the world from North America to India, Britain's forces were trouncing the French, adding vast tracts to her empire, creating fresh titles for the new king. The rich celebrated with jewels for wives and mistresses. The noble pranced well-corned chargers to review troops. The poor drank, brawled and wenched or whored uninhibitedly. At a time when the English laborer earned between fifteen shillings and a pound a week, while a million less favored or industrious made do on ten pounds a year, a few pennies on gin or trollops was the measure of the plain man's ebullience.

The *London Journal* of James Boswell—he was then a buck of strict financial limitations—tells how, to mark the anniversary of the king's birthday, he resolved to spend an evening on London. Arming himself with a stout stick, the common weapon of protection after dark, he made his way to St. James's Park, "picked up a low brimstone, called myself a barber and agreed with her for sixpence, went to the

bottom of the Park arm in arm, and dipped my machine in
the canal and performed most manfully. I then went as far
St Paul's Church-yard, roaring along, and then came to
Ashley's Punch-house and drank three threepenny bowls.

"In the Strand I picked up a little profligate wretch and
gave her sixpence . . . I was much stronger than her and
volens nolens pushed her up against the wall. She however
gave a sudden spring from me; and screaming out, a parcel
of more whores and soldiers came to her relief. 'Brother
soldiers,' said I, 'should not a half-pay officer roger for
sixpence? And here she has used me so and so.' I got them
on my side and abused her in blackguard style, and then
left them. At Whitehall I picked up another girl to whom I
called myself a highwayman and told her I had no money
and begged she would trust me." Boswell eventually arrived home "much fatigued."

Such bawdy candor was characteristic of a permissive,
high-spirited, turbulent age when few feelings were safe
from rough handling. A cartoonist thought nothing of depicting a member of the royal family being given an enema.
An army of satirists filled its quills with malice. No one
was too important, too powerful to avoid comment of a
caustic and Rabelaisian nature.

While costumiers and carpenters, chefs and musicians
worked and rehearsed for the coronation of George III,
visitors streamed into London for the occasion. For many,
the city—the background for the spectacle—must have
seemed a place of tumultuous, seething, altogether confusing
fermentation. It is worth sharing their impressions a moment before proceeding to the royal show.

Violence abounded in the capital. Riots and disorders
were commonplace, an even cheaper distraction for the
poor than drinking—though gin was advertised to get one
drunk for a penny, "dead drunk" for twopence—and drinking and rioting often went hand in hand. Crime in London,

as elsewhere, flourished openly. Due to inadequate police forces, it went largely unpunished. Yet when offenders were caught they were treated savagely. The theft of five shillings from a shop incurred the death penalty, and London was not inaptly described as "The City of the Gallows." Few entertainments in the capital drew a larger mob than a public execution.

Wrote Henry Fielding, the novelist and a Bow Street magistrate: "We sacrifice the lives of men, not for the reformation but the diversion of the populace." Someone estimated that fifty thousand people had been hanged at Tyburn, by Hyde Park, between the end of the twelfth century and the middle of the eighteenth.

It was only when that area of the West End began to become a fashionable residential quarter, and the crowds were unwelcome, that a movement was started to restrict the Tyburn hangings. Reaction was vehement. Even Dr. Samuel Johnson, London's literary lion of the day, and personally a kindly man, protested: "The age is running after innovation; all the business in the world is to be done a new way. Tyburn itself is not safe from the fury of innovation! No, Sir! It is not an improvement; they object that the old method drew together a number of spectators. Sir, executions are intended to draw the spectators."

Londoners swarmed to asylums and prisons to ogle the unfortunate inmates. The keepers of Bedlam, the notorious institution for the insane, did a brisk business in tips from the curious, while three thousand people visited Newgate prison in a single day to peer at one notorious highwayman. Many thousands more visited Bridewell Jail to gaze at the women there and to witness the floggings.

"We followed our noses," reported one visitor, "and walked up to take a view of the ladies, who we found shut up as close as nuns; but, like so many slaves, were under the care and direction of an overseer who walked about with a very flexible weapon of offence." From a quadrangle, spectators ascended a flight of steps to a spacious chamber where the court of punishment sat in somber grandeur, presided over by "a grave gentleman whose awful looks bespoke him some honorable citizen." The grave gentleman flourished a hammer.

Before this court, women, stripped to the waist, were whipped to the hoots and vulgarities of an avid crowd. When the judge decided the victims had had enough, he plied his hammer and the scourging ceased.

Animals, not surprisingly, fared worse. Cockfighting, bull-baiting and bearbaiting were favorite sports, the latter to be seen on Mondays and Thursdays at Hockley-in-the-Hole, near Clerkenwell.

> *Experienced men, inured to City ways,*
> *Need not the calendar to count the days,*
> *When through the Town with slow and solemn air,*
> *Led by the nostril, walks the muzzled bear.*

Those who provided dogs to toss into the ring at Hockley were admitted free, and few cared very much where the bear-fodder came from. Many dogs were stolen for the purpose.

In winter, the city's aspect could be grim. Such road names as Dirty Lane, Foul Lane and Melancholy Walk were expressive of an unwelcome abundance of mud, sewage and refuse. But in the spring and summer, London could still display rural charms. There was a farm—Capper's Farm —in the Tottenham Court Road, fields where later stood University College, and fruit gardens filled with blossom and singing birds.

Elsewhere, the noises were mainly human. "The attention of the newcomer to London," asserted Dr. Johnson, "is generally struck by the multiplicity of cries that stun him in the streets." London's cries, handed down from generation to generation, had, by the mid-eighteenth century, become more exuberant than musical. One writer, though able to admire the "sublime thunder" of a chorus of cucumber women in a narrow thoroughfare, admits to being confused by the overall cacophony. "There is a man at this moment under my window who cries 'Potatoes' to the very same tune that I remember when Cherries were in season, and it was but yesterday that a woman invited the publick to purchase shrimps to a tune which has invariably been applied to water-cress; as to spinage and muffins, I have so often heard them chanted in D that I defy any man to know which is which; matches too, have been transposed to the key of periwinkles, and the cadence which should fall upon 'rare' is now placed upon 'smelts' and 'mackerel' . . . In Radishes everybody knows that the *bravura* part is on the words 'twenty a penny,' but they swell these notes and shake upon 'radishes.' Sir, we have no ears, else we could not endure such barbarous transpositions . . . You may think lightly, Sir, of this matter, but my family shall starve ere I will buy potatoes cried in the treble cleff, or allow them to eat salad that has been sung out in flats. 'Soot-ho!' I will allow to be in alt, the situation of our chimneys justifies this; but certainly 'dust' ought to be an octave lower . . ."

For those who could stand the clatter—and had money—life was leisurely. "We rise at nine," wrote an eighteenth-century West End resident, "and those that frequent great men's levees find entertainment at them till eleven; or, as in Holland, go to tea tables. About twelve, the beau monde assembles in several coffee-houses . . . We are carried to these places in chairs, which are here very cheap, a guinea a week, or one shilling per hour, and your chairman serves you as porter to run on errands . . . if it is fine weather we take a turn in the Park till two, when we go to dinner . . . The general way here is to make a party at the Coffeehouse to go to dine at the Tavern, where we sit till six, when we go to the play, unless you are invited to the table of some great man."

This London preparing for the 1761 coronation was full of small-time remittance men, half-pay officers and garrulous freeloaders who eked out their incomes in the coffeehouses and cheaper taverns, living on their wit, their style and such persuasiveness as they could command in the presence of more substantial men. So popular had coffeehouses become by the second half of the century—at one time there were said to be three thousand of them in the capital—that an effort was made to suppress them on the grounds that "the great resort of the idle and dissipated persons in them have produced very evil and dangerous effects . . ."

Here such writers as Pope, Dryden, Addison and Johnson exchanged ideas not only with publishers and lesser literary lights, but with butchers, bankers and many other traders and professional men. "A man is sooner asked about his Coffee-house than about his lodgings," declared Defoe. "They smoak Tobacco, game, and read papers of intelligence; here they treat of matters of state, make League with Foreign Princes, break them again, and transact affairs of the last consequence to the whole world."

There was also a good deal of foppish play. A visitor to the Old Man coffeehouse, one of the larger establishments, spoke of a "room where a gaudy crowd of odiferous Town-Essences were walking backwards and forwards with their hats in their hands, not daring to convert them to their intended use lest it should put the foretops of their wigs into some disorder . . . their whole exercise being to charge and discharge their nostrils [with snuff, or 'snush'] and to keep the curls of their periwigs in their proper order. The clashing of their snush-box lids in the opening and shutting made more noise than their tongues. Bows and crimps of the newest mode were here exchanged 'twixt friend and friend with wonderful exactness. They made a humming like so many hornets in a country chimney . . ."

Women of the leisured classes were preoccupied with trivia. "The toilet," exclaimed Addison, "is their great scene of business, and the right enjoyment of their hair the principle employment of their lives. The sorting of a suit of ribands is reckoned a very good morning's work; and if they make an excursion to a mercer's or a toy shop, so great a fatigue makes them unfit for anything else all day after."

At the theater, performers of the caliber of David Garrick and Mrs. Siddons were great attractions in their own right, though, as could be said for other ages, fashionable London attended the playhouse at least as much to be admired as to admire the drama. Smollett's Roderick Random epitomized the man-about-town at the theater when he confessed that he "rose and sat down . . . twenty times between the acts," affecting to take snuff, flouncing his perfumed handkerchief, dangling his cane and adjusting his sword knot "in order to attract attention."

On a stratum of their own, above the general milieu, a small circle of families lived in opulence, dividing their time between London and the shires, their salons and carriages attended by liveried servants, the settings of their mansions arranged by such eminent landscape specialists as Capability Brown, the interiors furnished with pieces fashioned with due regard to Chippendale's *Gentleman and Cabinet Maker's Director*, walls hung with portraits in the "Grand Style" by Reynolds. A mere six hundred or so families in England had incomes of £2,500 and over; half of them upward of £4,000. In an age when £1,500 a year was the mark of a rich man, the spending power of the top three hundred families in the land was enormous, especially when, at the apex of the social order, the great lords could draw six-figure incomes from the rent rolls of their estates. Con-

gregated in breathtaking finery for that rare and most
resplendent of occasions, a coronation, they could put on
a show unsurpassed in the whole world. In September, they
had gathered in London to present it.

Thousands of people had slept the night in the open, and,
on the morning of the twenty-second, all London poured
forth to witness the spectacle. It could not have been a better day. The sun shone from a blue sky on an ocean of
heads, on the facades of buildings dressed entirely in
colored silks, on tapestried balconies, glittering troops, waving plumes and upon blazoned heraldry. The procession assembled at Westminster Hall, to which venue it was to return
for the banquet, proceeding on a carpet of blue cloth to the
Abbey for the ceremony. Of the peers in their velvet and
ermine, the Knights of the Bath in their plumed hats, the
judges in their scarlet robes, of the prelates in their vest-
ments, of the pursuivants and heralds, the flags and flaring
lusters, the poet Gray exclaimed, "the most magnificent
spectacle I ever beheld." Horace Walpole, who was present,
described the scene as a puppet show "worth a million."
"My Lady Harrington," wrote Walpole, "covered with all
the diamonds she could borrow, hire or seize, was the finest
figure at a distance. She complained to George Selwyn that
she was to walk with Lady Portsmouth, who would have a
wig and a stick. 'Pho,' said he, 'you will only look as if you
were taken up by the constable.' She told this everywhere,
thinking reflection was on my Lady Portsmouth." Outside
the ancient foundation of Westminster, the excited crowds
craned necks and fought for a glimpse of celebrities, who
were not only dressed with extravagance, but ornately
painted.
The Duchess of Bedford had applied make-up so luridly
that, according to the Duchess of Queensbury, her face

resembled the skin of an orange-peach, half red and half yellow.

Inside, the scene was splurged with purple, gold, crimson. All attention was fixed on the new king. He contributed, it seems, a nice theatrical touch for the occasion. His lofty deportment, particularly his studied manner of ascending and seating himself on the throne, was widely commended. One who was present, Bishop Newton, claimed that no actor in the character of Pyrrhus—not even Barton Booth, who was celebrated for it in the *Spectator*—ever took the throne with such grace and dignity.

George III was tall and well built, with a long nose and a solemn face; his queen, Charlotte of Mecklenburg-Strelitz, short, thin and pale with a tilted nose and a large mouth. Neither knew whether, having taken the vows to obey the laws of God and Parliament, they should remove their headwear for Communion at the altar. George asked the Archbishop of Canterbury, who did not know, and when the archbishop asked the Bishop of Rochester, who was assisting him, the bishop declared that he did not know either. Eventually, the king decided it would be proper to remove his crown and the queen's coronet.

Unfortunately, the prospect of removing the coronet without disarranging the queen's hair was daunting. Also, as the archbishop pointed out in a whisper, it might be difficult to replace the coronet afterwards. It was at last left in place on the queen's head, the king suggesting that it should be regarded as a purely decorative part of her costume.

George was most at ease in the spiritual aspects of the service. For a young man, his piety was striking. "In the religious offices," asserted a lady who was present, "his Majesty behaved with the greatest reverence and deepest attention . . . How happy that in the day of the greatest worldly pomp he should remember his duty to the King of Kings!"

The rest of the proceedings were beset by a singular series of accidents. After the long and demanding ceremony, the queen needed to retire in haste to a powder room provided nearby for her private use. In her rush, she almost bowled over the Duke of Newcastle, one of England's richest landlords, who had slipped inside, not expecting her arrival so quickly. In due course, she returned to the king's side. Slowly, the great host of noble and exalted persons in the Abbey made their way to the Hall for the banquet. Here, a dramatic lighting effect had been planned for Charlotte's entrance. "The instant the Queen's canopy entered," reported Gray, "fire was given to all the lustres at once by trains of prepared flax that reached from one to the other." The result was a sudden shower of burning flax which flabbergasted everyone. "For that half-minute it rained fire on the heads of all the spectators, the flax falling in large flakes; and the ladies, Queen and all, were in no small terror."

When the danger had passed, and the royal couple had recovered their composure, the king took his place with the queen on a dais at the head of the banqueting tables. Each table was heavy with gold plate. The smell of roast goose and venison filled the hall. The guests waited hungrily for the royal couple to sit down, but they could not, for someone had forgotten the royal chairs. When the king protested to Lord Effingham, the Deputy Earl Marshal, his lordship responded unhelpfully: "It is true, Sir, that there has been some neglect, but I have taken care that the *next* Coronation will be regulated in the exactest manner possible."

The person who would seem to have been largely to blame for the mishaps was the Lord Steward of the Household, William Earl Talbot. Talbot, a man of rude and swaggering demeanor who patronized prize fighters and was boastful of his own strength, was obsessed with economy in the royal household. This he had carried to the limit of reducing the number of places traditionally provided at the banquet. Among others, the Knights of the Bath, the aldermen of the city of London and the Barons of the Cinque Ports now found themselves without seating. They did not take it kindly.

"To us," Sir William Stanhope, a Knight of the Bath, told Talbot testily, "it is an affront, for some of *us* are gentlemen."

Exclaimed an alderman named Beckford, indignantly evoking a forthcoming occasion: "We have invited the king to a banquet which will cost us ten thousand pounds, and yet, when we come to court, we are to be given nothing to eat."

Angrily, Talbot ordered places to be set for them.

It was too late, however, to order more food, and the extra mouths stretched resources to an extent which did not please some of those present. The Duchess of Northumberland complained succinctly that there was "not the wherewithall to fill one's belly." The Barons of the Cinque Ports emerged with the poorest hospitality, for by the time he came to handle *their* protests, Lord Talbot was at the end of his patience. Far from accommodating the barons, he offered to fight them. "I am ready to give you satisfaction in any way you think fit," cried the earl. "I'm a match for any of you."

Due to his consequent unpopularity, one misadventure which befell Talbot during the banquet went down particularly well with the diners. As Lord Steward of the Household, it was part of his duty to ride on horseback to the royal dais, make an obeisance to the sovereign, then back his mount in a mannerly fashion from the great hall. The last part of the function being the most exacting, Talbot had devoted much time to teaching his horse how to back up. So well, indeed, had the animal learned its lesson, that it now persisted in entering the hall backwards and did its best, against the frantic efforts of its rider, to advance upon the king and queen hindquarters foremost.

Walpole described the endeavors of Lord Talbot as woeful. When the celebrated John Wilkes recalled the incident in his publication the *North Briton,* Talbot challenged him to single combat. They met by moonlight in the grounds of the Red Lion Inn, Bagshot, near London. Each fired a shot, and each missed.

One further and, to a superstitious populace, less amusing incident, occured at George III's coronation. In the course of the ceremony, a large and valuable jewel fell from the king's crown. For many, the mishap was symbolic. As one writer put it:

> *When first, portentous, it was known*
> *Great George had jostled from his crown*
> *The brightest diamond there,*
> *The omen-mongers one and all*
> *Foretold some mischief must befall;*
> *Some loss beyond compare.*

From the medieval sighting of Halley's comet, which had presaged the demise of Harold of Wessex, to this latest item of gossip, omen-mongers had sought analogous clues to high drama. Avidly, they now prognosticated the loss of something the nation held singularly valuable. Fate, in her humor, would contrive to prove the fools right.

CHAPTER 2

The Royal Family

If the circumstances which brought the Hanoverian Georges to the English throne were remarkable, they were not more remarkable than the Georges themselves. George I had been born in 1660 in Hanover, a small, independent kingdom of Germany which, save for the fact that it was destined to share the same king, had little in common with England. George had lived for half a century in his homeland when the death of Queen Anne of England jerked him somewhat rudely from his insularity. Anne, despite seventeen pregnancies, died heirless—all her children had expired in infancy—and the determination to avoid a Roman Catholic successor, especially the pretender James (son of the banished James II of England), forced Parliament in London to turn to a minor German state for a suitable Protestant candidate.

Parliament's knowledge of Hanoverian history was sketchy. In 1181, a duke of Saxony, Henry the Lion, had been placed under an imperial ban, and his duchy dismembered. Henry had been permitted to keep his hereditary possessions, a large part of Brunswick and Lüneburg. In 1520, the duchy of Lüneburg had been divided among three brothers, two of the resulting branches quickly fading, while the third established the line of Lüneburg-Celle. The dukes of Lüneburg-Celle took the name of Hanover, after the town (*Hohenufer*=high bank), and were the ancestors of the electors and kings of that house. Much of the history of Hanover was merged in that of Brunswick, which, due to the perpetual partitions of its territories and the internal squabbles of its princes, had not played a major part in German politics.

Englishmen might well have remained indifferent. George I's father, the elector Ernest Augustus of Hamburg, had been a dashing soldier in his youth, and a noted philanderer. But such qualities were hardly compelling. What interested London was that his heirs were a Protestant line. Emphasizing the strictly constitutional terms adopted on the expulsion of James II, the English leaders proposed that the elector's descendants should accept the throne of England. Doubtless flattered by the offer, Hanover accepted. One of her sons, however, was unimpressed. The first of the Georges never bothered to learn English, and had little inclination for kingship.

Both of George's parents had been affected in their time by melancholia, and though his mother, Sophia, a woman of intelligence and vigor, overcame the affliction to maintain her talents into old age, her husband was reduced earlier by severe nervous illness. George I was podgy, with a receding chin and bulging eyes, and possessed what his cousin, Countess Elizabeth Charlotte von Orleans, described as an "odd cranium." He was also oddly and incredibly stubborn. When his young wife, Sophia Dorothea of Celle, bored with her husband's company, had a love affair with one of her courtiers, George persisted in divorcing her, imprisoned her in the castle at Ahlden and refused to consider her repeated pleas for forgiveness. He took her children from her; he never allowed her to see them again; and he kept her a prisoner for the rest of her life. Nobody was allowed to mention the absent queen in George's presence. So far as he was concerned, he announced, she was dead. George's attitude was doubly deplorable in view of the standard he set himself. Like all the Georges, he had an insistent and restless libido. His preference was for hugely voluptuous women. Wrote Lord Chesterfield, whose perception was as sharp as the next man's: "The King loved pleasure and was not delicate in his choice of it. No women came amiss to him if they were very willing and very fat . . . The standard of his Majesty's taste made all those ladies who aspired to his favour, and who were near the suitable size, strain and swell themselves like frogs in the fable to rival the bulk and dignity of the ox. Some succeeded, and others burst."

The German king found England uncongenial, its people incomprehensible. His main aim, while using his station there to obtain petty advantages for his native principality and to fill the purses of his German mistresses, was to get away from the island as frequently as possible. "George the First was an honest, dull, German gentleman as unfit as unwilling to act the part of a King, which is to shine and oppress, lazy and inactive even in his pleasures, which were therefore lowly sensual," asserted Chesterfield. "He was diffident of his own parts which made him speak little in public and prefer in his social, which were his favourite hours, the company of wags and buffoons. Even his mistress, the Duchess of Kendal, with whom he passed most of his time, and who had all influence over him, was very little above an idiot. Importunity alone could make him act, and then only to get rid of it. His views and affections were singly confined to the narrow compass of his Electorate; England was too big for him."

Since George could speak no English, his ministers no German, the king did not bother to attend cabinet meetings. The result of this royal lack of interest in English politics was to encourage the Cabinet in its developing tendency to assert its independence of the monarch. As Prime Minister, the skillful parliamentarian Robert Walpole assumed powers almost regal in their increasing scope.

After the tradition of the absolutist German rulers—who tended, like dictators, to be jealous of their own heirs— George I was involved in a bitter feud with his firstborn son, George Augustus. The matter reached a head at the baptism of one of the prince's children. The Prince of Wales had selected one godfather; the king persisted in selecting a different one. Finally, the younger man turned in open anger on his father, was ordered into arrest and subsequently banished from St. James's Palace and all further court ceremonies. The prince moved to Leicester House, Leicester Square, and threw himself heartily into the opposition of his father and his ministers.

A pattern of father-son bitterness had been set which was to repeat itself uncannily in future generations, along with another family trait, more ominous, which showed itself in the later part of George I's existence. Following the death of his divorced and imprisoned wife Sophia, the king developed symptoms of depression much after the style of his forebears. He survived morosely to the age of sixty-seven, dying of apoplexy in a carriage traveling to his birthplace on a June night in 1727.

George II was an English-speaking version of his father. He looked like his father, shared his father's prejudices, and, being able to make himself understood to Englishmen, did so at considerable length and volume, discoursing in a clipped German accent on numerous subjects about which, for the most part, he knew little. He was particularly garrulous when annoyed, sometimes accompanying his anger by pulling his wigs and hats to pieces. Like his father, his heart was in Hanover and he did not have the highest regard for the English. According to one report, it was the king's declared belief "that no English cook could dress a dinner, no English confectioner set out a dessert, no English player could act, no English coachman drive, no English jockey ride, nor were any English horses fit to be ridden or driven. No Englishman could enter a room and no English woman dress herself."

Such sentiments were returned by his subjects in good measure. During one of the king's absences, an anonymous wit hung a notice on the gates of the palace. It read: "Lost or strayed out of this house, a man who has left a wife and six children on the parish; whoever will give any tidings of him to the church-wardens of St James's parish, so as he may be got again, will receive four shillings and sixpence reward. N.B. This reward will not be increased, nobody judging him to be worth a Crown."

Chesterfield, who knew him the best part of half a century, wrote of George II: "Everything in his composition was little, and he had himself all the weaknesses of a little mind, without any of the virtues or even the vices of a great one." Avarice was among his ruling passions, and it was said of him that he was never discovered in a generous action. Within limits, his understanding was clear and his conceptions quick, but the limits were narrow ones. He had the facility to seize and pronounce astutely on isolated propositions, especially unimportant ones, and admitted that little things affected him more than momentous ones. Complex problems demanding analysis, comparison and selection, defeated him. George II had none of the attributes of a ruler. He lacked both the intellect and the warmth of heart which might have inspired loyalty. Such friendships as he made withered beneath the triviality of his interests, the sterility of his conversation and the want of his amiability. He preferred the company of women to that of men, but chiefly of women who required little attention and less pay.

Declared one woman who knew him: "He looked on all

men and women he saw as creatures he might kick or kiss for his diversion."

Above all, perhaps, the king was methodical and regular, a compulsive habit-maker whose repetition often verged on neurosis. His urge to know at all times the precise state of his finances led to his constantly counting and recounting the coinage in his pockets. It was his boast that he never forgot a date. "Having done a thing today was an unanswerable reason for doing it tomorrow," an acquaintance said of him. "Every evening at the stroke of nine he went to his mistress, Lady Suffolk, and took a rapid walk with her back and forth down the corridor, his watch in hand, waiting for the final minute of the hour which was dedicated to this activity. From Hanover he wrote his Queen in England weekly letters of sixty and never less than forty pages, filled with nothing but meaningless trivialities, which were needless to write and completely useless to read."

The one great asset George II possessed which his father had lacked was a strong wife. Her name was Caroline Wilhelmina of Anspach. A woman of intelligence, with a broad and inquiring mind, Caroline regarded George's weaknesses with an unflinching, sometimes staggering, tolerance —she once exclaimed pungently of his repeated sexual recourse to other women that "she minded it no more than his going to close stool"—guiding him firmly and pragmatically in affairs both of household and state. It was the doughty, long-nosed Caroline who persuaded George, despite his early aversion for his father's minister, to espouse the cause of Walpole and uphold his continuance in office. In doing so, she showed her good sense.

Sir Robert Walpole, third son of Robert Walpole, M.P., of Houghton, in Essex, had been destined, as a young man, for the Church, but the death of two elder brothers had made him heir to an estate of £2,000 a year, and, in 1701, he had first sat in Parliament. During the reign of Queen Anne, Walpole's rigid Whig principles and personal zeal in opposition had brought him under fierce attack from his political opponents, who contrived his expulsion from the House on one occasion, and a spell in the Tower of London, on charges of corruption. The episode had done him no harm. His prison had become a Whig rendezvous, and his praises were sung in popular ballad.

After the accession of George I, the Whigs held control of English politics for nearly half a century, and Walpole's ambition, talent and popularity stood him in good stead. Having supported the Hanoverian succession, he had obtained the lucrative post of paymaster general of the forces. By 1720 he was regarded by the general public as the outstanding politician of the country, and, in 1721, had become First Lord of the Treasury and Chancellor of the Exchequer, remaining Prime Minister for the rest of the reign of George I. Neither that king, nor his premier, had been able to speak the other's language, and their conversations, in dog Latin, must have been curious.

Caroline listened to Walpole in most things, and if the calculating conservatism of the sagacious minister heaped mounting power upon the leading landowners of the country, emphasizing the political decline of the monarchy, the queen saw no alternative. She was realist enough to appreciate that a husband who could not rule his own family could scarcely rule a great nation. Caroline was in all things a woman of no nonsense, less concerned with feminine gossip than, among her other interests, physics and medicine. One of her minor triumphs was the exposure of a sensational hoax of the century, "The Rabbit Woman of Godalming"—alias Maria Toft. Mrs. Toft's bizarre claim to distinction was the allegation that she had given birth to rabbits; moreover, she promised to astound the nation by repeating the achievement for a suitable consideration.

Caroline commissioned her own investigation. When it was discovered that Mr. Toft, assisted by a renegade local doctor, was abroad in the countryside buying newborn rabbits, the queen's skepticism was vindicated.

To this incongruous royal couple, this blustering neurotic and his loyal and practical wife, there had been born at Hanover in January 1707 an eldest son, Frederick Louis. Frederick (Fred or Fritz, as his parents called him), maturing in his native land, was soon displaying the more scandal-inspiring of his blood traits. "The chief passion of the Prince," wrote a contemporary, "was women, but, like the rest of his race, beauty was not a necessary ingredient." Unlike his father and grandfather, on the other hand, Frederick had a degree of charm, a quiet gaiety, which enabled him to project his affairs with a certain grace. Though his oval face, with its large nose and bulbous lips, was not handsome, he was taller, more slender, altogether more physically attractive than his ancestors. Seated on a fine horse, his hat cocked to one side, a gauntleted hand on hip, he cut a dashing figure. He had been blessed, too, with an appealing amiability.

It is hard not to sympathize with Frederick. He was, among other things, a romantic fellow. When he was four, he had been betrothed to Wilhelmina, daughter of the King of Prussia, a cousin of George II. George disliked the Prussian monarch, and disapproved of the proposed marriage, but Frederick's affection for Wilhelmina increased as the years passed. When his parents had left Hanover to live in England, Frederick had remained in Germany, and, on coming of age, decided to negotiate a secret wedding. News of a conspiracy between Frederick and Wilhelmina's parents reached the ears of the British ambassador, who, though sympathetic to the romance, considered it his duty to report it to George in London. Furious that his son should presume such independence, George detached a

Colonel Launey from England, charged to return with the heir apparent.

On being hauled to England, a sulky prince found his father quivering with indignation. Caroline rallied to her husband. "He is such an ass," she cried of Frederick, "that one cannot tell what he thinks." Added her daughter, Amelia, who took the same side, "He is the greatest liar that ever spoke, and will put one arm round anybody's neck to kiss them and then stab them with the other if he can."

Blustered George himself: "My dear first born is the greatest ass, the greatest liar, the greatest *canaille* and the greatest beast in the whole world, and I heartily wish he was out of it."

Frederick seemed hardly the butt for such passions, his faults being rather less dastardly than negative. "Though there appeared nothing in him to be admired," admitted a report on his first reaching England, "yet there seemed nothing in him to be hated—neither anything great nor anything vicious. His behaviour was something that gained one's good wishes while it gave one no esteem for him . . ." Nevertheless, George's ill humor was exacerbated by the fact that the London crowds, deeming anyone better than the king himself, acclaimed Frederick enthusiastically, while the prince, it developed, was incensed that the income his father allowed him was inadequate.

Frederick had left Hanover in debt, and needed money urgently. He now sought the hand of an English girl, Lady Diana Spencer, granddaughter of a conveniently wealthy aristocrat, the Duchess of Marlborough, who agreed to a dowry of £100,000. The prince's problems would have been solved had not Walpole come to hear of the marriage plans. The duchess wielded considerable prestige in the country, and Sir Robert, jealous that his own influence over George might be prejudiced by the proposed relationship, presented it to the king in a bad light. George promptly intervened to upset his son's arrangements.

Gradually, ice formed on the once heated family relationship. King and prince rarely spoke. "Whenever the Prince was in the room with the King," declared a courtier, "it put one in mind of stories that one has heard of ghosts that appear to part of the company, and were invisible to the rest; and in this manner, wherever the Prince stood, though the King passed him ever so often, or ever so near, it always seemed as if the King thought the Prince filled a void of space."

Like his father before him, Frederick formed his own court, which quickly became a focus for the politically and socially disaffected. The royal rivalry even spread to the opera. While the king and queen patronized Handel at the Haymarket Theatre, Frederick and his friends supported Handel's rival, Buononcini, at Lincoln's Inn Fields. Society took the game seriously. An anti-Handelist was regarded as an anti-courtier. Voting against the court in Parliament was hardly a less remissible sin than speaking against Handel or going to the Lincoln's Inn Fields opera. Though Frederick's clique appears to have won the battle of the opera, the sovereigns were loath to give up. One evening, Chesterfield could report to the prince with some glee that he had been to the Haymarket Theatre and had found it almost empty save for the king and queen. "As I thought they might be talking business," he quipped, "I came away."

At the age of nearly thirty, and still unmarried, Frederick suggested testily that the king, having aborted two weddings, should be responsible for finding him a proper partner. Many people were disturbed by the prince's continuing bachelorhood, and George prudently condescended to act the marriage broker. His problem was the shortage of ranking Protestant princesses in Europe. After some searching, he came up with a demure sixteen-year-old named

Augusta, daughter of the duke of unimportant Saxe-Gotha, an inexperienced country girl whom the sovereigns had no doubts they could manage. On her arrival at Greenwich, George placed a prohibition on all demonstrations in her favor, and, having caused the child an anxious and protracted delay at disembarkation, eventually had her coach conducted to the palace by back streets. When Augusta not only failed to show the slightest irritation, but actually prostrated herself at the royal feet, even Caroline could not fault her.

The wedding took place the same evening in April 1736, with the minimum of publicity, and the newly married couple set up home at St. James's. The princess, "neither handsome nor ugly, tall nor short," as one report described her, was accommodating in all respects, content to bide her time. In Augusta lay the strength of a Caroline, but she was young and knew how to wait.

Frederick was an excellent catch for Augusta, but had to be accepted along with the more scandalous of the family traits. From the start, his wife turned a blind eye to his diversionary exploits, which, since his arrival in England, had been colorful. The first involved a maid of honor at court, Ann Vane, a young lady of beauty and sexual avidity. When she gave birth to a child in her palace apartment, a number of admirers claimed the honor of paternity, but Ann obstinately named the Prince of Wales. The ploy paid off. Frederick, turning to an older lover, Lady Hamilton, settled a house in Grosvenor Square and an allowance of £1,600 on the astute young mother.

Now married, Frederick moved Lady Hamilton into his household as a lady-in-waiting, perambulating the corridors between bedrooms as fancy and the demands of the respective ladies pressed him. But Lady Hamilton had a number of disadvantages as a paramour—in short, ten of them, her existing children. After a while, the affair palled and the prince turned to the talented but unlovely Lady Middlesex. Lady Middlesex duly shared his affections with an assortment of actresses and singers. All of which cost a great deal of money and plunged the impecunious Frederick deeply into debt with London's moneylenders. So much so that one of Caroline's favorites, Lord John Hervey, a courtier who had also enjoyed Ann Vane's favors and had no love for the Prince of Wales, actually warned the queen that the king's life was endangered "by the profligate usurers who lent the prince money on condition of being paid at His Majesty's death."

Furiously, George plotted in favor of the succession of his second child, William, Duke of Cumberland, while Caroline exerted her wits to discredit Frederick and any possible offspring of his marriage. For a while, she seems to have been convinced that Miss Vane's child was Hervey's, hopefully believing that Frederick was impotent. When Augusta's first pregnancy cast serious doubts on this, she became suddenly and suspiciously hospitable, inviting her son and daughter-in-law to stay with the king and herself at Hampton Court, the summer palace outside London. In this awesome pile, the scene of many a dark happening in the royal past, surrounded by the queen's minions, Augusta became understandably nervous. Caroline was determined to be present at the birth, and the pregnant woman feared for the safety and reputation of her baby.

"She cannot be brought to bed as quick as one can blow one's nose, and I will be sure it is her child," Caroline promised ominously.

Desperately, Frederick evolved a plan for the contingency. As soon as Augusta's labor pains started, the prince, his mistress and a friendly dancing master rushed the princess to a coach, cushions were tossed around her, and the party set off at a mad gallop for London. After ninety minutes of painful bouncing and bumping, the coach reached St. James's

Palace and Frederick sent requests to a number of cabinet members to turn out and witness the royal birth. It was ten o'clock at night. Since there was no clean bed linen in the palace, Augusta's bed was covered with tablecloths. The infant, a girl, was born an hour later and swaddled in the only thing handy, a table napkin.

When the news reached Hampton Court at two o'clock the same morning, George and Caroline were livid. "You see," the king ranted at his wife, "with all your wisdom they have outwitted you. This is all your fault. A false child will be put upon you, and how will you answer to it to all your children?" The queen was dressing too hastily to attend his argument. In half an hour she was on the road to London herself, accompanied by Hervey. Later, she declared that had Fred's child been a boy, she would "have gone about his house like a mad woman, played the devil, and insisted on knowing what chairman's brat he had bought." But sight of the little girl calmed her. "I don't doubt this poor ugly little she-mouse is the Princess's child," she told Hervey, who, to cheer her further, pronounced the infant no bigger than "a good large toothpick case."

Frederick, now frightened that he had gone too far with his parents, began excusing himself by letters to his father claiming that Augusta's labor pains had been premature and that there had been no midwife at Hampton Court. George was not having it. "The professions you have lately made in your letters of your peculiar regards to me are so contradictory to all your actions that I cannot suffer myself to be imposed upon by them," wrote the king. "You now plead surprise and tenderness for the Princess as the only motives that occasioned these repeated indignities offered to me and to the Queen your mother. This extravagant and undutiful behaviour in so essential a point as the birth of an heir to my crown . . . cannot be excused by the pretended innocence of your intentions, nor palliated or dis-

guised by specious words." Coldly, the king ordered his
son and daughter-in-law out of St. James's and gave notice
to the peerage, privy counselors and others that "whoever
goes to pay court to their Royal Highnesses the Prince and
Princess of Wales will not be admitted to their Majesties'
presence."

Caroline did not live to see another child born to Augusta.
In November 1737, less than four months after the hectic
night ride to London, she was operated on for strangulation
of the bowel, a condition she had borne without complaint
for some years. The surgeon, a Dr. Ranby, had recently left
his wife following a dispute. As he opened the incision, the
queen asked him grittily what he would give to have his
wife under the cutting blade. At the same time, an aged
doctor named Bussiere, who was holding a candle for Ranby,
set fire to his wig with the flame. The queen bore it all
bravely. Later, when it was clear that the surgery could
not save her, she was calmly philosophical, urging George to
marry again—mistresses, she told him, were not enough—
and trying to comfort him.

George was distraught at the loss of his helpmate. During
the last hours, he had refused Frederick's plea to see "his
poor dying mother," branding it another of "the scoundrel's
tricks." For months he suffered acute depression, weeping
uncontrollably and suffering drastic emaciation. For the rest
of his life, he refused to have Caroline's room touched.

Augusta's second child was already conceived when the
queen died. This time, with Caroline gone and the king
beyond caring, the confinement was a placid one. The boy
was born on June 4, 1738, and christened George William
Frederick. The infant who was to become England's outstanding royal George was a puny seven-months baby.

CHAPTER 3

Loss of a Father

The arrival of the premature George had been so unexpected that no arrangement for an *accouchement* had been made at Norfolk House, the home of the parents in St. James's Square since their expulsion from the palace. One bright June day, the mother was walking in the park; by eight o'clock the next morning she had given birth. That evening, in view of the infant's fragility, it was baptized by the rector of the parish. The child's speedy recovery of normal weight was largely due to Mrs. Mary Smith, wet nurse, "the fine, healthy, fresh-coloured wife of a gardener." Under other circumstances, a woman of higher birth would have been secured for a prince's sucking, but the emergency called for Mrs. Smith's accessibility as well as her robustly motherly talents. The lady made the most of them. When told the royal infant could not possibly sleep with her, she responded proudly: "Then you may nurse the boy yourselves." In the end, she had her way. "To her great attention," declared George in later life, "my having been reared is owing."

As George grew, the home filled with children, for, beside himself, his parents had seven others, and the nursery atmosphere was a happy one. "The Prince's family is an example of innocent and cheerful amusements," declared an observer. "All this last summer they played abroad, and now in the winter, in a large room, they divert themselves at baseball [an interesting early reference to the American game, believed to have originated from the English children's game rounders], a play all who are, or have been school-boys are well acquainted with. The ladies as well as gentle-men join in this amusement; and the latter return the com-pliment in the evening by playing for an hour at the old and innocent game of push-pin."

Amateur dramatics frequently occupied the children at the Prince of Wales's house. Frederick's romantic nature responded to theatricals, and he tried his moderate talent by writing lines for the juvenile actors and actresses. To instruct them, the prince hired the services of a celebrated professional, James Quin, who became a household favorite. Quin never forgot his court days, and the children never forgot Quin. "Ay!" he would boast later, when the young George had become king and made a good speech, "it was I who taught the boy to speak." George III paid the old actor a pension for the rest of his life.

At the age of six, George began his formal education un-der a Dr. Francis Ayscough. The doctor, described by a con-temporary as "an insolent man, unwelcome to the clergy on suspicion of heterodoxy, and of no fair reputation for integrity," had contrived to ingratiate himself with Frederick through the introduction of a brother-in-law, Lord Lyttelton. He was less than successful as a tutor, though the program he supervised was a busy one. The schedule was drawn up as follows:

The Hours of the Two Eldest Princes

To get up at 7 o'clock

At 8 to read with Mr Scot [the maths master] *'till 9, and he to stay with 'em till the Doctor comes.*

The Doctor to stay from 9 till Eleven.

From Eleven to Twelve, Mr Fung [language teacher].

From Twelve to half an hour past Twelve, Ruperti [dancing master]: *but Mr Fung to remain there.*

Then to be their play hour to 3 o'clock.

At 3 Dinner.

Three times a week, at half an hour past Four, Denoyers [violin instructor] *comes.*

At 5 Mr Fung till half an hour past 6.

At half an hour past 6 till 8, Mr Scot.

At 8, supper.

Between 9 and 10 in Bed.

On Sundays, Prayers, at exactly half an hour past 9 above stairs. Then the two Eldest Princes and the two Eldest Princesses, are to go to Prince George's apartment to be instructed by Doctor Ayscough in the Principles of Religion till 11 o'clock.

When, after a period of Ayscough's tuition, Augusta complained that George was a poor reader of English, the doctor quickly countered that her son could write good Latin verse. In this tight pedantic cocoon, the small Prince George, and his closest brother, Edward, learned little of what went on in the larger world. At home, Robert Walpole's star had waned and one of the most forceful statesmen and orators Britain had ever known, William Pitt, son of a governor of Madras, was climbing to eminence. Walpole had partially weakened his influence by a determined attack on excise evasion. He had proposed to counter smuggling and fraud through levying taxes on liquor and tobacco when these items left the warehouses for sale. His radical proposals proved extremely unpopular, and were abandoned. He had also lost popularity by his protracted opposition to the increasing pressures for war with Spain, whose pretensions in America and interference with British shipping had aroused the ire of the nation. Pitt's fighting policies were more in keeping with popular attitudes.

In European affairs, George II was causing widespread public resentment by devoting Britain's resources to Hanoverian interests in the War of Austrian Succession. English money and troops were being squandered needlessly whenever Hanover appeared in smallest danger. If Hanover's own troops were used, they were paid from British coffers, while violent differences between English and Hanoverian officers were frequent. In this disturbing situation, a threat struck the palace the terror of which penetrated even the young George's closet.

In 1745, Charles Edward Stuart, the legendary Bonnie Prince Charlie, grandson of James II, landed in Scotland from France. Rather more than half a century earlier, the Catholic James, last of the reigning Stuarts, had been forced to flee England by the arrival of William of Orange and his army, invited to Britain by a group of eminent citizens intent on redressing the nation's grievances. James's Catholic policies, supported by a large standing army, had so thoroughly alienated the country that even his daughter, Anne, and his best general, John Churchill, had been among the deserters to William's camp. Ever since James's departure, his adherents, the Jacobites, had awaited a restoration of the Stuart monarchy, their hopes resting first on his elder son, the Old Pretender, and later on the grandson, the Young Pretender. The young prince had been educated at his father's court in exile at Rome, and counted on foreign aid, especially French, in his plans to gain the British throne.

In the event, a series of storms caused a French invasion fleet to turn back, and Bonnie Prince Charlie arrived in Scotland almost alone. Within a short period, however, he had gathered a following of armed clansmen around him and marched triumphantly as far south as Derby, intent on seizing London. Panic gripped the capital. In an astonished city, laboring forces worked feverishly to throw up defenses, the banks opposed a stampede of withdrawals by refusing to pay out more than sixpence in the pound, and George II hastily dispatched the palace's gold tableware to Hanover, where it was regarded as a fine gift.

At this moment of crisis, the unsoldierly Frederick stepped forward to offer his sword to the nation. Let him, he petitioned the king in the best military fashion he could muster, lead the loyal forces against the invaders. George, perhaps wisely, declined the offer. Instead, he assigned the command to his favorite son, the Duke of Cumberland. Cumberland had little in common with his brother. A sturdy and ruthless man of action, ill tempered, boisterous and brutal, he was, if not the perfect general, at least the better candidate for the appointment, and was soon coping manfully with the emergency. In fact, the Pretender's advance was ill organized, his enthusiastic but poorly disciplined followers proving no match for the loyalists once the latter had recovered from their surprise.

By the beginning of 1746, the Pretender's force had been rolled back into Scotland, and here, at Culloden Moor on the morning of April 16, the two armies faced each other in the dawn mist. It was to be the last pitched battle on British soil, and a fateful one.

Charles had drawn his clansmen up in two lines to face the advancing Cumberland, who commanded the superior forces. Especially strong were Cumberland's cavalry and artillery, arms eminently suited to the desolate, gently undulating terrain. To the east of the Highland lines, the moor swept unbroken as far as the eye could see; to the southwest loomed the height of Dun Daviot. In the distance rose the towers and spires of Inverness, and the square bastions of Fort George, abutting on the Moray Firth. Slowly, the misty horizon began to thicken with the advancing army of Cumberland, "black or dim at first," wrote an eyewitness, "then gradually the lines of red-coats, black-gaitered and white cross-belted, with bayonets fixed and glittering, became distinctly visible. Closer and closer they came with drums beating and colours uncased."

The Duke of Cumberland is said in his memoirs to have adopted an array "the most prudent the mind of man was capable of contriving, because if one column failed a second supported; and if that failed, a third was ready. The rebels could no way take two pieces of cannon, but three must play directly upon them; nor break one regiment but two were ready to supply its place." Be that as it may, it seems to have been less the prudence of Cumberland than the imprudence of Charles which bore on the outcome, for, having watched his lines decimated for some thirty minutes by the enemy artillery, he gave a disastrous order for the right wing of his clansmen to charge.

Leaping the mangled bodies of their comrades, the Highlanders raced headlong into a withering storm of grapeshot and musketry. Those who survived staggered forward, and it was a token of their stubborn fury that they broke through two British battalions, cutting down more than two hundred men, before they were stopped by supporting fire. With the Highland right wing reduced to confusion, the left was ordered forward. One aging chieftain, and a few of his immediate kinsmen, advanced only to find that the rest of the clan remained stationary—an event unheard of in Highland history.

"My God!" cried the old man; "my God! Have the children of my tribe forsaken me?" Moments later, he fell, his body ripped by musket balls.

Realistically, the left echelon of the Pretender's army now wheeled about and, pipes playing, began to retreat in an orderly fashion. Among those of the clansmen who stood firm, few reached ultimate safety. Some, including an outstanding warrior named Gillies Macbane, made a stand by a stone wall. "Towering above the dead and dying who lay heaped about the wall, covered by his round shield, with his long hair streaming in the wind, as his bonnet had been shot away, and covered with wounds, he still faced the enemy. The Earl of Ancrum, who rode at the head of the 10th Regiment, cried, 'Save that brave fellow!' and offered him quarter, but Macbane disdained it." He was said to have unhorsed and killed thirteen troopers before he was brought down. Later, his head was found to be cloven, his body a mass of bayonet wounds.

Cumberland reacted to victory with an orgy of barbarity. Early reports have him riding through the bloody field, shouting repeatedly, "No prisoners—you understand me!" To their discredit, his men understood him all too clearly. Scouring the area, muskets in hand, they bludgeoned or bayoneted to death every wounded Highlander they could discover. Nearby cottages were searched and fugitives dragged out to be murdered. In one place, seventy-two were butchered together; in another, forty-two were burned to death in a hut. The rich dresses and trappings of Scottish noblemen were stripped off, their dirks, brooches, silver buttons and clasps looted, before they were slaughtered. Wrote a horrified observer: "The whole road to Inverness was strewn with the bodies of the slain; among them were many of the inhabitants who had come forth to view the battle."

The Duke of Cumberland returned to London to a hero's welcome and a reward of £25,000 a year. His popularity,

however, was short-lived. As word of his savagery reached
the English public, his reputation declined and he was re-
viled as a murderer. When it was proposed to confer on him
the freedom of one of the companies of London, a disgusted
alderman suggested that it should be the Butchers' Company. Nurses frightened their infant charges into obedience
by threatening to send for the Duke of Cumberland, and
even the duke's young nephew George was terrified of his
uncle. Once, when they were together, Cumberland attempted to amuse the boy by taking a sword off the wall
and drawing it from its sheath. To his annoyance, the child
turned ashen and quivered. At one time, Cumberland's
enemies claimed he was planning a coup d'etat. Such was
the feeling against him that many believed it. The king's
high plans for his second son were shattered.

Frederick, by contrast, grew increasingly popular.
Toward Charles Edward's supporters he showed a civilized
tolerance, obtaining the release of Flora Macdonald, the
young Scotswoman imprisoned for abetting the Pretender's
escape after Culloden, and fighting legislation to punish
Oxford University for sheltering Stuart sympathizers. He had
a certain flair for appealing to the populace. He had put
himself at the head of a league called the "Patriots," he had
advocated war for Britain's interests abroad, he had supported British products at home, he had done various good
works. Neither Frederick nor Augusta would wear clothes
manufactured in foreign materials, while, at one time, the
prince cleared Bath prison of all its debtors and made a
present of £1,000 toward a general hospital. In the world
of arts, he patronized the engraving firm of Thomson
and Vertue, employed the historian Freeman to write a
textbook for young George and his other sons, and was on
visiting terms with Pope, who then lived at Twickenham.

Much of Frederick's appeal lay in the traditional liking
of the ordinary Englishman for an underdog. It was gener-

ally considered that the king had ill treated him, and there was a disposition among the working classes to put the matter right. A popular verse expressed the indignation of many that the Prince of Wales should have been banished from the palace to a private house, without a sentry to protect him, while the Duke of Cumberland did not want for guards.

> *Some I have heard who speak this with rebuke,*
> *Guards should attend as well the prince as duke.*
> *Guards should protect from insult Britain's heir,*
> *Who greatly merits all the nation's care.*
> *Pleas'd with the honest zeal, they thus express,*
> *I tell them what each statesman must confess;*
> *No guard so strong, so noble e'er can prove,*
> *As that which Frederick has—a people's love.*

Nothing had irked Caroline more, before her death, than such fulsome sentiments. "My God," she had cried venomously, "popularity makes me sick; but Fritz's popularity makes me vomit."

Quite suddenly, in March 1751, Frederick died. He had caught a cold. The violinist Desnoyers was playing at his bedside. Suddenly the prince exclaimed: *"Je sens la mort."* He was dead of an acute pulmonary illness before help arrived. The king was enjoying a game of whist when he heard the news. *"Il est mort,"* he informed another player, the Duchess of Yarmouth, curtly, and retired to his rooms ungraciously. "I lost my eldest son," he said later, "but I am glad of it."

Frederick's death brought widely contrasting obituaries. One regarded him as "a tender and obliging husband, a fond parent, a kind master, liberal, candid and humane, a munificent patron of the arts, an unwearied friend to merit, well-disposed to assert the rights of mankind in general

son she could still control a key to the influence she coveted. At eight o'clock next morning, she began a meticulous examination of her late husband's papers, carefully burning the many that did not suit her purposes.

So far, Augusta's behavior, within the tricky circumstances of the family feud in which she found herself, had been largely circumspect. From the first, her manner to the king had been as conciliating as Frederick allowed, and George II had never disliked her as intensely as he had disliked his son. While Frederick lived, Augusta had kept her aims to herself, and one courtier spoke of her "most decent and prudent behaviour" during this time. A strait-laced, humorless manner passed in her for propriety; she had been a faithful wife in the face of provocation and was reckoned a good, if somewhat dominating mother. Behind all this, there was a calculating streak which had not escaped everyone. When a friend of her husband's, Lord Cobham, was asked what he considered the true character of Augusta, he replied: "Why, she is the only person I could never find out: all I could ever discover was that she hated those persons the most to whom she paid the most court."

George II, determined to exercise a close influence on the boy who was now to succeed him, lost no time in approaching the widow. At first, his gambit was an uncharacteristic paternal solicitude. Soon after learning of the death, he dispatched a messenger to Augusta with a message of condolence, following this with a visit in person. Waving aside a chair of state which was offered him, the king insisted on sitting beside his daughter-in-law on a sofa, and actually contrived to shed a few tears with her. When Augusta reappeared in public, he bestowed as many honors upon her as had once been enjoyed by his late wife. For a while he seems to have believed he was succeeding. "The King," wrote the Duke of Newcastle the month after

Frederick's death, "continues to be perfectly satisfied with the Princess, and is in raptures with the young Prince."

But in May, when a regency bill was put to Parliament as a precaution against the king dying while the prince was still a minor, it was Augusta who emerged in strength. The king and the Duke of Cumberland wanted a regency council with full executive powers. Instead, thanks considerably to the eloquence of Pitt, who took Augusta's side, the House agreed that the prince's mother should become effective regent while the council was relegated to an advisory capacity.

Pitt, at loggerheads with the king, had cultivated Frederick. It now suited him to cultivate the widow. Among his other objections to George II's policies, he was particularly disgusted by the monarch's practice of making the protection of Hanover the first principle of military strategy. Pitt's idea of war was to divert France, and draw troops from Germany, by surprise raids on the French and Flemish coast; also to engage in a naval campaign aimed at destroying the French fleet, capturing merchant ships and taking France's trading bases. Annexation appealed to him only when it embraced strategic bases or good trading prospects. These plundering concepts he knew how to decorate with eloquent invocations to patriotism and morality. The merchants of London and the provinces, convinced he had their welfare at heart, adored him. The king wished him elsewhere. George II had little enough time for the politicians who supported him—men such as the Duke of Newcastle and his brother, Henry Pelham, who had achieved a monopoly of power for the moment—let alone those who opposed him. By backing Augusta in her fight to dominate the royal heir, Pitt was looking to the future. The king's sympathy for the princess was short-lived. Far from continuing to be "perfectly satisfied" with his daughter-in-law, he was soon describing her as *"cette diablesse Madame la Princesse."*

The battle now moved to the classroom, not only the king and Augusta, but other political forces, vying to influence the prince through his tutors. Thirteen when his father had died, the youthful George had felt the loss more deeply than his years could express. He had cried for a long time. Later, it appeared to Ayscough that the bereavement had made the child unwell. "I feel," George told his tutor, "something here in my chest, just as I did when I saw two workmen fall from a scaffold at Kew." The subsequent struggle to capture his loyalty confused him and led to introspection. His daydreaming was noted unfavorably by his teachers. On one occasion, when the boy apologized for his idleness, the tutor rebuked him: "Idleness! Sir, *yours* is not idleness; your brother Edward is *idle,* but you must not call being asleep all day being idle."

If George was perplexed by the political shades of his governors and teachers, it is not to be wondered at. In 1750, a close friend of Frederick's, Francis, Lord North, had become the prince's governor. With Frederick gone, however, the king contrived to remove North and Ayscough, replacing them with two men of his own, Lord Harcourt and the Bishop of Norwich. Harcourt, described by a contemporary as a "sheepish peer," took an odd view of tutorial priorities. It was of considerable importance to him, apparently, that his pupil should "turn his toes outward." That he was put into the household as a cipher was generally recognized, and Augusta had a low opinion of him. He, in turn, was pointedly rude to her, and the memory of her husband. Of the Bishop of Norwich, who taught logic, Augusta was equally contemptuous. His thoughts, she observed, were too many for his words. As a logician, he seems to have suffered from the fundamental inadequacy of finding it hard to express himself. Not to be outdone by the king, his chief ministers, Newcastle and Pelham, inserted their own agent into the royal classroom in the person of sub-governor Andrew Stone, "a dark, proud man," as one who knew him had it, "very able and very mercenary." Stone had once been private secretary to the Duke of Newcastle, and was still his confidant. He joined another sub-governor named Scott, who had been appointed in the days of Frederick. When the sub-governors sided against the earl and prelate, Augusta supported the first pair.

In the general melee which followed, the bishop charged Stone with being a Jacobite, Stone charged the bishop with assaulting him, while Augusta accused Harcourt of avoiding her card parties and the bishop of perplexing her sons with his logic. Eventually, formal charges were drawn up by Harcourt and the bishop against the sub-governors, accusing them of infecting the mind of the heir to the throne with Jacobite philosophies. The matter was referred to a council of the Cabinet, which, to Augusta's immense delight, exonerated the accused, forcing Harcourt and the bishop to resign. The king next came up with a governor, the thirty-seven-year-old Lord Waldegrave—an amiable and honest peer but with no taste for office—who clearly knew what a task he was in for. "I am too young to govern," he moaned; "too old to be governed." Augusta replied by appointing Stephen Hales, a then aged but eminent physiologist famed for his experimental work on blood pressure. Waldegrave's blood pressure might have occasioned his professional interest. It rose alarmingly. "The mother and the nursery always prevailed," complained Waldegrave.

Through all this, the royal pupil endeavored to make headway with his studies and to prepare himself in a vague, idealistic fashion for the deadly earnest business of kingship. George had always been isolated from the hard world. According to one report of Augusta: "Such was the universal profligacy, such the character and conduct of the young people of distinction, that she really was afraid to have them near her own children." It was a strange preparation for

the duties the prince's father had spelled out for him, and
the youth increasingly escaped into himself. "He was shy
and backward," Augusta declared of him in his teens, adding that really "those about him knew him no more than if
they had never seen him." It was not until manhood that
George expressed an opinion of his tutors. He then described
Harcourt as "well intentioned but wholly unfit for the situation," dismissing Waldegrave, albeit somewhat unfairly, as
"a depraved, worthless man."

Surrounded by confusion and mistrust, George dreamed
of the day he would be able to sweep the board of his
tormentors. In history, his idealism found a parallel in the
life of King Alfred. Neatly, he wrote in his schoolbook:
"When Alfred mounted the throne, there was scarcely a
man in office that was not totally unfit for it, and generally
extremely corrupt . . . he got rid of the incorrigible, re-
claimed the others, and formed new subjects for to raise
his own glory, and with it the glory and happiness of his
country . . . no good and great Prince born in a free
country and, like Alfred, fond of the cause of liberty, will
ever despair of restoring his country to virtue, freedom and
glory, even though he mounts the Throne in the most
corrupted times, in storms of inward faction and the most
threatening circumstances without."

Lonely and anguished, the prince needed a mentor, a
friend to understand him. His younger brothers and nagging
mother were not enough. His adolescence demanded a
hero, a father-substitute to look up to. Much would depend
on the man he at last chose.

CHAPTER 4

Enter Lord Bute

John Stuart, Third Earl of Bute, Scotland, was handsome, ambitious and impoverished. According to one of his English detractors, of whom he had a surplus, "his bottom was that of any Scotch nobleman, proud, aristocratical, pompous, imposing, with a great deal of superficial knowledge such as is commonly to be met in France and Scotland, chiefly upon matters of natural philosophy, mines, fossils, a smattering of mechanics, a little metaphysics, and a very false taste in everything. Added to this he had a gloomy sort of madness which made him affect living alone, particularly in Scotland, where he resided some years in the Isle of Bute, with as much pomp and as much uncomfortableness in his little domestick circle as if he had been king of the island, Lady Bute a forlorn queen, and her children slaves of a despotick tyrant."

In short, he was a somewhat dour and thrifty Scot with an intellect many an English noble might have envied. His estate in Scotland provided a poor living, and his circumstances had not been improved by an early and prolific marriage. His wife was the only daughter of the wealthy but extremely miserly Lord Wortley Montagu, who, it appears, "had intended her for Lord Gower's son, whose great

estates marched with his own, but who had been born with
his legs backward." Bute, whoe legs were not only more
conventional but claimed by some to be his best parts, had
not impressed Wortley Montagu. When the young couple
eloped, his lordship refused to help them with a penny. In
reply to their pleas of poverty, he offered only the advice that
they should live economically.

In 1746, Bute moved south to try his luck in London. He
had not long to wait. Within a few months, chance had
thrown him into contact with Frederick, Prince of Wales.
Bute had taken a house at fashionable Twickenham, on
which he was spending an ill-afforded forty-five pounds a
year, when a neighbor drove him to a sporting event (said
by some to be a cricket match, others the races) patronized
by the king's heir. Due to rain, the event was postponed and
Frederick, proposing a rubber of whist, retired to the royal
tent. Only two other contestants could be found, but someone had learned that Bute was a card player and, dis-
covering him in his friend's carriage, invited him to make up
the table.

The prince was immediately drawn to the Scotsman. They
shared, he found, mutual interests in literature and the
amateur theater, while Bute was of a sufficiently romantic
understanding to flatter Frederick's temperament. In the
opinion of Waldegrave, the newcomer to the prince's court
had "a good person, fine legs, and a theatrical air of great
importance. There is an extraordinary appearence of wisdom,
both in his look and manner of speaking; for whether the
subject be serious or trifling, he is equally pompous, slow
and sententious."

That Frederick was not entirely deceived by the finely
featured Scot is evinced in his own description of Bute:
"a fine showy man who would make an excellent ambassador
in a court where there was no business." That, after all,
was much the situation in which the Northerner now found

himself; moreover, it suited the prince that his wife shared his liking for his new companion, for Frederick was at this time involved with Lady Middlesex and it was no inconvenience that Augusta should have someone to divert her. It was not until Frederick's death that the implications of Bute's insinuation in the houshold began to strike the nation. Then, with the late prince's friend playing consoler-in-chief to the princess, the people drew their own conclusions.

Augusta's popularity took a quick tumble. "The eagerness of the pages of the back-stairs to let her know whenever Lord Bute arrived," wrote an observer, "contributed to dispel the ideas that had been conceived of the rigour of her widowhood. On the other hand, the favoured personage, naturally ostentatious of his person and of haughty carriage, seemed by no means desirous of concealing his conquest. His bows grew more theatric; his graces contracted some meaning; and the beauty of his leg was constantly displayed in the eye of the poor captivated Princess . . . When the late Prince of Wales affected to retire into gloomy *allées* with Lady Middlesex, he used to bid the Princess walk with Lord Bute. As soon as the Prince was dead, they walked more and more, in honour of his memory."

Whether Bute and "the poor captivated Princess"—a singularly mistaken concept of so self-contained a woman—were lovers in deed is disputable. That most people thought so, is not. "I am as much convinced of the amorous connection between Bute and the Dowager as if I had seen them together," wrote Horace Walpole, while Waldegrave opined that the princess had discovered accomplishments in the Scot "of which the Prince, her husband, may not perhaps have been the most competent to judge." The ensuing disapproval of the couple derived less from their alleged physical intimacy—such situations were accepted as commonplace in high society—as from the fear that they were conspiring to use the heir apparent for their own ends. Bute further drew enmity on account of his nationality, regarded with suspicion in England at that time. Old boots and petticoats, crude symbols of the offending pair, were hung lewdly in the streets or burned on bonfires. Nor were the people entirely deceived in their anger, for Bute had discovered in the youthful prince a most tractable vehicle for his advancement and one expanding his ambitions to the utmost. "The Princess Dowager and Lord Bute," perceived Lord Chesterfield, "agreed to keep the Prince entirely to themselves. None but their immediate and lowest creatures were suffered to approach him." A new contender had entered the struggle for power over young George.

George had grown into a youth of some comeliness. He had a good physique and, though possessing the long nose and small chin of his ancestors, was distinguished by prominent blue eyes and generous lips. According to the tutor Scott, he was "a lad of very good principles, good-natured and extremely honest; has no heroic strain, but loves peace and has no turn for extravagance; modest and has no tendency to vice, and has as yet very virtuous principles." On the face of it, the picture was a distinct improvement on the free-living Hanoverian males of the past: so much so that the family seems to have shown apprehension for this gosling among royal ducks. Scott's "as yet" was significant. The prince's propriety appears to have cast doubts on his maturity. He was, declared Augusta, childish in his habits and backward for his years. What his tutors had taught him she knew not, but "to speak freely, she feared, not much."

"To tell the honest truth," a son of the future king could write later, "the impression on my mind has ever been that it was a very unfortunate circumstance for my father that he was kept as it were aloof, not only from his brothers, but almost from all young men of his own age." One of George's brothers asserted moreover: "No boys were ever brought up in a greater ignorance of evil than the King and myself. At fourteen years of age we retained all our native innocence." It thus became increasingly important to Augusta and her favorite, Bute, to project their relationship in a fashion undisturbing to the callow youth, with his pious and affectionate memories of his father. The task was not an easy one.

Since the Prince of Wales lived shut up with his mother and Lord Bute, their behavior toward each other was not free from frustration. Much as the princess might wish to be alone with Bute, the dread that her son should be out of her sight obsessed her. The dilemma was poignant. For his own part, Bute was content to work on the affections of the lonely boy. It was easier to gain the understanding of the youth than to attain ascendancy over a determined and experienced woman, and his lordship gradually gained the devotion of the quiet prince. George began to be remiss, on occasions, to his mother, and even dropped hints against women interfering in politics.

In an early letter to George, Bute faced the problem of his connection with Augusta. "It will sooner or later be whispered in your ear," he wrote, "don't you know Lord Bute was your father's friend and is strongly attached to the Princess, he only means to bring you under your mother's government. Sure you are too much a man to bear that. Hear Sir what Lord Bute will say—I glory in my attachment to the Princess, in being called your father's friend, but I glory in being yours too." George accepted it. The intense loyalty of his letters to Bute, soon "My Dearest Friend," revealed how totally he had succumbed to the spell of the Scot.

"My Dear Lord," George wrote Bute when he was eighteen:

> I have had the pleasure of your friendship during the space of a year, by which I have reap'd great advantage, but not the improvement I should if I had followed your advice; but

you shall find me make such a progress in this summer that shall give you hopes that, with the continuance of your advice, I may turn out as you wish. It is true that the Ministers have done everything they can to provoke me, that they have call'd me a harmless boy . . . They have also treated my mother in a cruel manner (which I will neither forget nor forgive to the day of my death) because she is so good as to come forward and preserve her son from the many snares that surround him. My Friend is also attacked in the most cruel and horrid manner, not for anything he has done against them but because he is my friend and wants to see me come to the throne with honour and not with disgrace, and because he is a friend to blessed liberties of his country and not to arbitrary notions. I look upon myself as engaged in honour and justice to defend these two friends as long as I draw breath.

I do therefore here in the presence of our Almighty Lord promiss that I will ever remember the insults done to my mother, and never will forgive anyone who shall offer to speak disrespectfully of her. I do in the same solemn manner declare that I will defend my Friend and will never use evasive answers, but will always tell him whatever is said against him, and will more and more show the world the great friendship I have for him, and all the malice that can be invented against him shall only bind me the stronger to him . . . I will take upon me the man in everything, and will not shew that indifference as I have as yet too often done. As I have chosen the vigorous part, I will throw off that indolence which if I don't soon get the better of will be my ruin, and will never grow weary of this . . . I hope my dear Lord you will conduct me through this difficult road and will bring me to the gole. I will exactly follow your advice, without which I shall inevitably sink. I am young and inexperienced and want advice. I trust in your friendship which will assist me in all difficulties. I know

few things I ought to be more thankful for to the Great
Power above than for its having pleas'd Him to send you to
help and advise me in these difficult times.

As the months passed, the almost abjectly dependent
tone of George's sentiments continued. Nobody but Bute,
he wrote, could steer him on his "difficult tho' glorious
path." Bute was his only true comforter, the one he esteemed
even beyond the greatest of stakes, the Crown of England.
"You are I believe sensible that besides having the greatest
opinion of your worth and judgement, I also have the greatest
love and friendship for you."

In political matters, Augusta's understanding of British
monarchy was hazy. Reared in the absolutist atmosphere
of the court of Saxe-Gotha, she lacked experience of constitutional rule. In her view, the monarch was omnipotent,
and she urged her son to grasp his destiny powerfully. "Be
a *King*, George," she spurred the heir apparent. Bute encouraged the same line, anxious to indoctrinate the prince
against established ministers. Be firm, he told George; be
unyielding, be resolute.

In 1754 Newcastle's brother and ally Henry Pelham had
died. George II's assertion at the time that he would now
"have no more peace" proved correct. Newcastle was inefficient, and two ambitious men with no undue deference for
the monarch, Henry Fox, an astute Whig politician, and
William Pitt, the most dynamic figure in Parliament, vied
for the vacant leadership of the Commons. While Newcastle struggled to hold a government together, Pitt pro-
jected himself to the nation as the white hope of exasperated
public opinion. The result was a state of confusion from
which Newcastle ultimately salvaged a proportion of his
former power only by accepting Pitt into his ministry on
equal terms in 1757. For the country, it was a timely compact, since Pitt was precisely the inspiration Britain needed

in the Seven Years War, which had just commenced, involving most of Europe, and in which England was again at grips with her old enemy France. For Newcastle, it meant life in the shadow of the stronger man. For the king, it meant a gloom of unrelieved prospects. Both his government and his heir had now eluded his flabby grasp, and the monarch concluded at length that his youthful namesake was spoiled beyond redemption. When the prince was eighteen, George II summoned him to his private chamber and questioned him on English and Hanoverian history. The lad was too flustered to make any proper sense. "You are fit only for reading the Bible to your mother," the king cried contemptuously, slapping his heir's face. George crawled miserably back to his friend Bute.

One facet alone of George's make-up seemed powerful enough to throw off Bute's domination: the marked sexual drive of the royal line. If the prince could only be persuaded to shed his inhibitions, declared the earl's enemies, the Scottish Svengali must lose his grip on that young mind. George touched on the matter in a letter: "You have often accused me of growing grave and thoughtful," he wrote Bute, "it is entirely owing to a daily increasing admiration of the fair sex, which I am attempting with all the philosophy and resolution I am capable of to keep under; I should be ashamed after so long having resisted the charms of these divine creatures now to become their prey; Princes, when once in their hands, make miserable figures . . . when I have said this you will plainly feel how strong a struggle there is between the boiling youth . . . and prudence."

There is some evidence that George had already been in love with a girl named Hannah Lightfoot. Hannah was a Quakeress of modest family. Her portrait, done later by Joshua Reynolds, reveals her as demure, serene and attractive, and she lived near St. James's Palace, where the

prince might well have spotted her on visits. The legend
of a love affair between George and the Quakeress flourished
later in his lifetime. It was touched upon in newspapers,
disseminated by word of mouth and came to be the subject
of a number of scandal sheets concerned with court secrets.
According to the story, Hannah was procured for George by
the notoriously brazen Elizabeth Chudleigh, a lady of the
court and afterwards the Duchess of Kingston. Of Miss
Chudleigh it was said that when she once complained to
Lord Chesterfield of being accused of having borne illegitimate twins, his lordship replied soothingly, "Good lady, I
only believe half what I hear."

Avid for scandal, many were prepared to believe far more.
Not only, it was asserted, had Hannah Lightfoot succumbed
to Miss Chudleigh's enticements, forsaken her home and
joined the lovelorn prince, she had allegedly married him—
some said at the ill-famed Curzon Street marriage mill—and
borne him children. At last, she was supposedly spirited
away by ministerial agents and hidden from her royal spouse.
So much for legend. It is true that Hannah suddenly stopped
attending Quaker meetings in 1754 after being a regular
worshiper. The minute book for the session January 1755
reported that she had been married at a non-Quaker ceremony, and that a committee had been formed to trace her.
It failed to do so. A year later, a "testimony of denial" was
made against her for marrying outside the rules of the
society. But the man Hannah Lightfoot married was not
the prince; he was a certain Isaac Axford. Furthermore,
George—sixteen in 1754—was still wrapped, on his brother's
evidence, in his "native innocence." One fact remains which
does need explaining. Thirty-four years later, when George's
mind was wandering in illness, he made repeated, if vague,
references to a romantic interest with a Quakeress. It seems
not unlikely that the boy prince fell in love with the vision of

the girl at St. James's. It seems most improbable there was more to it than a childish infatuation.

At all events, George's love life was not to be trusted to cupid. A few years later, increasingly discomforted by the hold Bute and Augusta were maintaining on the heir apparent, George II determined to divert his grandson willynilly with a pretty wench. During a visit to his Hanoverian dominions he had become aware of the developing attractions of the eldest daughter of the Duchess of Brunswick-Wolfenbüttel, the Princess Sophia Caroline Maria. "Beautiful, sensible, modest and accomplished," Sophia set the sovereign's own ageing pulse thumping, and he resolved to introduce her to George with a view to their marriage. "The Prince of Wales," observed Waldegrave of the plan, "was just entering into his eighteenth year, and being of a modest, sober disposition, with a healthy, vigious constitution, it might reasonably be supposed that a matrimonial companion would be no unacceptable amusement."

Augusta prepared to do battle. "Surely the King would not marry my son without acquainting me with it, so much as by letter," she remonstrated. "I shall let him know how ill I take it, and I shall not fail to tell him fairly and plainly it is full early." Of Sophia, she exclaimed: "She will never do here . . . Her mother is the most sarcastical, satirical person in the world and will always sow mischief wherever she comes." Not only were she and Bute appalled by the influence a comely young princess might obtain over George, but, for Augusta, there were unpleasant financial implications. As she was not slow to point out, she had seven other children for whom she hoped the king would make provision before disposing of her eldest son—especially since, if George had children, their interests would take precedence over those of her own brood.

As a first defense, she warned George earnestly that his grandfather's motive in the match was to further the interests of Hanover. As a second, she slandered Sophia ruthlessly. "The suddenness of the measure and the little time left for preventing it," wrote a contemporary, "at once unhinged all the circumspection and prudence of the Princess. From the death of the Prince [Frederick], her object had been the government of her son; and her attention had answered. She had taught him great devotion, and she had taken care he should be taught nothing else. There was no reason to apprehend from his own genius that he would escape her, but bigoted and young and chaste, what empire might not a youthful bride assume over him? The Princess thought that prudence now would be most imprudent. She immediately instilled in her son the greatest aversion to the match."

Accordingly, the charming Sophia was represented to the youth as the very last person with whom he would wish to be intimate. "The young Princess," reported Waldegrave, "was most cruelly misrepresented. Many even of her perfections were aggravated into faults, his Royal Highness implicitly believing every idle and improbable aspersion." Added Horace Walpole: "Her ladyship's boy declares violently against being *bewolfenbuttled*—a word I do not pretend to understand as it is not in Mr Johnson's new Dictionary." In the end, the king's plan was foiled. George II was forced to forget the alluring Sophia with a last wishful side-glance. "I remember his telling me," recalled Waldegrave, "that had he been twenty years younger, she should never have been refused by a Prince of Wales, but should at once be Queen of England."

Backed by his ministers, the monarch now turned to another scheme to lure George from Augusta. The youth would come of age at the end of his eighteenth year, and Waldegrave was sent by the king to inform him that it was time to depart his mother's house, in consideration of which the king had consented to settle on him an income of

£40,000 a year and to renovate suitably princely apartments in St. James's and Kensington Palace. The response was stubborn but not undiplomatic. George would gratefully accept the allowance, he replied, but "I hope I shall not be thought wanting in the duty I owe your Majesty if I humbly continue to entreat your Majesty's permission to remain with the Princess my mother; this point is of too great a consequence to my happiness for me not to wish ardently your Majesty's favour and indulgence in it." As one report had it, the youth expressed appreciation of the King's kind intentions, at the same time dwelling feelingly "on the great affliction which a separation from his mother would entail upon both."

Such tactics placed the government in an awkward position. Was the offer of money to be revoked because the prince had a natural affection for his mother? Was the choice to be taken to its logical conclusion and a young man, of age by act of Parliament, to be taken by force and detained a prisoner in the palace? Could such a measure possibly be justified to the public?

True, there was a precedent insofar as the king himself, when Prince of Wales, had been placed under arrest for insubordination. But George II had then been an impertinent and rebellious son. His grandson, by contrast, was polite and sympathetic, his only crime a boy's love for his mother. The predicament of the king's ministers was evident in the silence which surrounded them. For about a month, they took no further action. Meanwhile, prompted by the lean and forceful Augusta, Prince George followed up his advantage by suggesting that Lord Bute should be appointed his groom of the stole, the head of his household. The king, cursing "that puppy Bute," groped for a countermove. Several weeks after the first message, the best he could manage was a second one inquiring ominously of the prince if he still stood by his desire to remain with his mother and his demand for the Bute appointment.

George stood his ground. Yes, he replied, since the king did him the honor of asking, he did hope to have leave to continue to live with his mother. Her happiness depended on it. And, yes, he did desire to have Lord Bute in attendance. He had a high opinion of his lordship.

At this stage, the ministers admitted to losing the game, and, with an eye to ingratiating themselves with their future sovereign and his formidable mother, persuaded the king with some difficulty to agree to his grandson's requests. The king, growing in infirmity, fumed at his impotence. So objectionable to him was the elevation of Bute that instead of personally handing him the gold key of his new household office, as was customary, he sent it by messenger. The messenger, the Duke of Grafton, dropped it unceremoniously into Bute's pocket, advising him not to make anything of the affront. The advice was unnecessary. Bute could afford to wait for the ceremonial niceties. His obedient pupil had already intimated his intention of making his "Dearest Friend" first minister on the king's death.

CHAPTER 5

Mr. Pitt Is Put Out

At one o'clock on the morning of September 13, 1759, a
flotilla of flatboats took the waters of the St. Lawrence
river, Canada, drifting quietly downstream toward Foulon
cove, beneath the Plains of Abraham, Quebec. Aboard
were troops of the Master of Lovat's Highlanders, the Louisbourg Grenadiers and four battalions of the British Line.
For two months and a half, their frail young general, the
thirty-two-year-old James Wolfe, a junior under Cumberland at Culloden, had been seeking a way of taking the
city from the French commander, the Marquis de Montcalm. Wolfe's losses in the attempt had been heavy. Failure
to make headway had broken his fragile health, driving his
troops to the brink of despondency. But Wolfe was tenacious.
"I will never return home to be exposed, as other unfortunate
commanders have been, to the censure and reproach of an
ignorant and ungrateful populace," he promised. Finally, he
had evolved a daring plan of action.

Quebec was defended by French positions on all sides
save one. That single aspect, the heights giving onto the
Plains of Abraham, was held sufficiently formidable in its
own right to deter an invasion. Its base was awkward of
access; its precipice daunting. Wolfe decided to try and

scale it in darkness. As the laden boats plowed deeply through the water, the general's men huddled between the gunwales. Hopes for a safe landing were based on information that the French were expecting a fleet of provision vessels that same night and that river movements would not unduly alarm them. Suddenly, from the wooded shore, came the voice of a sentinel.

"*Qui vive?*"

"*La France!*" returned a British officer.

"*À quel régiment?*"

"*De la Reine.*" This was the regiment expected to form part of the supply convoy.

"*Passe, monsieur!*" And the troops in the boats heard the sentinel uncock his musket. Further downstream, there came another challenge. When the same procedures had been followed, the second sentry shouted suspiciously:

"*Pourquoi est ce que vous ne parlez pas haut?*" (Why don't you speak more audibly?)

"*Camarade, tais toi, nous serons entendus!*" rasped the officer. (Hush, we shall be overheard!) For a moment, Wolfe's men gripped their guns apprehensively, but there was no more trouble from the bank, and the boats drifted silently inshore, grounding at Anse du Foulon, later known as Wolfe's Cove.

Wolfe examined the precipice, which towered into the darkness. "I don't know what the chances are of getting up," he told his officers, "but you must do your best." The Highlanders went first. Slinging their muskets, some climbing with swords in their teeth, the Scots scrambled up the steep and wooded precipice, grasping the roots of trees, tufts of grass, rocks and whatever else might aid their ascent. Reaching the summit, they rushed a French defense post and secured a narrow path, enabling their comrades of Louisbourg and the Line to reach the plateau more easily. They were 250 feet above the river.

By dawn, Wolfe had his entire attacking force in battle array on the heights. Ahead lay the "soft" side of Quebec and the open battlefield the British general had been seeking. Below stretched the mighty coils of the St. Lawrence. It had not been possible to haul artillery up the cliff, nor was the scope for retreat very comforting. In the event of defeat, Wolfe's position was desperate, but at least his men, now advancing in line with fixed bayonets, had their spirits up.

Taken by surprise, Montcalm responded precipitately, rushing his numerically superior forces into action before they were thoroughly organized. The first to meet Wolfe were Indian and Canadian irregulars, husky sharpshooters clad in hunting shirts and moccasins. Concentrating on the outstanding targets presented by the scarlet-clad British officers, their fire was galling but too ragged to upset the attacking force. Wolfe, struck in the wrist by a Canadian shot, wrapped a handkerchief round the shattered limb and continued to give encouragement and orders. His instructions were that his men should avoid emulating the uncontrolled outbursts of the enemy, but should hold their fire until the critical moment. "A cool, well-levelled fire," he asserted, "is much more destructive and formidable."

About midmorning, the main body of Montcalm's army advanced, shooting confusedly. Wolfe's warriors fingered their triggers and waited. Then, with the two lines at some forty yards distance, they opened up. The French onslaught was stopped in its tracks. Huge gaps appeared in Montcalm's ranks, and their opponents prepared to use their bayonets. At that moment, Wolfe, at the head of the Louisbourg Grenadiers, received a shot in the stomach and another in the chest. With blood streaming from the wounds, he collapsed into the arms of a subordinate, Captain Currie. As Wolfe fell back dying, the whole British line was charg-

ing. "They run! See how they run!" shouted Currie, but
Wolfe's sight was failing.

"Who run?" he asked.

"The French. They are giving way in all directions."

Wolfe's last words characterized the professionalism of
a new breed of young officers which had emerged in the
British Army since the conflict with Charles Stuart. "Then
go one of you," he said calmly, "to Colonel Burton and
tell him to march Webb's regiment to the river St Charles
to secure the bridge and cut off the retreat of the fugitives."

Within four days, Quebec had surrendered. As Wolfe
would have wished, for the massacre at Culloden had
sickened him, the defeated were treated with honor.

The central epic of the conquest of Canada, the capture
of Quebec symbolized the astonishing change in Britain's
fortunes abroad once William Pitt had come to power
in Westminster. Pitt was a remarkable statesman. He fawned
neither to kings nor to princes, looking rather to the people
for his mandate. Essentially a man of sensitivity, he had developed at an early age a shield of striking haughtiness well
suited to the lofty estimation accorded him by his supporters.
Tall and handsome, he had an arched nose, down which he
could peer with considerable disdain at those who offended
him. He was a lifelong sufferer from gout, and pain added
an austere touch to his features. In maturity, Pitt indulged
in few social recreations, devoting himself passionately to
affairs of state. His pleasures were simple ones. He took
long, solitary rides on horseback, chased butterflies or
engaged in exploratory rambles on the Dorset coast.

Pitt's father, Robert, had been born in India, the son
of a notorious and rough-hewn governor whose dealings
had involved the acquisition of a gigantic diamond of
410 carats. Yet Robert was never rich. After making a
number of voyages to China, he had settled in England and
married Lady Harriet Villiers, a relative of the dukes of

Buckingham. All but one of their seven children were to show signs of mental instability in later life, and William was not the exception. William had been a gentle and delicate child whose early consignment to Eton had proved hard on him. Due to his attacks of gout, he had been unable to participate in sports and other physical activities. Yet his grandfather had perceived a resilience in the boy, for he once wrote reassuringly to Robert: "He is a hopeful lad and no doubt but will answer yours and your friends' expectations."

Among Pitt's contemporaries at Eton had been George Grenville, who was to figure prominently in George III's reign. Grenville was a nephew of the influential Sir Richard Temple, Viscount Cobham. Lord Cobham's stately home at Stowe, in Buckinghamshire, had become the focus of an impressive circle of politicians, aristocrats, soldiers and intellectuals, and here, amid magnificent settings and hospitality, the young Pitt had made his earliest social contacts. in 1731, thanks to Cobham, Pitt had been appointed a cornet in the King's Own Regiment of Horse, popularly known as "Cobham's" after its colonel. The commission provided further introductions to court and public life.

As a strenuous opponent of Robert Walpole's ministry, Cobham had marshaled his group for an attack in the Commons, where it had enjoyed the patronage of Prince Frederick. Pitt, spreading the wings of a natural eloquence and a developing flair for publicity, entered Parliament in 1735, where he had become a member of the Patriots, as Frederick's friends liked to be known. On the occasion of the prince's marriage to Augusta, Pitt had delivered a maiden speech so scathing in its references to George II that Walpole described him as "that terrible cornet of horse" and gave orders that he should be dismissed from the Army. He could scarcely have done Pitt a better turn. The budding statesman had immediately become the Patriots' martyr, evincing his aptitude for showmanship by touring the country to display the poverty forced on him by his sacking.

In 1737, the year Frederick and Augusta were expelled from St. James's Palace, Pitt had been made a groom of the bedchamber to the banished prince at a salary of £400 per annum. The money was welcome, but he had made it clear he had not sold his independence. "I am in the service of one of the branches of the Royal Family," he declared. "I think it an honour to be so; but I should think otherwise were I not as free to give my opinion upon any question which happens in this house as I was before I possessed such a place." Pitt's interests were elsewhere than in the royal family. Increasingly, he addressed himself to the country, projecting his personality beyond the bounds of Parliament to the many people who felt ill represented there.

Expanding his talents as an orator with an instinctive sense of the histrionic, Pitt repeatedly had invoked the "voice of England." In particular, he claimed to speak for the commercial sectors of the populace, and for the absent colonists. In 1746, long since the acknowledged leader of the Patriots, he had been appointed paymaster general of the forces. In this post he proceeded to increase his reputation by renouncing the customary perquisites of the office and living solely on his salary. Such novel scruples were worthy of wide comment. The country had been duly impressed by his efficiency and honesty.

The commencement of the Seven Years War provided the lofty, Roman-nosed Pitt with the opportunity he had awaited. Primarily, the war was a European one. Russia, Austria, France, Sweden and Saxony had formed an alliance against Prussia with the intention of smashing, or much reducing, the power of Frederick the Great. As it happened, they were to prove unsuccessful, Frederick's Prussia, against most predictions, resisting them to lay the foundations of what became modern Germany. But there was a far-reaching offshoot. England, joining Prussia in her struggle, became again the open enemy of France. The situation presented Pitt with a ready-made pretext for assailing French pretensions overseas.

For a long time he had advocated attacking France through her colonial possessions, where she was most vulnerable, and where British naval power would pay dividends. Relentlessly, he had chastised the government for its alliances and subsidies to Hanover, calling one Secretary of State "a Hanover troop minister . . . who seems to have renounced the name of an Englishman." Popular demand for the man the people came to call the Great Commoner grew by leaps and bounds. Supremely confident, with his shrewd eye for public relations, Pitt declared grandly: "I know that I can save this country and that no one else can."

In July 1757, George II had put the boast to the test. Pitt was called to the helm of the nation and entrusted with full conduct of the so-far disastrous war. The task was an awesome one. Against seven million Britons were arrayed twenty-seven million French, linked through the Bourbon dynasty with ten million Spaniards. Britain's survival called for a reorganization of her forces to the point of utmost efficiency. Pitt approached the job thoroughly. Leaving first the Duke of Devonshire, and then the Duke of Newcastle, to control affairs of patronage as nominal heads of the ministry, he devoted himself to the war. Reviving the national militia, he shaped it into a useful defense force. He re-equipped and reorganized the Navy, and he filled top army posts with young men of daring and enterprise. Among them were Wolfe and General Amherst, whose successful campaign against Montreal subsequent to the fall of Quebec was described as "one of the most perfect and astonishing bits of work which the annals of British warfare can show."

In Parliament, the Great Commoner repeatedly laid

emphasis on the importance of America, her skills and her fantastic potential wealth—vital ingredients, as he saw them, to empire. "The succour and preservation of my dominions in America," he wrote into the king's address to Parliament, "have been my constant care. And, next to the security of my kingdom, they shall continue to be my great and principal object: and I have taken measures which I trust, by the blessing of God, may effectually disappoint the designs of my enemies in those parts." Elsewhere, Pitt enthusiastically supported the East India Company and its "heaven-born general," Robert Clive, in its successes against its French rivals.

With victories beginning to take the place of defeats abroad, Pitt attained unchallenged power in England's government. Careful to lay stress on individual liberties, he avoided any popular outcry his autocracy might have raised, and the millions hailed him as a hero and patriot. But, to his political opponents, he was otherwise. None resented him more than Prince George, who saw Pitt as a direct challenge to his plans for Lord Bute. "I can't help feeling," wrote the prince as the great uplift of morale swept the country, "that every such thing raises those I have no reason to love." When the prince volunteered to accept a command in the Army, only to have his offer blocked by the statesman, he wailed to Bute: "I am not much supriz'd at this insolence of Pitt's, he has long shown a want of regard both to you, my Dearest Friend, and consequently of myself."

For his own part, Bute was inclined to compromise. Early in 1760 he attempted to negotiate with Pitt for his future appointment to First Lord of the Treasury, but the nation's leader was not impressed by such temerity. "I cannot be dictated to," declared Pitt, intimating that Bute's inexperience, plus the fact that he was a Scottish peer, rendered such a posting unacceptable. Both George and Bute were infuriated by the slight. "The late instance of the transaction with Mr P.," fumed the prince to his favorite, "is perhaps the strongest that ever happened to a man of your strong sensations; he has shown himself the most ungrateful and, in my mind, the most dishonourable of men; I can never bear to see him in any future Ministry; what I still flatter myself is that some method may turn up of regulating affairs, which may still make the Treasury not unpalatable to you; if that should not happen, you will for all that be Minister, for all men will find the only method of succeeding in their desires will be by first acquainting you with what they mean to request before they address themselves to me . . . whilst my Dearest is near me I care not who are the tools he may think necessary to be in Ministry provided the blackest of hearts [Pitt] is not one of them."

George II, now seventy-six, doddered toward death unaware of the depth of animosity around him. Thanks to the promotion of Pitt, the old king had found a new affection in the hearts of the masses and, though partially deaf and blind, still enjoyed the comforts of his mistress, Lady Yarmouth. On the morning of October 25, 1760, he died of a heart attack. "The King is dead," wrote Gray, the poet. "He rose this morning about six—his usual early hour—in perfect health, and had his chocolate between seven and eight. An unaccountable noise was heard in his chamber. They ran in and found him lying on the floor. He was directly bled, and a few drops came from him, but he expired instantly." Lady Yarmouth was called, but, in the name of decorum, failed to answer the final summons.

Early on the morning of his grandfather's death, George, now twenty-two, had set out on horseback from Kew Palace intent on riding to London on private business. Not far from Kew Bridge, he was stopped by an anxious messenger, who handed him a piece of paper bearing the name of George

II's German valet. The news was that the king had met with
an accident which threatened to prove fatal. After the
initial shock, the prince's first thought was for Bute. Together, they must snatch what forewarning they had to
plan for the contingency. Accordingly, he misrepresented
to his attendants that his horse was lame and turned back
to Kew, where he hastened by a back path to the earl's
house. At nine o'clock, word arrived from the prince's aunt,
Amelia, confirming that the king was in fact dead. George
and Bute set out by royal coach for London.

Amid the splendors of an autumnal countryside, George
must have recalled Augusta's exhortation to decisiveness:
"Be a king, George! Be a *king!*" George II had depended
on a Whig oligarchy, that is, a government dominated
by the seventy or so great Whig families which exercised
the power and patronage of the state. Opposed to these
were the Tories, the landed gentry, whose influence was
spread widely in the provinces. Could he, the new king, a
royal innocent, rise above the politicians to rule in his own
right? Could one so young and unworldly alter the destiny
of the British monarchy? His first test was not far ahead.
Suddenly, the horses were halted with a flourish. Blocking
the road ahead stood a magnificent coach and six, manned
by servants in blue and silver liveries. It was Pitt on his
way to bring news of George III's accession. As the two
parties talked, the atmosphere was frigid. There must be an
early meeting of the Privy Council, said Pitt, who offered
to advise and to pass on the new king's instructions.

The Privy Council comprised the leading men of the
country, princes, archbishops, principal officers of state and
notable private citizens. It was, however, by this time
dominated by the Cabinet, whose officers were *ex officio*
members. When George told Pitt stiffly that he was already
on his way to deal with things, the great man ordered his
coach reversed and followed. The next moves involved an

astonishing wrangle. While Pitt arranged for the Privy Council to meet at Savile House, George changed the venue to his mother's residence, Leicester House. Some members went to one, the rest to another, and the affair was finally switched to a third place.

Meanwhile, George had politely insisted on treating the Duke of Newcastle, First Lord of the Treasury—but only nominally head of the ministry—as first minister rather than Pitt, the leader acclaimed by the nation. Thomas Pelham-Holles, Duke of Newcastle, was the elder son of Thomas, Lord Pelham, by Lady Grace Holles, both the Pelham and Holles families having accumulated great fortunes in the previous two centuries. At the age of fourteen, Thomas had inherited the wealth of his mother's family, and the following year had come into his father's title and vast estates. By seventeen he had been one of the richest landowners in Great Britain. This wealth and influence he had immediately employed in supporting the succession of George I and the political ascendancy of the Whigs. In the family tradition, he had soon strengthened his connections by marrying Lady Henrietta Godolphin, the daughter of another leading Whig family. In 1724, Walpole had made him Secretary of State, an office he was to hold almost continuously until becoming Prime Minister in 1754, when he had been created Duke of Newcastle. Newcastle had served both George I and George II with faithfulness and diligence. Now, an efficient political schemer if somewhat timid for a man of such wealth and influence, the old man was uncomfortable, especially when George remarked artlessly: "My Lord Bute is your good friend; he will tell you my thoughts."

What followed left everyone more than uncomfortable. The king's declaration, which should properly have been drafted by members of the Council, was clearly the work of the Scottish earl. It started innocuously. Toward the conclusion, however, the eminent members suddenly heard their glorious foreign campaigns denounced as "a bloody and expensive war" which the king intended to "prosecute in the manner most likely to bring on an honourable peace." Pitt's countenance is said to have "betrayed an expression of mingled indignation and astonishment singularly ominous of that strong personal dislike which, in common with most of his Whig colleagues, he apparently ever afterwards entertained towards George the Third." Hardly able to credit his hearing, Pitt asked Newcastle to repeat the king's words. "God knows," wrote the incredulous Newcastle afterwards, "the distress I am in."

Bute realized that so long as Pitt, supported by the Whig oligarchy, was in charge of a triumphant war, it would be impossible for the new king to gain control of the government. Throughout the next day, the Scotsman and Pitt argued over the wording of the declaration that should go on public record. Eventually, to the chagrin of George, who clung to the memory of his father's advocacy of peace, Bute agreed to amend the offending passage from "a bloody and expensive war" to "an expensive but just and necessary war." On November 18, 1760, the day of the new king's first speech to Parliament, a fresh controversy exploded. George's duty was simply to read the lines prepared for him by the government. He added a few more—again on the posthumous advice of his father. "Convince this nation," Frederick had preached in his testament, "that you are not only an Englishman born and bred, but that you are also this by inclination." George determined to do so. In deference to Bute, however, he widened the term of nationality. "Born and educated in this country," he extemporized, "I glory in the name of *Briton*." The reference not only annoyed the Cabinet, who saw it as Bute's work, but offended other sections of the nation. "When you affectedly renounced the name of Englishman," wrote one commen-

tator, "believe me, Sir, you were persuaded to pay a very
ill-judged compliment to one part of your subjects at the
expense of another."

But not everyone took the new king's first efforts in
bad part. For many, the general permissiveness and easy-
going morals of the time were a cause for anxiety, and an
early proclamation from George in favor of piety and virtue,
deploring and promising to punish "vice, profaneness and
immorality," was received by such people with eagerness.
At last they had a sovereign with an untarnished moral
reputation. "Thank Heaven!" wrote one, "that our King is
not a hero, a wit and freethinker, for in the disposition of
the present times we should soon have seen the whole nation roaring blasphemy, firing cannon, and jesting away all
that is serious, good and great. But religious as this young
monarch is, we have reason to hope God will protect him
from the dangers of his situation, and make him the means
of bringing back that sense of religion and virtue which
has been wearing off for some generations."

Mary Lepel, Lady Hervey, the wife of Caroline's favorite,
Lord Hervey, had known George from childhood and had a
high opinion of the young man. "So much unaffected good
nature and propriety appears in all he says and does that it
cannot but endear him to all; but whether anything can
long endear a King, or an angel, in this strange factious
country I cannot tell. I have the best opinion imaginable of
him; not from anything he does or says just now, but because I have a moral certainty that he was in his nursery the
honestest, most true and good natured child that ever lived,
and you know my old maxim that qualities never change.
What the child was, the man most certainly is, in spite of
temporary appearances." Even Horace Walpole, who, to
use his own expression, was "not apt to be enamoured with
royalty," compared the new king favorably with his predecessors. "His person is tall and full of dignity, his counte-

nance florid and good-natured, his manner graceful and
obliging. He expresses no warmth or resentment against
anybody, at most coldness . . . I saw him yesterday and
was surprised to find the levee-room had lost so entirely the
air of a lion's den. The Sovereign does not stand in one
spot with his eyes fixed royally on the ground, and dropping
bits of German news. He walks about and speaks freely
to everybody. I saw him afterwards on the throne, where
he is graceful and genteel, sits with dignity and reads his
answer to addresses well."

Amid a flurry of comment and speculation, the nation
paid its last respects to the late George. Before his death,
that monarch had instructed that, when the time came, his
body should be embalmed with as little delay as possible
and with double the normal quantity of perfumes. Also
that one side of the late queen's coffin should be removed
and that his body, with a corresponding side of his own
coffin removed, should be placed beside hers so that their
remains might mingle. These requests were observed dutifully by the new king. For some reason, perhaps because
of the strong scent, one of the grooms of the bedchamber, a
Mr. Clavering, refused to sit up at night with the royal
corpse. The young George promptly sacked him. In
George II's private cabinet were found six thousand pounds
in bank notes with a request that they should be delivered
to his mistress. In another drawer was a further wad of two
thousand guineas. His grandson lumped the two sums together and had the lot sent to Lady Yarmouth.

The funeral took place on November 11, at Westminster
Abbey. It was an impressive ceremony. Every seventh
guardsman in the turn-out carried a flaming torch, the
officers wore crepe sashes, drums were muffled, bells tolled,
minute guns fired a solemn accompaniment. At the entrance
to the Abbey, the procession—the coffin draped in purple—
was received by the dean and chapter in rich robes, the

choir and almsmen bearing torches. The Abbey was so fully illuminated that its tombs, long aisles, fretted roof and other aspects, had seldom been seen to better advantage. The Duke of Cumberland, clad in a cloak of black cloth with a train of some five yards, was an outstandingly tragic figure. A paralytic stroke had distorted his bloated face, and he limped on an injured leg. He bore himself sternly.

By comparison, the Duke of Newcastle's behavior was burlesque. He burst into a fit of weeping the moment he entered the chapel, flinging himself theatrically into a stall, where a cleric hovered over him with smelling salts. After a couple of minutes, his curiosity got the better of his hypocrisy and he ran about the chapel, mopping his eyes with one hand and holding a spyglass in the other, taking stock of who was, or was not there. At one stage, the Duke of Cumberland, sinking from exhaustion, felt himself weighed down, and, turning round, discovered the Duke of Newcastle standing on his train to avoid getting chilled feet.

As the old king was laid to rest, the sycophants salvoed their eulogies to the new king. Burbled one:

> *Another George! ye winds convey*
> *Th' auspicious name from pole to pole:*
> *Thames catch the sound and tell the subject sea*
> *Beneath whose sway its waters roll*
> *The heavy monarch of the deep*
> *Who soothes its murmurs with a father's care,*
> *Doth now eternal Sabbath keep,*
> *And leaves his trident to his blooming heir.*

CHAPTER 6

Georgian England

At the beginning of the eighteenth century, England had been a land of small towns and a widespread population, still poorer than France or Holland, but steadily developing her agricultural and industrial resources, the latter boosted by the growing use of her coal and the protected markets of her empire in America. Mounting prosperity increased the belief in overseas trade, her ports became busier, her merchant shipping more numerous. By the end of the first decade of the century, Britain seemed set for world ascendancy in commerce. As trade grew, and with it industry, the populace began to cluster more and more at the points of commercial activity.

The story of George's reign would be incomplete without a wider look at his island realm. While London was still by far England's most populous and important city, other urban centers were growing rapidly at the time of George III's accession. Bristol, widely regarded as the second city of Britain, was certainly second only to the capital as a port. The merchant vessels in Bristol's expanding docks hailed from the snows of Russia to the sunny Mediterranean, from the New World of America to the old of Holland and Hamburg. Houses had risen in thousands over a few decades, and with them came such amenities as a new parade and theater. Liverpool and Newcastle had both more than doubled their populations since the turn of the century, Manchester had established itself as a great textile center, and a new canal bringing cheap coal to Birmingham was hastening that city's industrial growth.

With the expansion of the towns and cities went an increase in traveling. Stage and mail coaches, and private carriages, ran between the larger conurbations, carrying the news of London swiftly to the provinces, and vice versa. On the crack coaches, the horses were usually of high caliber and well attended, though this was not always the case. John Woolman, the American Quaker, traveled from London to Yorkshire on foot rather than witness more of the cruelty to animals he had experienced in coaches. "Stage coaches frequently go upwards of one hundred miles in twenty-four hours and I have heard Friends say in several places that it is common for horses to be killed with hard driving and that many others are driven till they go blind," Woolman wrote. "So great is the hurry in the spirit of this world that in aiming to do business quickly and to gain wealth the creation at this day doth loudly groan."

There were many things to groan about. The roads themselves, though improving as the century progressed, were appalling, and coaches frequently bogged down, overturned, lost wheels or broke axles. In winter, the circuit judges refused to travel to Lewes, the county town of Sussex, because of the shocking roads. To the west, there were no roads beyond Exeter, Devon, fit for carriages or coaches. In spring, road plows were dragged over the main highways to scrape up the winter's mud, and stones were tipped into the ruts and the potholes. It did not help much. And it did not improve the temper of travelers to have to pay tolls about every five miles to local authorities for the alleged maintenance of the highways. Many travelers

avoided the toll gates by diverting through fields or by-
ways. At intervals, aggravated mobs attacked the turnpike
houses and sacked them.

To add to the hazards of the road, there was always the
prospect of robbery and violence, especially at night. "The
roads grew bad beyond all badness, the night dark beyond
all darkness, the guide frightened beyond all frightfulness,"
wrote Horace Walpole of a journey in Kent. Walpole's guide
knew that law officers were hopelessly thin on the ground,
and that highwaymen, though less plentiful than in the
preceding century, were a very real prospect. Walpole was
himself robbed by one Captain McLean, the son of a clergyman, and something of a romantic, who stole the wallets
of the wealthy and the hearts of respectable young ladies.
Another notorious character, Jack Rann, flaunted a scarlet
coat, white silk stockings, a laced hat and a bouquet of
flowers at his shoulder. Eventually sentenced to death after
robbing a royal chaplain, he spent his last night in Newgate
dining with a bevy of pretty girls.

But most highway robbers, many of them soldiers dis-
charged from the wars, were ruthless and desperate, and
travelers rightly went in fear of meeting them. "We provided
ourselves with an armed servant on horseback," wrote one
foreign visitor of the menace, "because my Lady Hunting-
don had been robbed a few days previously in these parts.
We remained close together in our three carriages and
divided our party so that we drove in pairs." Some people
hid their money in secret compartments of their coaches
while traveling; others carried two purses, one containing a
small amount of money specially for handing to highwaymen. Later in the century, the advent of paper money,
checks and a better police force drove the highwaymen
off the roads. Meanwhile, they remained a consideration.

Beside the rutted roads, and especially on the outskirts
of the expanding towns, whose centers were deteriorating

into dense slums, stood the homes of the prosperous. The Georgian house of the middle classes was a simple, upright structure—less picturesque than the Elizabethan and Jacobean dwellings; less beautiful than those of the reign of Anne—characterized by a fine and uncluttered balance of proportions. Its appearance was at once solid and elegant, its rooms tall and well lit with large sash windows, its interior walls decorated brightly in contrast to the wooden paneling of earlier times, which was going out. Bedrooms were becoming more plentiful than before, and the children of the family, once accustomed to be lumped together at night, were in many instances able to enjoy their own rooms.

The big old inglenook fireplace of the past was absent from the new house. Except in the grander dwellings, the Georgian fireplace was a relatively small grate, often finely wrought in iron or steel, and framed by a marble surround. It was more attractive than it was efficient. Most of the heat went up the chimney, and drawing room temperatures seldom rose above 50° F in the winter. A Swedish visitor to an English middle-class home complained that it was as cold indoors as outdoors. Plumbing was as primitive as the heating. Most houses of moderate proportions had one cold-water tap, in the kitchen, fed by a hand pump from a well, a pond or a river. A few of the larger places pumped water to a roof cistern, from where it ran by gravity to one or more points in the house. Bathrooms were almost unknown to the Georgian gentry, and privies were generally of the outbuilding type, comprising a hole connected by a brick drain to the city sewer, or, in the country, a cesspool. Occasionally, the device was linked to slow-running water. More often, it had to be swilled with a bucket.

But if the mechanics left something to be desired, the furnishings did not. Georgian furniture, lighter, more graceful and charming than the older styles, had an elegance of design which has rarely been achieved since. Spindle-legged sofas and chairs, satin wood cabinets, charming little tables and elegant sideboards in mahogany or with walnut veneers which took a lustrous polish, graced rooms of superbly accommodating proportions. When, in 1754, the Yorkshireman Thomas Chippendale published *The Gentleman and Cabinet Maker's Director,* at the expensive price of two pounds and eight shillings, it became a pattern book for all that was fashionable in furniture throughout the country. Suddenly, it was possible to obtain the most modish and stylish designs in most places, for everywhere lesser-known cabinetmakers produced copies from the *Director,* or their own variations. The result was a commonly high standard of taste, enhanced during the Georgian years by such other designers as Sheraton and Hepplewhite.

Upon the furniture, and in the niches of gentlefolks' houses, were displayed finely made china, glass, statuary, gilded birdcages and even perfect miniature replicas of their own furnishings. Relatively mundane articles such as tea caddies, snuffboxes and work cases were designed to delight the eye in exotic woods, inlaid with ivory, tortoiseshell and mother-of-pearl. Thomas Tompion, the "father of English clockmaking," had died some years earlier, but his simple, elegant timepieces, usually cased in ebony or walnut, kept the hour in many a prosperous British home.

In the first part of the century, porcelain from China, France, Italy and elsewhere was eagerly collected by the ladies of fine houses, who sometimes paid the dealers with discarded gowns and silk petticoats. By the middle of the century, however, the first English china was appearing in English homes. Chelsea ware, dating from 1745, was highly regarded, some of it in the form of animals, birds and vegetables, some beautifully painted with flowers, and yet more, perhaps the best known, taking the form of such smaller articles as scent bottles, bonbonnières and patch boxes. At Bow, a few years later, English craftsmen had discovered the advantages of adding bone ash to soft paste to produce fine bone china. Bristol added soaprock to the ingredients to give a greater resistance to high temperatures and to make it particularly desirable for use with hot beverages. By the accession of George III, no English home of pretensions was without its display of lovely English porcelain.

Wealthy people who could afford the grand tour of Europe brought back classical statuary to grace the alcoves of their fine homes. Not all of it was genuine, but it looked impressive and was usually expensive. The tourists also arrived back with "pictures"—Titians, Raphaels, Vandykes and Canalettos. In families of more modest means, the ladies not infrequently painted their own pictures, usually watercolors, which were often decorative and sometimes even accomplished. Prints and silhouettes, less expensive than paintings, adorned the walls of the middle class, the silhouette raised to a fine standard by some artists working on card, glass or plaster. Intricate family groups, and profiles of royalty, were popular.

On the whole, a little money went a long way. James Woodforde, diarist and country parson, kept four servants, three horses and entertained handsomely on an income of something like £400 a year. The middle classes could afford to take holidays at such spas as Bath, Tunbridge Wells and Harrogate, and to spend money on silks and satins, silver and plate. They represented a ready market for the quality manufacturer, and the reign of George III would be a buoyant one for English craftsmen. In many ways, the life of Georgian gentility was as bright as the superb English cut glass which appeared in the period, shimmering and sparkling in the candle glow which still illuminated the Georgian home after nightfall.

All but the poor of the time ate prodigiously. It was

normal to serve two courses in a meal, each course comprising from three to nine meat dishes and as many side dishes. Woodforde served four guests with a dinner of "leg of mutton boiled and capers, a boiled fowl and a tongue, a batter pudding, a fine turkey rosted, fried rabbits, tarts, custard and jellies. Almonds, raisins, oranges and apples after. Port wine, mountain, porter and ale, etc." Another time, "We had for dinner some pike and fried soals, a nice piece of boiled beef, ham and a couple of fowls, peas and beans, a green goose rosted, gooseberry pies, currant tarts, the charter, hung beef scraped," and so on. Diaries of the day dwell obsessively on food and eating. When Woodforde's sister died, he wrote: "It makes me very miserable indeed. *O tempora quo modo mutantur! In his temporibus, quid desdirandum!* Dinner today a fine turkey rosted."

For those living in the country, food was readily available for all who could pay for it. In the expanding cities and towns, however, increasing demand and transport difficulties raised problems. Urban populations could no longer live off the immediately surrounding countryside. Meat often had to be driven long distances on the hoof and was tough on arrival. Fish, especially in warm weather, was in a poor condition by the time it had been carted slowly along the rough roads to inland areas. And milk and vegetables produced and vended in cities were of very suspect quality. Cabbage and spinach grown in the smoke of London had, declared one visitor, "a very disagreeable taste." Town cows were kept in appallingly unhygienic conditions, their milk hawked from door to door in open buckets. By the middle of the century, the inferior quality of much of the food that reached the kitchens had helped to spread the fashion for French cuisine, with its heavy use of sauces and relishes. "Everything," complained one conservative

Englishman, "is dressed in Masquerade, seasoned with slow Poisons."

The amount of food consumed in Georgian homes was matched by the quantities of liquor. Drunkenness at all levels of society was commonplace, and regarded with tolerance, though men of the day seemingly could hold huge amounts without being much the worse for it. Dr. Johnson saw no reason to disbelieve that Dr. John Campbell had taken thirteen bottles of port at a sitting, and Addison spoke of a man who estimated he had imbibed four tons of wine in twenty years. Water was regarded as an unhealthy drink, and people were brought up to take alcohol from childhood. Imported wine, varying from five to eight shillings a gallon for medium quality in the first half of the century, was not regarded as cheap, and, even in wealthy homes, women made their own wines from red currants, raisins, oranges, turnips and other ingredients.

They also made cordials with such flavors as mint, caraway, ginger and aniseed. These were less innocent than they sound, the base being usually of a strong spirit. Even Georgian lemonade had a kick in it. One mid-century recipe for lemonade specified half a lemon to equal parts of brandy, wine and water. Other drinks served to guests in Georgian homes were punch, based on rum or brandy, with fruit and spice; bishop, made of hot port wine and roasted oranges; and negus, a milder hot drink with a wine base, either red or white. Many people reduced the cost of their entertaining by buying smuggled wine to avoid the import tax. Woodforde bought regular quantities of wine, rum, brandy and gin from his local blacksmith, John Buck, known as "Moonshine" Buck for his smuggling activities.

Another drink which invited smuggling was the increasingly popular beverage tea. Once as much as £3. 10s. a pound, it had dropped to less than half that price by mid-century—still sufficiently expensive to be bought by the ounce where housekeeping budgets were modest, and kept under lock and key. Most families used it sparingly, sometimes only when entertaining, and seldom for the benefit of children or servants.

Until the eighteenth century, there had not been any theaters in the provinces, but now provincial theaters were appearing apace, and Georgian families in most parts of the land could occasionally see a play, perhaps even one performed by London players. Larger provincial centers also had assembly rooms for such social activities as card parties, ridottos, routs and musical concerts, as well as their town bands, choral groups and recitalists on harpsichord or spinet. In fine weather, band concerts in parks and pleasure gardens drew large crowds. In some cases, the musicians played from stands; in others, they were concealed in pits among bushes and shrubs so that the music appeared to arise from the earth itself. Summer had begun to see a gathering of fashionable families by the seaside for bathing, a habit at first indulged for the cure of aches and pains, but, later, simply for pleasure.

Though most sporting activities were coarse and brutal, a number of genteel recreations, including quoits and ninepin bowling, was popular. Golf was spreading south from its birthplace in Scotland. When the weather was inclement, the literate diverted themselves with the reading of a mounting production of books, magazines and periodicals. The advent of the novel had greatly stimulated the nation's reading habits, and three notable works of this description, Samuel Richardson's *Pamela*, Tobias Smollett's *Roderick Random* and Henry Fielding's *Tom Jones*, had appeared in the forties.

It was an age much concerned with personal appearance, upon which, not infrequently, hinged personal fortune. Beauty, in both sexes, was a highly prized attribute, and might, regardless of others, make a duchess of a servant

girl, or marry a down-and-out coxcomb to an heiress. Men
and women alike assiduously painted their faces, blanching
the skin with mercury water and smarming their cheeks with
poisonous white lead. That the result was often disastrous
to their complexions, that their hair fell out, and that some
even died as a consequence, did not deter them. Cosmetic
was applied to hide the ravages of cosmetic, as well as to
conceal the pits of smallpox and to disguise the signs of early
ageing. Women compounded the risks by painting not only
their faces, but their necks, arms and the large area of their
breasts exposed by the low décolletage required by current
fashions.

Complexions, ruined by overeating and overpainting, were
spotty, and both sexes used patches to cover imperfections.
The rich town-dweller probably bought her ointments,
salves and other beauty aids expensively from a cosmetic
specialist. The middle-class countrywoman made her own.
Recommended ingredients included herbs, vegetables, fat
and spirits. One popular spot remover contained finely
minced meat. Another called for "seven or eight White
Pigeons" minced and saturated in an alumbic.

Freckles and suntan were universally frowned upon, and
women maintained a desired pallor by avoiding the sun,
when necessary by using parasols, straw hats and sometimes masks. Men and women powdered heavily. Ground
rice, or wheat meal, was often used, and wigs were greased
to make the powder stick. On the whole, men were more
conservative in the color of their powder, content to use
gray or white, while women launched out into blue, brown
and yellow. Hair powdering was done at least three times
daily, and powdering rooms, complete with puffs, dredgers
and covering gowns, were found in most places where
people gathered socially. Titivation was as endless as the
methods were objectionable. Hair lines were plucked to give
a fashionably high forehead, and a mixture of vinegar and

cat dung applied to prevent the hair growing low again. Depilatories, in wide use, contained quicklime, and must have caused severe discomfort, to say the least.

Many women had their eyebrows plucked and false ones fitted, tooth whiteners were used to disguise the ravages of dental neglect and leather stretchers were used on the face to eliminate wrinkles. Strong perfumes of civet, musk and ambergris were liberally applied as an alternative to personal hygiene, and men and women carried scent and used it repeatedly, especially in company.

Such was the so-called Georgian elegance, the age of grace and splendor. The good taste, if superficial, was real enough, but behind it was a harshness, an earthiness, a callousness, a violence belied by the splendid clothes, the delightful furniture, the gracious palaces of Kent and Adam and the landscapes of "Capability" Brown. The few who had wealth made no bones about preserving and increasing it; the multitude, who had little or nothing, erupted periodically in orgies of burning and looting which, during the first half of the century, had verged at times upon minor civil war. Preserving law and order was a constant challenge to government. In 1756, a Shropshire mob, incensed by its inability to afford the price of food, gave itself the title of The Levelers—"and so they were indeed," wrote an eyewitness, "this night the gentlemen muster'd up several hundred men, to supress them, they were all arm'd and marched up our railway. They made a formidable appearance; they met with the mob at Ketley and they stood three fires before they fled."

It was only one of the repeated riots of a period when millions lived in squalor, misery and filth. In the cities, they swarmed the cellars and tenements, huddled together for warmth in the winter, in summer embraced by the stench of sewage and refuse. In the country, they lived in hovels of mud and straw, a few old boards nailed together for a table, a floor of bare earth and a bed of rushes in the corner. "How wretched the miseries of the cottagers appear," wrote an observer, "want of food, want of fuel, want of clothing! Children perishing of an ague! and an unhappy mother unable to attend to or relieve their wants, or assuage their pains . . . whilst the worn-down melancholy father, pinched by cold and pining with despair, returns at evening close to a hut devoid of comfort, or the smallest renovation of hope."

While the few stuffed their bellies and powdered their periwigs, an army of beggars overran the countryside, preferring starvation to the death by disease which often awaited in the workhouse. In one year at a Sunderland workhouse, 126 out of 220 inmates died of "putrid fever." Parishes wrangled continuously about the fate of their poor, trying to thrust responsibility for them elsewhere. A pauper named Mary Mann was dragged seven miles in bitter weather to appear before the magistrate of another parish. She was so exhausted that she had to be supported in court by two persons, "for which hard usage, Mary Mann died." True, there were people of charitable impulse who did their best to help, some of them influential, but the strong were largely concerned with acquisition. Where the strong entered, the weak were unceremoniously bundled out. Small, struggling farmers were dispossessed by the great landowners and rich merchants, forced to renew the search for a livelihood among the ragged hordes of the cities, where men, women and children alike were glad of any work, however poor the pay and conditions.

It was a time when a generous farmer paid his men eight pounds a year, when dairymaids received £3. 10s., and small boys labored like adults for twelve months to receive thirty shillings. Women could be hired to pick stones from the land in midwinter for sixpence a day and an extra sixpence for every twenty bushels. It was a time when grazing was so expensive that the laborer could not afford the customary cow to give milk for his family, and when fuel was so scarce he often had to pay a penny to cook on his neighbor's fire. It was a time when death was never very far away, and must have seemed to many, a friendly escape from a cruel life. Such was the England George III inherited.

CHAPTER 7

A Romantic Interlude

While Pitt fumed and Newcastle dithered, the majority
of Whigs awaited developments less with alarm than amusement. What, they asked, might this sheltered king and his
Scottish hanger-on do against the great Whig houses of
Russell, Lennox, Fitzroy, Cavendish, Manners, Bentinck,
Wentworth and Pelham; against such Whig dukes as
Argyll, Bedford, Devonshire, Grafton, Richmond, Montagu
and Dorset, and such Whig earls as Harrington, Sandwich
and Bath? "I laugh," said Paymaster General Henry Fox,
a realist and cynic among Whig politicians, when he heard
that George intended to make Tory appointments.

The names Whig and Tory had been introduced in the
previous century during the struggle between those who
had opposed and favored the accession of the Roman Catholic James II. A whig was the common name for a cattle
or horse thief, and was connected with Presbyterianism
and rebellion. It came to be applied to those who wished to
keep James off the throne. The word tory, in its popular
form, meant a Papist outlaw, and was used to abuse those
who approved James's accession. Following the defeat of
James in 1688—an achievement shared by Whigs *and* Tories, for the king had upset most factions—and his flight to

France, the political differences between the parties became blurred. With the exception of extremists, both sides now accepted the principle of a limited constitutional monarchy. Socially, however, there was considerable antipathy between the parties. Toryism stood for the rural squirearchy; Whiggism for the great landowners, the aristocrats and the city business interests.

With the accession of George I, there had commenced half a century of rule by the Whigs, the Tory diehards discredited as Jacobites. In fact, Jacobitism never really caught hold in England, where, for the most part, it remained a pretty empty sentiment. "The principle difference between Whigs and Tories," says one historian of the period, "is that the Whigs were in office, while the Tories coveted it, and that the Tories, once their Jacobite passions had subsided, would have employed power in all essential respects as it was employed by the Whigs." Nevertheless, the rivalry between the parties was fierce and enduring. "Pray, Mamma," the daughter of a famous Whig family is supposed to have asked her mother, "are Tories born bad or do they become so?" To which the answer came quickly: "They are born bad, my dear, and they become worse."

Fox, who had grown as unpopular with his fellow Whigs as with Tories for his overweening avarice, was the son of a successful parvenu named Sir Stephen Fox. Stephen Fox had risen from plebeian beginnings to die a well-to-do courtier, and his boy, Henry, had consolidated the family's new status by marrying Caroline Lennox, daughter of the Duke of Richmond and great-granddaughter of Charles II. The marriage of the commoner Henry to the semi-royal Caroline had scandalized society no less than many of Fox's noted attitudes. His self-confessed creed, "Never do today what you can put off till tomorrow," did not extend to his pecuniary instincts. He seldom delayed where the chance to make money was evident. As paymaster general during most of the Seven Years War, Fox accumulated a fortune. Some £49,500,000 passed through his hands in this period, and his position entitled him quite legitimately to use this money as would a private banker, retaining the interest and such capital profit as he might make by investment. Fox exploited the advantage to the utmost. Some of the money was still in his account years after his resignation, and the city branded him "the public defaulter of unaccounted millions."

But for all his cynicism as businessman and politician, Fox had a softer, romantic side to his character. His marriage was wholly successful, and he was remarkably indulgent to his children. A child, he said, should never be given a command or be thwarted in its pursuit of happiness. "Let nothing be done to break his spirit. The world will do that business fast enough." It was his opinion that "Young people are always in the right, and old people in the wrong." When his son Charles, who was to outshine his father's fame, desired to destroy a gold watch, or to throw his father's dispatches on the fire, Henry observed, "If you must, I suppose you must," and watched him do it. Once, when Charles was disappointed at not having witnessed the demolition of a wall on the Fox estate, Henry had the wall rebuilt and dynamited a second time. He gave the boy five guineas a day for the express purpose of learning to gamble in good style. Such behavior could not have seemed more inexcusable to the earnest George. But now Fox laughed at the young king's predicament.

As Fox knew better than most, the Whigs had Parliament sewn up. At this stage of its history, the votes of members were purchasable commodities, and the Whig managers held the purse strings. In the last decade of Walpole's administration, the allocation of "secret service" money had cost the nation nearly a million and a half pounds. It was said that there was hardly a member of the House of Commons who, if he happened to dine with Sir Robert when his vote was wanted, would have expected to find less than £500 tucked into the folds of his table napkin. Walpole boasted that there were only three members of the House of Lords whose "price" he did not know. Even now, as George III took the throne, the borough of Sudbury, Suffolk, was actually advertised to be sold to the highest bidder.

What, people speculated, could the new king hope to achieve against so much? He had led an abnormally isolated life, had traveled little and had held few responsibilities, not even an army command. Among his limited enthusiasms, he liked the countryside and took an interest in the botanical gardens his mother was developing at Kew. He also found some pleasure in tinkering with watches and other mechanical instruments. Declared Samuel Johnson: "The young man is hitherto blameless, but it would be unreasonable to expect much from the immaturity of juvenile years and the ignorance of princely education. He has long been in the hands of the Scots, and has already favoured them more than the English will contentedly endure. But perhaps he scarcely knows whom he has distinguished, or whom he has disgusted." As Chesterfield saw it, George had been "lugged out of the seraglio by the Princess and Lord Bute" and propped on the throne "like a new Sultan."

"Secluded from the world and attached from his infancy to one set of persons and one set of ideas," observed a newspaper, "he can neither open his heart to new connections nor his mind to better information." Within four months of the accession, Attorney General Pratt was predicting "a weak inglorious reign." Lord Waldegrave, admitting the new monarch's earnestness, prophesied: "He will seldom do wrong except when he mistakes wrong for right; but as often as this shall happen it will be difficult to undeceive him, because he has strong prejudices." As another who knew the young king summed it up: "He is very obstinate."

Stubborn indeed was George in his youthful ideals and aversions. However much he was abused and obstructed, this bright-eyed youngster with the quiet manner was resolved to restore to the Crown the powers which had passed to the nation's great families. Like Bolingbroke's "Patriot King" he dreamed of becoming the supreme chief, the friend and father of his subjects, and not merely a frontpiece for political factions, be they Whig or be they Tory. His was a naïve but at least honorable concept in which he imagined himself selecting as his ministers the wisest and straightest men—men, as he saw it, like his "dearest friend" Bute—and re-establishing the incorruptibility of Parliament. Wrote Sir Joseph Yorke, scion of a family eminent in the judicature, shortly after George's accession: "In what way the new Parliament will be chosen we shall soon see. I hear the fashion at Court is to say it shall be a Parliament of the people's own choosing; which, in these times, may open the door to new cabals and difficulties, though the principle of it may be wise and honest." Fox went on laughing. He had a special reason to indulge his amusement.

At twenty-three, George was almost certainly a virgin, a psychological strain on the system unknown by the earlier males of the house of Hanover, whose sexual adventures had started at less advanced ages. George's strict conscience had bade him wait for marriage, and now, as king, he urgently needed a queen and wife. Embarrassingly enough, he had already fallen headlong in love with the daughter of a Whig family, Lady Sarah Lennox, a young sister-in-law of that connoisseur of irony, Henry Fox. Not only was Sarah one of the loveliest products of England's ruling families, she was herself of royal descent, being the great-granddaughter of Charles II through his mistress Louise de Kéroualle, the Duchess of Portsmouth, and had as a young child been a great favorite with George II. She had first met the late king in Kensington Gardens, where, skipping away from her governess, she had accosted him happily: *"Monsieur le roi, vous avez une grande et belle maison ici, n'est pas?"* Delighted by her bravado, the sovereign had contrived to see her frequently up to 1751, when Sarah had been sent to stay with a sister in Ireland, Lady Kildare.

Eight years later, now a pretty young lady of thirteen, she returned to England and was quickly invited to the court to renew her acquaintance with the old king. Unfortunately, George II still treated her as the small child he had once known, and Sarah, her dignity offended, failed to respond. "Pooh!" exclaimed the monarch unfeelingly, "the girl's grown quite stupid." Whereupon, according to a contemporary biographer, the Prince of Wales, who was present, was "struck with admiration and pity" for the red-cheeked Sarah and fell in love on the spot. His taste was commendable, for Lady Sarah had delicate, classical features, a slender grace, a poise beyond her years and the spirit of a thoroughbred filly. "Her beauty," declared Henry Fox, "is not easily described otherwise than by saying she had the finest complexion, most beautiful hair and prettiest person that ever was seen, with a sprightly and fine air, a pretty mouth and remarkably fine teeth, and excess of bloom in her cheeks . . . This is not describing her, for her great beauty was a peculiarity of countenance that made her at the same time different from and prettier than any other girl I ever saw."

Horace Walpole was equally enthusiastic. "There was a play at Holland House [Fox's London home]," he wrote in 1761, "acted by children; not all children, for Lady Sarah

Lennox and Lady Susan Strangways played the women
. . . the two girls were delightful and acted with so much
nature that they appeared the very things they represented.
Lady Sarah was more beautiful than you can conceive . . .
no Magdalen of Corregio was half so lovely and expressive." To Fox's delight, his young relative was staying at
Holland House in the early months of the new reign. The
old mansion was in close proximity to the king's residence
and George, riding out, would often see Sarah in the grounds.
To leave the coast clear for romance, the wily politician
departed from time to time to his seaside house at Isle of
Thanet. The girl displayed herself prettily. "Though Fox
went himself to bathe in the sea, and possibly even to disguise his intrigues," said Walpole, "he left Lady Sarah at
Holland House, where she appeared in a field close to the
great road in a fancy habit making hay."

Doubtless, she was flattered to have the king's eyes on
her, but he was by no means her only admirer and she
treated him coyly. At a Twelfth Night ball which was held
at St. James's, he plucked up enough courage to take her
apart from the other guests and ask her about her stay in
Ireland. "Tell me about your sister's household," he said.
"Does Lady Emily or Lord Kildare govern? Either a husband or wife must take the lead." Replied Sarah pertly: "I
think any husband who allowed his wife to govern would
be very foolish." Then, maliciously: "Everybody says you
are governed by your mother."

"And do you not think parents are the best people to
govern?"

"Yes, sometimes. But a German woman is not the best
person to govern the King of England."

Sarah carried off the indiscretion by making a virtue of
her truthfulness. She would not, she said, lie to anyone.
"But you would not mind telling a white lie?" asked George.

"Indeed I would, Sir!" said Sarah.

George was a hesitant lover. Fettered both by his own innate shyness and his fear of the reactions of Bute and his mother, he conducted the romance with reticence. He lost no chance to ride past the broad meadow in front of Holland House in the hope of glimpsing his beloved. He even considered extending the royal estate to link up with Fox's grounds and facilitate casual meetings. And he postponed his coronation in the hope that a queen might be crowned with him. But, in Sarah's company, he lost courage and became gauche. When, in February 1761, he nerved himself sufficiently to make what appears to have been a proposal, it was not put directly to Sarah but suggested obliquely through her friend Lady Susan Fox-Strangways, with whom he had an odd conversation:

"You are going to Somersetshire; when do you return?" George asked Susan.

"Not before winter, Sir, and I don't know how soon in winter."

"Is there nothing will bring you back to town before winter?"

"I don't know of anything."

"Would you not like to see a coronation?"

"Yes, Sir. I hope I should come to see that."

"I hear it's very popular, my having put it off . . . Won't it be a much finer sight when there is a queen?"

"To be sure, Sir."

"I have had a great many applications from abroad, but I don't like them. I have had none at home. I should like that better. What do you think of your friend? You know who I mean. Don't you think her fittest?"

"Think, Sir?"

"I think none so fit."

For a moment, Susan had imagined that the king was

proposing to her. Her embarrassment dissolved when he continued: "I mean your friend Lady Sarah Lennox. Tell her so from me." Fox, on learning of the message, thought the method "strange," but was in no doubt about the meaning. "His Majesty is not given to joke," he pointed out, "and this would be a very bad joke." Three days later, the king entertained at court. Though Sarah was not enamored of George's lack of gallantry, Fox persuaded her to attend. "Has your friend told you of my conversation with her?" George asked.

"Yes, Sir."

"And what do you think of it?"

Snapped Sarah angrily: "Nothing!"

The king sighed. "Nothing comes of nothing . . ." And he turned away dejectedly.

George had made the move at a bad time. While the royal lover fumbled for a way to the girl's heart, Sarah was being wooed by a smooth young buck named Lord Newbattle, an experienced turner of female heads. That Sarah found Newbattle's forceful ways more congenial than those of the timid monarch was all too apparent to Fox, who, a day after the abortive court meeting, removed his relative to Goodwood, in Sussex, where he hoped she might reconsider her attitude without Newbattle's interference. When his ardent lordship followed her to Goodwood, Fox moved Sarah even further into the country, to Bruton in Somerset. His brother, Lord Ilchester, had a house there. At this stage, Fox had a stroke of luck. Here, in March, Sarah fell from a horse while hunting and broke a leg, to be laid up for six weeks. During this period of indisposition, it seems that Lord Newbattle cooled off. At all events, Sarah's own feelings grew markedly frigid when she heard that he had observed of her accident: "It will do no great harm. Her legs were ugly anyhow."

Meanwhile, George grew increasingly lovelorn. Unable to keep the pain to himself, he had confided desperately to Bute:

> I do not write expecting any alleviation to my present misery except that of opening my soul to a sincere friend; but finding my melancholy increases and feeling culpable in having kept you so long in the dark, I resolv'd to acquaint you with it, who I am sure will pity me. What I now lay before you I never intend to communicate to anyone; the truth is the D. of Richmond's sister [Sarah] arriv'd from Ireland . . . I was struck with her first appearance at St James's, my passion has been increas'd every time I have since beheld her. Her voice is sweet, she seems sensible, has a thorough sense of her obligations to her sister Lady Kildare; in short she is everything I can form to myself lovely.
>
> I am daily grown unhappy, sleep has left me, which never before was interrupted by any reverse of fortune; I protest before God I never had any improper thought with regard to her; I don't deny often having flatter'd myself with hopes that one day or other you would consent to my raising her to a Throne; thus I mince nothing to you; the other day I heard it suggested that the D. of Marlborough made up to her. I shift'd my grief till I retir'd to my chamber where I remained for several hours in the depth of despair. I believe this was said without foundation, at least I will flatter myself so.
>
> Having now laid the whole before you I submit my happiness to you who are the best of friends, whose friendship I value if possible above my love for the most charming of her sex; if you can give me no hopes how to be happy I surrender my fortune into your hands, and will keep my thoughts even from the dear object of my love, grieve in silence, and never trouble you more with this unhappy tale;

for if I must either lose my friend or my love, I will give
up the latter, for I esteem your friendship above every
earthly joy; if on the contrary you can devise any method
for keeping my love without forfeiting your friendship, I
shall be more bound to you than ever, and shall thank
Heaven for the thought of writing to you on this subject.

If this remarkable reflection of George's humbleness before Bute gave the Scottish earl any satisfaction, it was
considerably less than the dismay both he and Augusta
experienced at the prospect of the king's marriage to a will-
ful Whig beauty. They had not frustrated George II's plans
to marry his grandson off for this. The prospect was appalling. Not only would they have to contend with a
seductive bride, but also with the intrigues of Henry Fox
and his like, whose greatest pleasure would be to see them
banished from the king's councils. For all George's assur-
ances, Bute played it cautiously.

"I will carry your letter with me to the country," he
replied, "weigh every circumstance, and then like an honest
man, a devoted servant and a faithful friend, lay the
whole before you." At the same time he hinted broadly at
the outcome. "Think, Sir, in the meantime who you are,
what is your birthright, what you wish to be, and prepare
your mind with a resolution to hear the voice of truth, for
such alone shall come from me; however painful the office,
duty and friendship and a thousand other ties command
me and I will obey tho' death looked me in the face."
When the "voice of truth" was at last raised, it sounded
emotionally against the marriage. Any such course, warned
Bute, would wreck the dowager princess' health. Augusta,
for her part, dispatched a secretary to search the European
courts for a more suitable wedding candidate. George
obeyed her summons to consult the latest lists of German
princesses. He had spent an evening, he told Bute, "look-

ing in the New Berlin Almanack for Princesses where three new ones have been found, as yet unthought of . . ."

Fox and his camp were not finished. "They talk very strongly," he wrote gloomily on April 7, "of a white Princess of Brunswick about fifteen, to be our new Queen, and so strongly that one can hardly help believing it." But, a week later, he had perked up. "On Sunday I heard from good authority that the report of his Majesty's intended marriage with a Princess of Brunswick was entirely without foundation, and that he was totally free and unengaged." To his added satisfaction, Sarah, infuriated by Newbattle, had veered toward the king in her sympathies. In May, she returned from the country to Holland House, meeting George at the theater the same month and at a reception at St. James's at the beginning of the next. On both occasions the king showed his delight at seeing her, and she responded pleasantly.

On June 4, they met at the king's birthday ball. It was a sumptuous occasion—a setting for the most gorgeous gowns, jewels, wigs and uniforms in the land, and all eyes were on Sarah. "The birthday," asserted a contemporary, "exceeded the splendour of Haroun Alraschid and the 'Arabian Nights,' when people had nothing to do but to scour a lantern and send a genie for a hamper of diamonds and rubies. Do you remember one of those stories where a prince has eight statues of diamonds, which he overlooks because he fancies he wants a ninth, and, to his great surprise, the ninth proves to be pure flesh and blood, which he never thought of? Somehow or other, Lady Sarah is the ninth statue; and, you will allow, has better white and red than if she was made of pearls and rubies." Conscious of her mending leg, Sarah was not dancing. Instead, she sat beside the king, and the two talked all evening, he gradually edging his chair closer to hers. At one point, they discussed a dance called the Betty Blue.

"It was taught me by a lady," George declared coyly. "A very pretty lady that came from Ireland November was a twelvemonth . . . I am talking to her now. She taught me at the ball on Twelfth Night."

"Indeed, Sir. I did not remember it," said Sarah.

"That may be, but I have a good memory for whatever concerns that lady. I had got a pretty new country dance of my own for the late King's birthday, if he had lived . . . I named it the 'Twentyfifth of February' [Sarah's birthday]."

The battle between the pro- and anti-Sarah factions, which had so far occurred behind the scenes, now came into the open. On Bute's instructions, his wife trailed Sarah whenever she appeared at court and refused to leave her and George alone together. Augusta and her eldest daughter, Princess Augusta, waged a war of nerves on the poor girl, maliciously laughing at her, sometimes to her face. Toward the end of May, George had told Bute that, of the German princesses, the one he most favored was Charlotte of Mecklenburg-Strelitz. She was "not in every particular as I could wish, but yet I am resolv'd to fix there." Nevertheless, his behavior was equivocal, and the "nursery powers" were taking no chances. On June 18, at a palace reception, the king contrived to speak privately to Sarah once more. "I was told you were to go out of town. If you had gone I should have been miserable," he whimpered. "For God's sake think of what I said to Lady Susan Strangways before you went to the country! And believe I have the strongest attachment."

Urged on by the Foxes to force George's hand, Sarah was now steeling herself for the final act. "I must show I wish it to be explained, without seeming to expect any other meaning. What a task it is! God send that I may be able to go through with it," she wrote her friend Susan. "I am working

myself up to consider what depends upon it that I may
me fortifier against it comes—the very thought of it makes
me sick in my stomach already." Twice more, on June 21
and July 2, she met George at court, but Augusta and Bute
gave her no chance to tackle him privately. Then, suddenly,
the secret was out. The Privy Council had been convened
to meet on July 8 to hear George's intention to marry Princess Charlotte. The king's behavior toward Sarah was con-
demned widely for its cowardice. In fairness, he had plainly
made his decision only after a long inner struggle—the sort
of self-torturing process that was to play so dramatic a role
throughout his life. As one writer of the age put it: "Edward
the Fourth or Henry the Eighth, in his situation, would
have married and placed her [Sarah] on the throne. Charles
the Second, more licentious, would have endeavoured to
seduce her. But the King . . . subdued his passion by the
strength of his reason, his principles, and his sense of public
duty."

All the same, George had not shown up gallantly, and
Sarah made a poignant heroine. It was maintained by
many, not unjustly, that he owed her at least an explanation, if not an apology. The young lady got neither.
"I assure you nothing was said," she informed Susan, writing
of her astonishment. "He always took pains to show me
some preference by talking twice, and mighty kind speeches
and looks; even last Thursday, the day after the orders
were come out, the hipocrite had the face to come up and
speak to me with all the good humour in the world, and
seemed to want to speak to me but was afraid. There is
something so astonishing in this that I can hardly believe
. . . In short, his behaviour is that of a man who has neither
sense, good nature nor *honesty.* I shall go Thursday sen-
night [to court], I shall take care to show that one can
vex anybody with a reserved, cold manner, he shall have it

I promise him. I did not cry I assure you, which I believe you will as I know you were more set upon it than I was. The thing I am most angry at is looking so like a fool, as I shall for having gone so far for nothing, but I don't care much; if he was to change his mind again (which can't be, tho'), and not give me a very good reason for his conduct, I would not have him, for if he is so weak as to be govern'd by everybody I shall have but a bad time of it. Now I charge you, dear Lady Sue, not to mention this to anybody . . . to any mortal, for it will be said we invent stories, and he will hate us all anyway, for one generally hates people that one is in the wrong with and that knows one has acted wrong, particularly if they speak of it . . ."

The lines revealed shrewdness and bravery in a girl of fifteen, albeit a worldly one. Sarah was as good as her word. After attending court on July 16, she further informed her friend: "I went this morning for the first time. He looked frightened when he saw me, but notwithstanding came up with what countenance I don't know for I was not so gracious as ever to look at him: when he spoke, our conversation was short. Here it is. 'I see riding has begun again, it's glorious weather for it now.' Answer. 'Yes, it is very fine,' —and add to that a very cross and angry look on my side and his turning away immediately, and you know the whole."

Swore Fox: "The King shall behold your pretty face and repent." And there is some evidence that such was the case. Certainly, Charlotte of Mecklenburg was no substitute for Sarah in good looks. Seventeen years of age, she was short with rather homely features dominated by a tip-tilted nose and a wide mouth. According to Thomas Gray, her complexion inclined to yellow, with little other color, while she possessed "dark and not large eyes, hand and arm not perfect, very genteel motions, great spirits and much conversation." Charlotte reached London at three o'clock one

afternoon the following September and was married the
same day. Ironically, Lady Sarah was chief bridesmaid. On
the word of an eyewitness, she held George transfixed.
"During the ceremony he never took his eyes from Lady
Sarah, or cast them once upon his bride." Next morning,
when Lord Hardwicke—"the most consummate judge who
ever sat"—observed slyly that "it was a very fine night," the
king seemed upset.

As time passed, the philosophy of Lady Sarah Lennox
mellowed. She led a full and sometimes turbulent life, in
1781 making "a match of her own choice" with the sporting
baronet Sir Thomas Bunbury. Later, after this union had
been dissolved, she married the Honorable George Napier,
by whom she had eight children, two of her sons becoming
national figures in their own right, Sir Charles James Napier,
the soldier, and Sir William Francis Napier, the military
historian. "I declare that I have for years reverenced the
Queen's name, and admired the judgment of Providence in
placing so exalted a character in a station where my miserable one would have been a disgrace!" she wrote in middle
age. "I see she has chosen to punish the poor King's faults
by her ambitions and conduct instead of *me* by my faults,
and I still rejoice I was never Queen, and so I shall to my
life's end; for, at various events in it, I have regularly
catechised myself upon that very point, and I always preferred my own situation, sometimes happy, sometimes miserable, to what it would have been had that event ever taken
place."

Finally, she put her seal on the subject:

> In the year 1759 . . . I ought to have been in my nursery,
> and I shall ever think it was unfair to bring me into the
> world while a child. *Au reste*, I am delighted to hear the
> King is so well, for I am excessively partial to him. I
> always consider him as an old friend that has been in the

wrong; but does one love one's friend less for being in the wrong towards oneself? I don't, and I would not value the friendship of those who measure friendship by my deservings. God help me if all my friends thought thus.

CHAPTER 8

A *Taste* of *Marriage* and *Politics*

On July 8, 1761, the day appointed for "the most urgent and important business" of the Privy Council, George had told its members solemnly: "Having nothing so much at heart as to procure welfare and happiness of my people, and to render the same stable and permanent prosperity, I have, ever since my accession to the throne, turned my thoughts towards the choice of a Princess for my consort; and I now with great satisfaction acquaint you that, after the fullest information and maturest deliberation, I am come to a resolution to demand in marriage the Princess Charlotte of Mecklenburg-Strelitz, a princess distinguished by every eminent virtue and amiable endowment." Nobody questioned this assessment. "Perhaps," wrote one, "there were not six men in England who knew that such a Princess existed . . . Lord Harcourt is to be at her father's Court, *if he can find it,* on the 1st of August, and the coronation of both their Majesties is fixed for the 22nd of September."

Only when the marriage negotiations had been thoroughly completed was Charlotte acquainted with her destiny. So far, her life had been something less than a preparation for

so exalted a station. "She described her life at Mecklenburg as one of extreme retirement," said a friend she made
later:

> They dressed only *en robe de chambre* except on Sundays,
> on which day she put on her best gown and, after service,
> which was very long, took an airing in the coach and
> six . . . She had not "dined at table" at the period I am
> speaking of. One morning her eldest brother, of whom she
> seems to have stood in great awe, came to her room in
> company with the Duchess, her mother. He told her to
> prepare her best clothes, for they were to have *grand
> couvert* to receive an ambassador from the King of England,
> and that she should for the first time dine with them. He
> added: "You will sit next him at dinner; mind what you say,
> and *ne faites pas l'enfant*"—a favourite expression of his—
> "and try to amuse him, and show him that you are not a fool."
>
> She then asked her mother if she was to put on her blue
> tabby "*et mes bijoux?*"—"*Mon enfant,*" said the Duchess,
> "*tu n'en as point.*" And the Queen produced her garnet ear-
> rings, about the size of a half-crown, which were then in
> fashion, but which, as she said, a housemaid of these days
> would despise. Thus attired, she followed her mother . . .
> and Mr Drummond [resident British minister at the
> court] was introduced to her . . . In a few minutes, the
> folding doors flew open to the saloon, which she saw
> splendidly illuminated; and there appeared a table, two
> cushions, and everything prepared for a wedding. Her
> brother then gave her his hand and, leading her in, used
> his favourite expression: "*Allons, ne faites pas l'enfant—
> tu vas être Reine d'Angleterre.*" Mr Drummond then ad-
> vanced. They knelt down. The ceremony, whatever it was,
> proceeded. She was laid on the sofa, upon which he laid his
> foot; and they all embraced her, calling her "*la Reine.*"

These formalities over, the girl was given a week to recover from her surprise, then whisked to the coast, where a royal yacht, freshly painted and renamed the *Charlotte*, awaited her. The voyage, from Cuxhaven to Harwich, was a rough one, but Charlotte turned out to be a good sailor. "They had a most hazardous voyage, and at one time feared not making England; but while the other ladies were crying, she was undaunted; consoled them, prayed, sang Luther's hymns and, when the tempest a little subsided, played 'God Save the King' on her guitar." Like Sarah, it seems, she was a young woman of spirit. On the road to London, the ladies sent to fetch her wanted to curl her toupee. She retorted promptly that it looked as good as any of theirs and would do as it was. When informed of the king's preferences in female attire, the princess exclaimed tartly: "Let him dress himself, I shall dress as I please."

The result was individualistic. "She was hideously dressed in a blue satin quilted jesuit, which came up to her chin, and down to her waist; her hair twisted up into knots called a *tête de mouton,* and the strangest little blue coif on the top. She had a great jewel like a *Sévigné,* and earrings like those worn now with many drops, a present from the Empress of Russia, who knew of her marriage before she did herself." Charlotte's costume for the wedding in the chapel royal was sumptuous if eccentric. "An endless mantle of violet-coloured velvet—lined with ermine and attempted to be fastened on her shoulder by a bunch of huge pearls—dragged itself, and almost the rest of her clothes, half-way down her waist," observed Walpole. "The spectators knew as much of her upper half as the King would himself." If Charlotte were afterwards tired by the ordeal of the day, it was not evident. While waiting for supper at St. James's Palace, she entertained the wedding guests by singing and playing the harpsichord, at intervals chatting brightly with her husband, until the early hours of the morning. It did not appear said a witness, that they would be the two most unhappy people in England.

Indeed, in many ways they were well matched. Both were linguists, fluent in more than one language; both were musicians, Charlotte particularly fond of Bach, and both made a virtue, even a ritual, of domestic life. In this last respect, Charlotte was admittedly circumscribed by the frequency of her pregnancies—she bore George fifteen children before she was forty—but appears to have had little real taste for public activities, content to pursue her queenliness mainly in the household. George rose regularly before five in the morning, lit a fire in their room, then returned to bed until the air had warmed up. He next washed, dressed, and went to his study to work on memoranda while the queen had her hair combed by her wardrobe woman. Meticulous, if not always grammatical, in his letters, the king fastidiously noted the hour and minute of the day upon each one. At about seven-thirty, Charlotte dressed, the wardrobe woman handing each garment to a lady-in-waiting, who placed it on her mistress. Having breakfasted, the king and queen repaired to chapel for prayers, after which George attended public business while Charlotte coped with domestic details. An extremely frugal young man—he ate one piece of toast for breakfast for fear of growing fat—her husband was particularly insistent on economy in the kitchens.

At a quarter to one, the queen changed into more formal dress. "We help her off with her gown," reported the diarist Fanny Burney when she became lady-in-waiting, "and on with her powdering things, and then the hairdresser is admitted. She generally reads the newspapers during that operation . . . if she is grave, and reads steadily on, she dismisses me . . . but at all times she never forgets to send me away while she is powdering, with a consideration not to spoil my clothes that one would not expect belonged to her high station. Neither does she ever detain me without making a point of reading here and there some little paragraph aloud. When I return . . . I find her then always removed to her state dressing-room, if any room in this private mansion [the Windsor residence] can have the epithet of state. There, in a very short time, her dress is finished. She then says she won't detain me, and I hear and see no more of her till bedtime. It is commonly three o'clock when I am thus set at large."

For the rest, there were court functions, concerts, the theater, or simply relaxed evenings at home when George would play the flute and Charlotte accompany him on the harpsichord. In many respects, life at court was far from luxurious. The royal residences, especially Windsor, were drafty, ill-heated places, not improved by the king's ruling penchant for economy. When Miss Burney first joined the court at Windsor, a garrulous equerry, Colonel Goldsworthy, warned her emphatically of palace life. "How do you like it ma'am? though it's hardly fair to ask you yet, because you know almost nothing of the joys of this sort of life. But wait till November and December, and then you'll get a pretty taste of them! Running along in these cold passages; then bursting into rooms fit to bake you; then back into all these agreeable puffs! Bless us! I believe in my heart there's wind enough in these passages to carry a man of war! And there you'll have your share ma'am, I promise you that! You'll get knocked up in three days, take my word for that."

The colonel elaborated gloomily on the palace drafts, detailing those which Miss Burney would face between her room and the queen's. The first, he said, was upon opening her door; the second, at the bottom of the steps leading from it, which were exposed to the wind from the garden door downstairs; the third, as she turned the corner to enter the passage; the fourth, gusting from the hall door; the fifth, fit to knock one over, as she turned to the upper passage; the sixth, on the last corner before the queen's room; and the seventh, and last, a minor hurricane from the king's stairs—enough to blow one a half mile.

"Stay till Christmas; only stay till then, and let's see what you'll say," warned Goldsworthy dismally. "You'll be laid up as sure as fate, take my word for that. One thing, let me caution you about—don't go to early prayers in November; if you do, that will completely kill you! Oh ma'am, you know nothing yet of all these matters!—only pray, joking apart, let me have the honour just to advise you this one thing, or else it's all over with you, I do assure you!"

George liked the earthy, uncomplicated country activities, and would hunt or hike tirelessly, seeming to take an almost penitential satisfaction in mud, rain and blizzard. Goldsworthy groused volubly at such hardships, but considered the final insult to be the king's abstemiousness, notably with alcohol—a habit which tended to be forced upon others. "After all the labours of the chase," complained the colonel, "all the riding, the trotting, the galloping, the leaping, the—with your favour, ladies, I beg pardon, I was going to say a strange word, but the—the perspiration—and—and all that—after being wet through overhead, and soused through under feet, and popped into ditches, and jerked over gates . . . after all this, fagging away like mad from eight in the morning till five or six in the afternoon, home we come, looking like so many drowned rats, with not a dry thread about us, nor a morsel within us—sore to the very bone and forced to smile all the time! and then, after all this, what do you think follows?

" 'Here, Goldsworthy,' cries his Majesty: 'Sir,' says I, smiling agreeably, with the rheumatism just creeping all over me! but still expecting something a little comfortable, I wait patiently to know his gracious pleasure, and then, 'Here, Goldsworthy, I say!' he cries, 'will you have a little barley water?' Barley water in such a plight as that! Fine compensation for a wet jacket, truly!—barley water! I never heard such a thing in my life! Barley water after a whole day's hard hunting!"

At the extremities of George's empire, events marched favorably. At eight o'clock on the morning of January 16, 1761, the white standard of France was lowered against a brilliant eastern sky at Fort Louis, Pondicherry, on the Coromandel coast of India. For eight months, the French commander, the Count de Lally, an Irish soldier of fortune in the French service, had held out against forces treble the strength of his own under the British leader, Colonel Eyre Coote. Unable to renew their food supplies, Lally's men had first resorted to eating elephants and camels, and, eventually, dogs, cats and rats. Finally, Pondicherry, capital of the French Indies, together with military equipment worth two million pounds, had fallen to France's colonial rivals.

First Quebec, and now this! Pitt's victorious ministry was at its zenith, his genius toasted not only throughout the armed forces of Britain, who crowned him with their confidence, but by the masses of ordinary people for whom he was *Mr.* Pitt, the splendid commoner. Who but Pitt could have turned national humiliation and defeat into conquest and triumph? Could have raised the commerce of England to par with her military renown? Could boast that he owed his power not to the favor of kings, but to the people of the nation? Could have remained above bribe and reward, without garter or ribbon to vie with his natural brilliance? So exceptional was his supremacy in the House of Commons that he was accepted as its virtual dictator. "The deference which they paid him," it has been written, "was manifested not only in the vast sums they voted him without inquiry and without a murmur, but also in the awe

against Newcastle. They had been safe too long, and the dangers of their actions escaped them.

The opportunity was not lost on Bute. In January, in concert with his friend the young king, he moved against one of the weaker links in the government, the somewhat ineffectual Earl of Holderness, who shared with Pitt the title of Secretary of State. At the end of that month, an apprehensive Newcastle told his fellow Whig the Marquis of Rockingham: "We have received a message from the King, of great importance; he wishes that the Earl of Holderness may resign the place of Secretary of State for the Northern Department, and receive in lieu of it the Wardenship of the Cinque Ports, and that the Earl of Bute may be appointed Secretary of State for the Northern Department, in place of the Earl of Holderness." This thrust found the administration divided, part in favor of placating the new king by accommodating his favorite, part maintaining that such an appointment would prove merely the thin end of the wedge. The first faction prevailed; the second would be proved right.

The not inconsiderable Tory minority in Parliament now found an influential champion in the wily Bute, athirst for nothing less than the crushing of Whig power. Bute's plan was based on exploiting the influential peace movement which had gathered way in the country. While the proletariat stood largely behind Pitt and his successful war, the middle and upper classes were a good deal less unanimous. Hostilities had cost the country dearly. The annual supplies charge, £19.5 million that year, had risen to more than three times the prewar level, £12 million had to be borrowed, and Newcastle was frightened of imposing new taxes. True, commercial interests had prospered, but families dependent on land—taxed particularly high in wartime—and inherited wealth badly wanted a relaxation of levies, and they were important in Parliament. Some con-

sidered the continuing price justified. "The war," wrote
Lady Hervey, "has cost us a great deal . . . but then we
have had success and honour for our money. Before Mr
Pitt came in we spent vast sums only to purchase disgrace
and infamy." But more were eager for a way out before the
nation was ruined by its victories.

When, in mid-1761, the French offered to negotiate an
armistice on the basis of Britain retaining the bulk of her
gains, the offer was warmly welcomed by the peace party.
Bute clamored for acceptance, and the king backed him.
Cabinet ministers were ready to resign if Pitt would not
talk peace. Into this turmoil, the great man dropped a
bombshell.

Behind the scenes, France had persuaded Charles III of
Spain to join her in a secret treaty, the so-called Family
Compact, in which the French and Spanish wings of the
house of Bourbon pledged to make common cause against
England. Pitt, who had received intelligence of the treaty,
not only failed to respond to peace pressures, but now
actually proposed attacking the Spaniards. "I submitted,"
to use his own words, "to a trembling Council my advice
for an immediate declaration of war with Spain." Bute was
the first to object, denouncing such a course as "rash and
unadvisable," urging diplomacy. George applauded him
warmly: "I highly approve the part my Dearest Friend
took yesterday, it was the only way of keeping up the
honour of the British Crown, of acting with justice, and of
overturning Mr Pitt's black scheme. I thank Heaven that
you know him so well, that being the case his venome is not
to be feared; were any of the other Ministers as spirited as
you are my Dearest Friend, I would say let that mad Pitt
be dismissed, but as matters are very different from that we
must get rid of him in a happier minute than the present
one."

In the event, Pitt saved George and Bute the trouble

of contriving his dismissal. All his power and prestige could not persuade his cabinet colleagues to take the awesome step of declaring war on Spain. Alone among them, his brother-in-law, Earl Temple, shared his views on the issue. On October 5, too fixed in his attitude to compromise, Pitt made the grand gesture of resigning. "It is difficult to say," remarked Horace Walpole, "which exulted most on the occasion, France, Spain or Lord Bute." The British nation did not. It was, Walpole added, "thunderstruck, alarmed, indignant." Throughout the city of London, votes of thanks and condolence were passed for the ex-minister, and it was even proposed to display black drapes and hold a period of general mourning.

A few days later, a subdued populace learned that the Great Commoner had deigned to accept from the king a peerage for his wife and a pension of £3,000 a year for his family. Bute, alarmed by manifestations of Pitt's popularity, jumped at the chance to discredit him in public. An unusual statement of his retirement and the favors accepted was published in the *Court Gazette*, while caricaturists and pamphleteers under the influence of the Scotsman poured scorn on the ex-minister for allegedly turning his back on the people. Lady Hester Pitt, who took the title of Baroness of Chatham, was dubbed Lady Cheat'em. One propaganda verse ran as follows:

> *Three thousand a year's no contemptible thing*
> *To accept from the hands of a patriot king,*
> *(With thanks to the bargain for service and merit),*
> *Which he wife and son, all three shall inherit*
> *With limited honours to her and her heirs.*
> *So farewell to old England. Adieu to all cares.*

Less publicized was the fact that George and Bute had quietly tried to get Pitt to stay on in a lesser role and assist them. Face to face at last with the prospect of real power, Bute was jittery. The king had asked Pitt what sort of terms would tempt him. For one thing, the ex-minister had replied, Bute must support him at all times. George, having listened with impatience, had retorted that rather than accept, "I will first put my Crown upon your head and next submit my neck to the axe." There was to be no co-operation. Changing tack, George had endeavored to place Pitt under obligation, first offering the governor-generalship of Canada at £5,000 a year, then a rich sinecure, the duchy of Lancaster. Pitt had refused both posts. He was a wealthy man and did not need money, nor was he seeking favors for himself. But he held for his wife a great affection, and, finally, had been tempted for her sake.

As a sympathizer wrote in Pitt's defense: "The sum that was given was undoubtedly inadequate to his merits; and the *quantum* was rather regulated by the moderation of the great mind that received it, than by the liberality of that which bestowed it." Pitt was quick to put his own case: "Finding, to my great surprise, that the cause and manner of my resigning the seals is grossly misrepresented in the city, as well as that the most gracious and spontaneous remarks of his Majesty's approbation of my services, which marks followed my resignation, have been infamously tra-duced as a bargain for forsaking the public, I am under the necessity of declaring the truth of both those facts in a manner which, I am sure, no gentleman will contradict. A difference of opinion with regard to measures to be taken against Spain, of the highest importance to the honour of the Crown, and to the most essential national interests (and this founded on what Spain has already done, not on what that court may further intend to do) was the cause of my resigning the seals. Lord Temple and I submitted in writing, and signed by us, our most humble sentiments to his Majesty; which being overruled by the united opinion of all the rest of the King's servants, I resigned the seals on the 5th of this month, in order not to remain responsible for measures which I was no longer able to guide."

Though it was not George who had got rid of Pitt so much as a conflux of events culminating in the so-far disputable policies of France and Spain, the resignation, coming within months of the accession, appeared a royal triumph, a portent of the newly powerful monarchy, the personal rule the king cherished. "If you can be without war," his father had written, "let not your ambition draw you into it." George had lost no time in keeping faith, and the gratification of the peace party at events, combined with the momentary fall in popularity of Pitt, seemed to cast George's ideals in a favored light. Disillusion awaited him.

CHAPTER 9

The Wickedest Age

The fog cleared, the sun shone on St. Paul's and London
Bridge, the old capital was caught in a festive mood. Flags
and bunting adorned the streets, troops of cavalry clattered
to appointed posts, coaches and trappings were given a
final shine, huge decorated barges floated on the Thames
like multicolored beetles, and everywhere wine and beer
flowed freely. From dock to dock, office to office, ale house
to ale house, celebrating parties rollicked and stumbled.
London's cries were punctuated with hiccups, her dignitaries
wore their hats at fancy angles, her wenches giggled. At
Lambeth Palace, even His Grace the archbishop was dispensing claret with munificence. The king might drink
barley water, but not his subjects, for this was Lord Mayor's
Day—November 9, 1761, just over a month since Pitt resigned—the day the Corporation and citizens of London
traditionally let their hair down.

At about noon, the pageantry began in earnest. From
St. James's to the Guildhall, where the royal party and
leading politicians were due to be banqueted that evening
by the city, crowds swarmed the streets; windows and
balconies brimmed with gaily dressed spectators. So jammed

with traffic was the three-mile route down the Strand, past Garrick's house, the Turk's Head coffeehouse, New Church, St. Clements, Temple Bar, the Mitre Tavern, into Fleet Street and Ludgate Street, past St. Paul's and Child's coffeehouse to Cheapside and Bow Church, that some coaches took four hours to traverse the distance. In glorious chaos, bodies of brightly clad troops and flunkies, interspersed with the carriages of the famous, piled up on each other's heels and spent longer marking time than marching forward. Everyone strained to see who was coming next. When the lady mayoress poked her head from the window of the mayoral coach, her immense hat caught in the sash and a footman had to release it before she could withdraw again.

For its public figures, Lord Mayor's day was an unnerving test of popularity. The crowds responded exuberantly to their favorites, leaving those who displeased them in very little doubt of it. The latter could be excused for approaching the procession with apprehension. The journey could prove extremely harrowing. Both Bute and Pitt were among the guests invited to the Guildhall, and, while Pitt had no qualms about his reception, Bute was distinctly fearful for his safety in the London crowds. "My situation, at all times perilous," he wrote to a fellow peer, "has become much more so; for I am no stranger to the language held in this great city." As a safety measure, he had arranged that his coach should be accompanied by a squad of strong-arm men headed by a one-eyed bruiser named George Stephenson.

To Bute's surprise, the main part of his ride through the noisy streets went smoothly. On Ludgate Hill there was even applause and shouts of greeting. It was not until the last lap of the journey that it became evident the spectators thus far had failed to recognize him. Suddenly, near St. Paul's, a voice shouted angrily: "By God, this is Bute! Be damned to him!" At this, the crowd erupted with hoots, yells and hisses. Cries of "No Scotch rogues!" and "No Butes!" resounded about the coach while a barrage of mud was unleashed at it from all sides. The liveries of the coach-man and footmen were smothered. Stephenson and his bruisers waded into action, but the mob was too numerous for them, and, as the coach turned into King Street, its guards were overpowered by a determined forward surge. The situation had grown critical. People were attempting to cut the traces and release the horses, when a strong body of law-enforcement officers fought its way to the rescue and escorted the coach with difficulty to Guildhall. Though Bute had displayed bravery in front of the hostile crowd, he prudently accepted the offer of a lift home from the Lord Chancellor.

George wrote angrily of "the wicked designs of the mob this day; I am ready to put any plan in execution to rid my D. Friend of apprehensions that must every hour attend him, and shall be most happy if the changing his situation shelters him from what there is at present too much reason to fear; this is, I believe, the wickedest age that ever was seen; an honest man must wish himself out of it; I own I begin to be heartily sick of the things I daily see; for ingratitude, avarice and ambition are the principles men act by." Toward Pitt, on the other hand, London's affection was manifest. The first flare of resentment at his pension had dwindled, and now, as his carriage followed Bute's in the procession to Guildhall, he was applauded rapturously, his footmen congratulated, even his horses kissed.

Finally, the crowd showed its feelings for the king him-self. Preceded by upwards of twenty carriages of the royal party, the heavy gilt state coach bearing George and Char-lotte was escorted by Grenadier Guards, Yeomen of the Guard and a corps of Horse Guards. The whole was a brilliant sight. But, as the king passed, he was met with a chilling hush. Few people waved, and fewer cheered. At the Guildhall, there was an equally frigid reception as George was led to his seat by the Lord Mayor; little applause as he toasted the Corporation of London, whose members had prospered under Pitt. Moreover, many aldermen had not forgotten their treatment at the coronation banquet. George had brought with him a royal party of at least fifty, and, even in an age of royal freeloaders, the host regarded such numbers as presumptuous. Throughout the procession and the feast and ball that followed, the young king remained composed and aloof to the indignities thrust on him. At midnight, the royal coach driver was found drunk. George waited patiently for him to sober up, but the man still contrived to hit a gatepost at St. James's on the return trip.

For just one revealing moment that day, amid the revelry of "the wickedest age that ever was," the king had dropped his air of sobriety and shown a flash of real enthusiasm. It had come at the home of David Barclay (one of the founders of Barclay's Bank) near Bow Church in Cheapside, on whose balcony the royal family had paused awhile to view the scene and take refreshment. The Barclays were a conscientious Quaker family, their house a haven of peace in the tumultuous city. Here was no slopping of ale or popping of champagne corks, no ostentatious show of jewels or costume finery, no roistering, no maudlin sentiment. The Barclay family, which included four sons and ten daughters, greeted the king and queen with simple courtesy, dressed in the plain garb of the Society of Friends. So overwhelmed, it appears, was George by this homely picture that quite suddenly and impulsively he embraced Mrs. Barclay and those of her grown daughters present, kissing each with unrestrained emotion. It was a remarkable outburst of feeling from the young monarch. Embarrassed by his own performance, George quickly drew Barclay to one side and spent the rest of their time together discussing religion.

At the opening of Parliament, a month after Pitt's resignation, the king's speech emphasized the resolve of the court party to pursue peace to a happy conclusion. But in Spain all was not well. The Earl of Bristol, in Madrid attempting to iron out Anglo-Spanish differences, was shocked by a Spanish proposal to seek the helpful arbitration of France—with whom England was still in a state of hostilities. This was followed by a request on Britain's part for information regarding the Family Compact. When the Spaniards refused to clarify the issue, Bristol was recalled to London and, on January 2, 1762, George was forced to admit that peace with Spain was no longer maintainable. Two days later, war was declared. It was a harsh blow to the peaceful dreams of the young king, and it became clear to those near him that he was deeply disturbed by the turn of events. His manner was distant, his countenance melancholy. After a time, so completely had he shut himself away from the country, secluded in one or another of the royal homes, that one poet compared him to an oriental monarch:

> *Our sons some slave of greatness may behold,*
> *Cast in the genuine Asiatic mould,*
> *Who of these realms shall condescend to know*
> *No more than he can spy from Windsor's brow.*

The war with Spain was a spendid vindication for Pitt; a distinct loss of face for Newcastle, now First Lord of the Treasury, and Bute, Secretary of State. Not only had Pitt's warning to the nation proved correct, but the English victories which followed in rapid sequence—the capture of Martinique, Granada, St. Lucia, St. Vincent, Havana and the Philippines—were justifiably attributed to the preparations he had taken while still directing operations. "Give me leave," wrote Bishop Warburton to Pitt in March, "to congratulate you on the success at Martinico. I do it with singular propriety; for it is the effect of an impulse (I hope not yet ceased) which your glorious administration had imparted to the whole political machine." Declared another ecstatically: "Do you think Demosthenes or Themistocles ever raised the Grecian stocks two per cent in four-and-twenty hours? I shall burn all my Greek and Latin books; they are histories of little people. The Romans never conquered the world till they had conquered three parts of it, and were three hundred years about it. We subdue the globe in three campaigns; and a globe, let me tell you, as big again as it was in their days." In Britain, Pitt was more popular than ever; on the Continent, his powers were regarded with awe.

In the meantime, Bute had become first minister in everything but name. The only obstacle which remained between him and the premiership was the aged Duke of Newcastle, who clung pathetically to office in the face of the most blatant hints and insults from George and his favorite. Newcastle, who for nearly half a century and in three reigns had held the highest offices of the state, deeply offended the ideals of the young king. George despised the old man as a jobbing, corrupting, unprincipled politician—all the things he wished to expurgate from government. He had lost no time in making his feelings known. As early as November 1760, Newcastle had written: "The King has been remarkably cold and ungracious, insomuch that I could hardly get one word, or the least mark of approbation, at my proposal of raising twelve millions for him." Again: "For myself, I am the greatest cypher that ever appeared at Court. The young King is hardly civil to me; talks to me of nothing, and scarce answers me upon my own Treasury affairs." Later, he told the Duke of Bedford that, with one exception, "I don't remember a single recommendation of mine which has taken place since his Majesty's accession to the Crown."

In April of 1762 the king wrote Bute of the tottering premier: "The more I know of this fellow the more I wish to see him out of employment . . . I flatter myself that will soon be the case." As, indeed, it was. For, next month, Newcastle at last accepted the inevitable and resigned. The king had recently created seven new peers without consulting him. It was an insult not even the aged Whig could bear. When he told George of his intention to retire, the king observed coolly: "Then, my Lord, I must fill your place as well as I can." No one was in any doubt as to how he would fill it. Bute, his ambition firmly in his grasp, did not pretend to commiserate with the fallen minister. "He never requested me to continue in office nor said a civil thing to me afterwards while we remained together," complained Newcastle. Nor did his fellow politicians, disinclined to risk their own necks, raise their voices to comfort him. "The Duke of Newcastle," observed a contemporary, "has spent half a million, and made the fortunes of five hundred men, and yet is not allowed to have one real friend."

Thus Bute became first minister, George Grenville, formerly treasurer of the Navy, succeeded to Bute's old post, while Sir Francis Dashwood, in a most extraordinary and inexplicable appointment, became Chancellor of the Exchequer. Of Dashwood, a notorious profligate who had been a friend of Frederick Louis, it was said that "a figure of five digits was an incomprehensible mystery" to him. One commentator described him as a vulgar fool "with the familiarity and phrase of a fishwife." Dashwood was at least under no misapprehensions. "People will point at me in streets and cry, 'There goes the worst Chancellor of the Exchequer who ever appeared,'" he said. "I think I am equally fit to be the head of the Church as of the Exchequer."

"The new Administration begins tempestuously," reported

Walpole. "My father was not more abused after twenty years than Bute after twenty days. Weekly papers swarm and, like other insects, sting." Particularly assailed was Bute's installation as a Knight of the Garter after four months of office. "All England, to hang him, would give him both garters," exclaimed one wit. "And, oh! how the rabble would laugh and would hoot, Could they once set a swinging this John Earl of Bute." Rhymed another:

O Bute! If, instead of contempt and of odium,
You wish to obtain universal eulogium,
From your breast to your gullet transfer the blue string,
Our hearts are all yours at the very first swing.

Cartoons depicting the intimacy of Bute and Augusta continued to proliferate, customarily displaying the former clad in a petticoat. Bute hit back through his own propagandists. "I am beset with a host of scribblers," he asserted, "and I must acknowledge that I can discern great talent in some of their productions . . . I am, however, by no means without literary talent on my side; most of our best authors are wholly devoted to me, and I have laid the foundation for gaining Robertson [historian William Robertson] by employing him for the King in writing the history of England; he must be pensioned." Tobias Smollett and Dr. Johnson were on Bute's payroll. But Boswell was indignant at any hint to Johnson's corruptibility:

"I have taken care to have it in my power to refute these malicious stories, from the most authentic information. Lord Bute told me that Mr Wedderburn, afterwards Lord Loughborough, was the person who first mentioned this subject to him. Lord Loughborough told me that the pension was granted to Johnson solely as the reward of his literary merit, without any stipulation whatever, or even tacit understanding, that he should write for the Administration. His Lordship added that he was confident the political tracts which Johnson afterwards did write, as they were entirely consonant with his own opinions, would have been written by him though no pension had been granted to him."

Bute came to power pledged to obtain peace for England, and started by having to declare war with Spain. Thanks to the disasters inflicted on the nation's enemies, however, it soon looked as though negotiating a peace with them might well be easier than steering it through the British Parliament. He was also committed to strengthen the royal prerogative and establish government on a less corrupt basis. That Bute was himself quickly forced to spend substantial sums to win support, and did not fail to feather his own nest, was perhaps less a reflection against his relative integrity than on the general mores of contemporary politics. "Bute made himself immediately Secretary of State, Knight of the Garter, and Privy Purse: he gave an English peerage to his wife, and the reversion of a very lucrative employment for life to his eldest son," recorded Chesterfield. "He placed and displaced whom he pleased; gave peerages without number and pensions without bounds; by those means he proposed to make his ground secure for the permanency of his power."

But money alone could not control the House of Commons —experienced management was needed. And now, with the Whigs retrenching behind Pitt to repulse peace proposals, Bute began to feel distinct pangs of inadequacy. He was "inexperienced," he admitted privately in September. "The weight and labour of his office," wrote a confidant, "were too much for him." Soon afterwards, he pored forth his heart to George Grenville. He had only accepted office, first as Secretary of State and later as premier, he maintained, under pressure from the king. He had quickly tired of the former post, he admitted, and was now weary of the latter. He would like to revert to private life, but so upset had been the king by this suggestion, that he had sat for hours, head on arm, without speaking a word. Those near to the king had begged him (Bute) to stay in office for the sake of the royal mind, and he could not, he was resolved, abandon the king to the mercy of the "Great Families" at this critical moment.

The burden of responsibility, plus the bitter antagonism of public opinion, had taken its toll of Bute. His nerves were in a bad state. Somehow, the court party had to achieve an effective majority, and the answer hit upon by the Scot was Henry Fox. Fox, beguiling, brilliant and ambivalent, distrusted as much by his fellow Whigs in the past as by the Tories, was the one man who could hold his own in debate with William Pitt. He was quick-witted, lucid and logical. According to a contemporary comparison of the two politicians, "Fox always spoke to the question, Pitt to the passions; Fox to carry the question, Pitt to raise himself; Fox pointed out, Pitt lashed the errors of his antagonists." More important, the round-faced, smiling Fox was as accomplished a schemer, as shrewd a manipulator of political forces, as the deposed Newcastle, and not averse, as Bute now discovered, to work for the king at a price. The price agreed was a peerage. "His Majesty," wrote Fox dryly, "was in great concern lest a good peace, in a good House of Commons, should be lost, and his authority disgraced for want of a proper person to support his honest measures and keep his closet from that force with which it was so threatened. *I was that person who could do it.*"

To George, the proposition was thoroughly abhorrent. Not only was the employment of Fox's cynical methods at variance with all his ideals for a "purified" Parliament, a negation of his satisfaction at Newcastle's departure, but his very nature was offended by Fox as a person. In this engaging, often scintillating, art-loving libertine—a man who had personally arranged the introduction of his much-loved sons to the fleshpots of Paris—George saw everything inimical to his own cloistered, moralizing propensities. To use Fox would be for the first time to compromise his ideals. Not to do so might be to see them vanquished by his enemies. For the young monarch, the dilemma was profoundly upsetting. At last, he admitted resignedly: "We must call in bad men to govern bad men."

Fox's behavior in his new role, though exaggerated by his enemies, was undoubtedly thorough. Ousting much of the Newcastle following, he proceeded to introduce fresh and trusty personnel to most branches of the government. According to Walpole, he approached individual members of the Commons "with so little decorum on the part of either buyer or seller, that a shop was publicly opened at the Pay Office, whither the members flocked, and received the wages of their venality in bank-bills, even so low a sum as two hundred pounds." The Secretary of the Treasury subsequently claimed that twenty-five thousand pounds was issued from the public exchequer on a single morning for persuasive purposes. In other instances, intimidation was employed. The Duke of Devonshire—the "Prince of Whigs" as Augusta dubbed him—was dismissed from the office of Lord Chamberlain with neither warning nor explanation. Returning from a brief visit to the country, he had called at the palace to pay his respects to the sovereign. "Tell him that I will not see him," the king ordered a page-in-waiting testily. "Go to him and tell him in those very words."

On December 9, the day of the peace debate in Parliament, a thick crowd gathered at Westminster, abusing Bute and Fox as they entered and waiting to demonstrate loyalty to Pitt. For some time, Pitt had been sick, and it was not certain that he would be able to attend. As the hour advanced, and he failed to appear, members of the court party in the House grew increasingly optimistic. Then a burst of cheering was heard in the distance, shouting and applause drew nearer to the chamber, the doors were thrown open, and a striking figure, supported by two attendants, stood in view of the assembly. Pitt was clad in black velvet, his face deathly pale. "He had the appearance," wrote an eyewitness, "of a man determined to die in that cause, and at that hour." Taking frequent drinks of cordial, Pitt addressed the House for three hours and forty minutes, speaking against a peace which, he claimed, would be inadequate, insecure and conducive to further threats from Spain and France. Then, exhausted, he was assisted from the House, not waiting to hear the next speech, by Fox. Pitt's appearance had been dramatic, but Fox had prepared the ground well and was confident. While the Great Commoner received the cheers of the London crowd, his opponent received the votes—three hundred and nineteen against a mere sixty-five.

The court was triumphant, the Whig grip on it shattered. "*Now* my son is King of England," crowed Augusta. A delighted George ordered a ball in honor of the victory, and Bute declared that he wished for no better epitaph than that of peacemaker. But the popularity he might have expected failed to materialize. To help defray the expenses of peace negotiations, a tax was placed on cider—supposedly because the incompetent Dashwood was unable to understand an alternative scheme to tax linens. It was received as a dastardly imposition on the poor, for whom cider was the cheapest of potent drinks. The mistake cost Bute yet more insults. One cartoonist had him flaying Britannia with thistles, another depicted the roads to London jammed with ragged Scotsmen, while a third pictured the king asleep in his mother's lap as Bute and Fox stole his scepter and wallet. Ran a popular epigram:

Say, when will England be from faction freed?
When will domestic quarrels cease?
Ne'er till that wished-for epitaph we read,
"Here lies the man that made the peace."

Weary of abuse, afraid for his own health, Bute decided to relinquish the burdens of office. "When you, Sir," he wrote Fox, "with a spirit and generosity that I can never forget, gave us your help to save this poor country in its extreme peril, honor, gratitude, duty and affection made my stay necessary; but now, thanks to kind providence, the vessel's safe in harbour." George proclaimed his dismay at his friend's news. "My D. Friend must not be surprised that the seeing him resolved to quit the scene of business is the most cruel political blow that could have happen'd to me." But he was not so disconsolate, some believed, as all that. The king had served his apprenticeship. He had been introduced to political realities. He had been freed from the Whig cabal, and had learned to make his wishes felt. He certainly did not share Bute's gratitude to Fox, as the following lines to his favorite establish:

I am ever hurt when my D. Friend and myself are in the least of different opinions, 'tis what I ever strive to prevent; but in the case of Mr Fox I fear we shall never think alike. I have one principle firmly rooted in my mind from the many seasonable lessons I have receiv'd from my D. Friend [namely] never to trust a man void of principles. If any man ever deserved that character 'tis Mr Fox; the seeing him at the head of the House of Commons was very unpleasant to me: but I consented to it as that was the only means of getting my D. Friend to proceed this winter in the Treasury; if he resolves to quit that situation the only consideration that could make me bear Mr Fox is vanished . . . 'tis not prejudice but aversion for his whole mode of government that causes my writing so openly my thoughts to my only friend; has this whole winter been anything else but a scene of corruption? and I am persuaded were he [Fox] the acting Minister this would appear in more ways than he is now able to accomplish; for my D. Friend's heart is too upright and his principles too well grounded to approve of this; they are the true sources of his dislike to his present employment, which has given him too many proofs of the baseness of the present age.

In April 1763, following the Treaty of Paris, Bute resigned, quickly followed by Fox, who duly claimed his peerage. As George grew more knowing, his understanding more complex, so mounted his obstinacy. The king faced the future determined to redeem the royal heritage, to force his personal will on the government.

CHAPTER 10

Country Gentlefolks

Queen Charlotte's first child was born on August 12, 1762. By the afternoon, she was in labor, and, at twenty-four minutes past seven that evening, she was delivered. "The Queen scarce cried out at all," wrote Lady Northumberland, who was present. The excited messenger who brought the news to George, told the king he had a daughter. But when George reached the bedchamber, he discovered not an infant girl but "a strong, large, pretty boy." The pretty boy, christened George Augustus Frederick, was to prove a gift of the devil to his father. Before long, Bishop Richard Hurd, the prince's tutor, would see fit to prophesy that his young charge would be "either the most polished gentleman or the most accomplished blackguard in Europe—possibly both." The youth's scandalous and dissipated career began, in fact, well before he became of age, representing a regression with a vengeance to the style of his profligate ancestors. There was some excuse for his wayward behavior. In an age of great liveliness and adventure, of compellingly extrovert enthusiasms, the fearfully dull and parsimonious life of his parents could hardly have failed to produce a youthful reaction.

Life beyond the court was full of zest and temptation.

Rich men devoted fortunes to drinking, gambling and women. Intellectually, the scene was stimulating and alive. At one end of the smart scale, a man might belong to the Hell Fire Club, renowned for its orgiastic vulgarity; at the other, to the Dilettanti, famed for the knowledge of its members and their good taste. Out of doors, the ubiquitous sportsman did nothing by halves. Cricket and horse racing were the fashionable interests; the former, spreading from the Weald of Kent in the sixties, becoming almost as popular a field for financial speculation as the older sport. Enthusiasts such as Sir Horace Mann of Canterbury thought nothing of backing a cricket team to win at £1,000 a game. Soame Jenyns, the poet and moralist, bemoaned that England's "well bred heirs" were "Gamesters and Jockeys turned, and cricket players." They also played the tables with zestful abandon. Fox's son Charles ran up gaming debts of £100,000. But the spirit of the age was not always so fatuous. The same lust for excitement and action was prompting men such as James Cook to gamble their lives in ocean exploration; James Watt to pit his brain against the problem of harnessing steam. All over Europe, there was mounting scientific activity. Prince George Augustus would grow up at a time when Joseph Priestley contrived to isolate oxygen, Karl Scheele discovered chlorine, when Torbern Bergman riveted Uppsala with his treatise on carbon dioxide and carbonic acid. Others explored the heavens or dined out on talk of the latest play or the stirring new world of British art. Society was stamped with gusto and expectation.

By contrast, the court was incredibly dreary and insular. The queen's first party after her son's birth was described as a "gingerbread affair" to which a mere dozen or so couples were invited, and they were not given supper. Observers wrote of the "recluse life" led by the royal pair, carried to "an excess of privacy and economy." The palace drawing rooms, it was reported, were abandoned. "Lady Buckingham was the only woman there on Sunday . . . In short, one hears of nothing but dissatisfaction, which, in the city, rises almost to treason." Fox noted the general feeling. "A young, civil, virtuous, good-natured King might naturally be expected to have such a degree of popularity as should for years defend the most exceptional Favourite," he declared, yet "his Majesty from the very beginning was not popular."

For all his virtues, George lacked the "common touch," that ability to get across to his fellow mortals which could have worked wonders for his personality. He was well meaning but out of sympathy with the age. In childhood, he had shown a precocious feeling for religion, learning by heart, it was said, several pages of Doddridge's *Principles of the Christian Religion* before he was six. Most days of his life, he spent an hour reading the Scriptures. He once reinstated a palace under-gardener who had been dismissed as a religious crank. "Why should he be turned away?" George exclaimed. "Call me Defender of the Faith and turn away a man from his religion!" Though prejudiced against Roman Catholicism, he had an enduringly soft spot for Nonconformists. "The Methodists are a quiet good kind of people and will disturb nobody. If I can learn that any persons in my employment disturb them, they shall be immediately dismissed."

The puritanical side of the king's nature was vividly exemplified in a letter he wrote to Archbishop Cornwallis after hearing that the prelate's wife had held a ball. "I could not help giving you this notification of the grief and concern with which my breast was affected at receiving an authentic information that routs have made their way into your palace. . . . I must signify to you my sentiments on this subject, which hold these levities and vain dissipations as utterly inexpedient, if not unlawful, to pass in a residence for many centuries devoted to Divine studies, religious retirement, and the extensive exercise of charity and benevolence—I add, in a place where so many of your predecessors have led their lives in such sanctity as has thrown lustre upon the pure religion they professed and adorned. From the dissatisfaction with which you must perceive I behold these improprieties, not to speak in harsher terms, and still more pious principles, I trust you will suppress them immediately; so that I may not have occasion to show any further marks of displeasure, or to interpose in a different manner. May God take your grace into his Almighty protection."

When Dr. Thomas Wilson, Prebendary of Westminster, sought to ingratiate himself with the king by delivering a sermon flattering the monarch, George rebuked him: "I go to church to hear God praised and not myself."

To society in general, shortly after his accession, he addressed a somewhat garbled but revealing proclamation:

> We most seriously and religiously considering that it is an indispensable duty on us to be careful above all things to preserve and advance the honour and service of Almighty God, and to discourage and suppress all vice, profaneness, debauchery and immorality, which are so highly displeasing to God, so great a reproach to our religion and government, and (by means of the frequent ill examples of the practices thereof) have so fatal a tendency to the corruption of many of our loving subjects, otherwise religiously and virtuously disposed, and which (if not timely remedied) may justly draw down the Divine vengeance on us and our kingdoms— we also humbly acknowledging that we cannot expect the blessing and goodness of Almighty God (by Whom king's reign and on which we entirely rely) to make our reign happy and prosperous to ourselves and to our people, without a religious observance of God's holy laws—to the intent

thereof that religion, piety, and good manners may (according to our most hearty desire) flourish and increase under our administration and government, we have thought fit, by the advice of our Privy Council, to issue this our royal proclamation, and do hereby declare our royal purpose and resolution to discountenance and punish all manner of vice, profaneness and immorality in all persons of whatsoever degree and quality within this our realm, and particularly in such as are employed near our royal person; and that, for the encouragement of religion and morality, we will, upon all occasions, distinguish persons of piety and virtue by marks of our royal favour.

And we do expect and require that all persons of honour, or in place of authority, will give good example of their own virtue and piety, and to their utmost contribute to the discountenancing persons of dissolute and debauched lives, that they, being reduced by that means to shame and contempt for their loose and evil actions and behavior, may be therefore also enforced the sooner to reform their ill habits and practices, and that the visible displeasure of good men towards them may (as far as it is possible) supply what the laws (probably) cannot altogether prevent.

It was the cry, even down to the hint of pessimism in the last of its tortuous lines, of one who loved humanity in the abstract, but found it harder to accept in reality. "We must walk about for two or three days to please these good people," George told Charlotte at the beginning of a seaside holiday, "and then we may walk about to please ourselves." People and pleasure were often at odds in the king's world. On the whole, he did not delight in company, and his subjects knew it. Perhaps, in part, this was due to a naturally nervous and awkward manner which, in public, was overcome by undue self-consciousness: what was once termed his "putting on the King." In private, he talked extremely rapidly, punctuating his speech with spasms of "What? What? What?" and seldom staying still for very long. Sir Nathaniel Wraxall, a diligent recorder of events and personalities, talked of "the oscillations of his body, the precipitations of his questions, none of which, it was said, would wait for an answer, and the hurry of his articulation." Observed Johnson: "His Majesty is multifarious in his questions, but thank God he answers them all himself."

George could display a brusqueness, a lack of tact and grace, which probably derived from the same lack of confidence. Thus, to a Yorkshireman at a levee:

"I suppose you are going back to Yorkshire, Mr Stanhope? A very ugly county, Yorkshire."

"Sir, we always consider Yorkshire a picturesque county."

"What? What? What? A coal-pit a picturesque object! What? What? What? Yorkshire coal-pits picturesque! Yorkshire a picturesque county! What? What? What?"

On occasions, he could certainly seem cruel to subordinates. Shortly after he decided to transfer the mastership of his staghounds from Lord Bateman to the Marquis of Carnarvon, Bateman, who knew nothing of the decision, called to ask when the king wished the hounds to be turned out. "My Lord, I cannot exactly answer that," said George swiftly, "but I can inform you that your Lordship was turned out an hour ago." Yet the king was far from an unfeeling man. His rudeness seems largely to have been an expression of embarrassment. There was about him a poverty of imagination, an inability to unbend, which often rendered his deeper compassion inarticulate. He did not know when to relax in the presence of subordinates, or how generously to waive the formalities of court etiquette. Once, when Pitt was suffering from gout, the king kept him standing for two hours without inviting him to sit down.

Another time, Mrs. Siddons, summoned to read a play at

the palace, was kept on her feet until she almost collapsed from fatigue. As one commentator put it:

La! Mrs Siddons is quite faint indeed,
How pale! I'm sure she cannot read:
She somewhat wants her spirits to repair,
And would, I'm sure, be happy in a chair.

This unbending attitude rubbed off on Charlotte, who, asked at one time if Lady Townshend, then pregnant, might sit in her presence, answered primly: "She may stand—she may stand." The Duchess of Ancaster, a most resourceful woman, went so far as to marshal a line of troops in front of her so that she could rest unseen on a bench at another royal occasion. Fanny Burney, writing to her mother, cast a wry sidelight on the behavior expected at court by the king and queen:

In the first place you must not cough. If you find a tickling in your throat, you must arrest it from making any sound; if you find yourself choking with the forebearance, you must choke—but not cough. In the second place, you must not sneeze. If you have a vehement cold, you must take no notice of it; if your nose-membranes feel a great irritation, you must hold your breath; if a sneeze still insists upon making its way you must oppose it by keeping your teeth grinding together; if the violence of the repulse breaks some blood-vessel, you must break the blood-vessel, but not sneeze.

In the third place, you must not, upon any account, stir either hand or foot. If, by chance, a hat pin runs into your head, you must not take it out. If the pain is very great, you must be sure to bear it without wincing; if it brings tears to your eyes, you must not wipe them off; if they give you a tingling by running down your cheeks, you must look as if nothing was the matter. If your blood should gush from your head by means of the pin, you must let it gush; if you are uneasy to think of making such a blurred appearance, you must be uneasy, but you must say nothing about it. If, however, the agony is very great, you may, privately, bite the inside of your cheek, or of your lips, for a little relief; taking care, meanwhile, to do it as cautiously as to make no apparent dent outwardly. And with that precaution, if you even gnaw a piece out, if will not be minded, only be sure either to swallow it, or commit it to a corner of the inside of your mouth till they are gone—for you must not spit.

The most publicized of George's foibles was his parsimony. Cartoonists depicted the royal couple preparing their own meals in the kitchens from the most frugal ingredients, or working on the royal farm to save their money. One drawing by Isaac Cruikshank pictured George churning butter in the dairy while Charlotte counted the takings brought home by the market maid. "Good Heavens!" exclaimed Cruikshank's horrified queen, "is it possible the people can be so unreasonable these plentiful times to expect six eggs for a groat! You shall tramp to London next market day!" George's meanness very likely had its origins in his father's financial recklessness. Frederick had often been desperate for money, and the fact cannot wholly have escaped his children. George, in his own philosophy, liked to compare himself with the simple, honest peasant.

"What do they pay you?" he inquired of a stable boy at Windsor.

"Nothing but food and clothes," groused the youngster.

"Be content," said the king, "I have no more."

Raised in a royal vacuum, George had little idea how the rest of the world lived. In his mind, a kind word from the sovereign, a mark of royal approval, was a more desirable reward to his subjects than silver. Mrs. Siddons, who was appointed preceptress in English reading to the royal daughters when they arrived and grew to school age, was not paid a salary. Nor was she remunerated for the many readings and recitations she gave at court. She came out of the palace, it was said, "as rich as she went in." Thomas Lawrence, the painter, fared no better when summoned as a young man to paint a portrait of the queen. "No money was paid," reported a member of Charlotte's staff. "The King told him to remove it to town and have it engraved. When that was done, the portrait was to be sent to Hanover, and then the King proposed to pay. But Lawrence had no money, and could not risk the engraving at his own expense." The picture remained in his studio, and was not sold until after the artist's death. When the Empress of Russia asked for a portrait of the British monarch by the fashionable and expensive Joshua Reynolds, George sent her a likeness by a less expensive artist.

So determined was George that his farming hobby should pay its way, that satirist John Wolcot, alias Peter Pindar, wrote sardonically:

> Of Kings who cabbages and carrots plant
> For such as wholesome vegetables want;
> Who feed, too, poultry for the people's sake,
> Then send it through the villages in carts,
> To cheer (how wondrous kind!) the hungry hearts
> Of such as only pay for what they take.

A perhaps apocryphal, but nevertheless characteristic, anecdote involving a workman who was surprised to be tipped twice as handsomely by the king's son as by the king himself, related how George explained solemnly: "You should consider I have a large family to provide for; he is but a single man, and has nobody to provide for but himself." Lord Carlisle recalled that the king once "stopped all

the hunt to give an old man something for opening a gate at
Bray Wick: after a long search for his purse he produced
a penny from it and bestowed it on the man. He gave a
fête in the Castle to all the Eton schoolboys. It consisted
of a very long concert of sacred music with nothing to
eat or drink."

Another aspect of George's character which aroused comment was his dull taste. Like many well-meaning men of
puritan concepts, the king was disturbed by real talent, preferring a homely and modest mediocrity. Though he supported the foundation of the Royal Academy, he liked the
painting of Benjamin West better than that of Reynolds. He
collected an extensive library, but was more taken, it was
said, by the bindings of the books than by their contents. He
patronized the theater, yet considered Shakespeare "sad
stuff" and, on disapproving a passage in a play, could instruct Charlotte, "Don't look, it's too much."

In music, he found pleasure and solace, but his choice
was limited and those around him complained of the lack of
variety in his concert programs. Of outstanding men in
many fields he held a deeply felt suspicion. For politicians
such as Pitt and Fox, the king displayed an aversion beyond
reasonable proportions; he said Sheridan should be hanged;
he could not bear to look at the drawings of Blake, and, on
one occasion, he contradicted Sir John Pringle, President
of the Royal Society, on a scientific matter of which the
king knew nothing. Conversely, he could be happy with
relative nonentities. Declared one satirist maliciously:

> To circles of pure ignorance conduct me;
> I hate the company that can instruct me;
> I wish to imitate my King, so nice,
> Great Prince who ne'er was known to take advice!
> Who keeps no company (delightful plan!)
> That dares be wiser than himself, good man!

Charlotte might well have developed, in different circumstances, a taste for greater stimulation and brilliance. The possibility, however, was overwhelmed, both by the initial dominance of Augusta and by the nature of George himself, almost from the moment of her marriage. "Soon after," wrote a contemporary, "Buckingham House was purchased, and bestowed on her Majesty, St James's not seeming a prison strict enough."

Asserted another: "Except for the Ladies of the Bedchamber for half-an-hour a week in a funereal circle, or a cermonious drawing-room, she never had a soul to speak to but the King. This continued till her first child, the Prince of Wales, was born; then the nurse and governess, Lady Charlotte Finch, coming into the room was a little treat; but they had still for years no other society, till by degrees the Ladies of the Bedchamber came far more frequently, and latterly the society, for various reasons—the children growing up, the journeys, etc.—was much increased. Expecting to be Queen of a gay Court, finding herself confined in a convent, and hardly allowed to think without leave of her husband, checked her spirits, made her fearful and cautious in the extreme, and when the time came that amusements were allowed, her mind was formed in a different manner of life."

In retrospect, Charlotte took it in good part. "I am most truly sensible to the dear King's great strictness at my arrival in England," she maintained, "to prevent my making many acquaintances; for he was always used to say that, in this country, it was difficult to know how to draw a line on account of the politics of the country and that there never could be kept up a society without party, which was always dangerous for any woman to take part in, but particularly so for the royal family; and with truth do I assure you that I am not only sensible that he was right, but I feel thankful for it from the bottom of my heart."

Royal life was at its most relaxed in the rustic setting of Kew Palace, where formalities were kept to a minimum.

"There is no form of ceremony here of any sort," wrote Fanny Burney. "Her [the queen's] dress is plain, and the hour for the second toilette extremely uncertain. The royal family are here always in so very retired a way, that they live as the simplest country gentlefolks. The King has not even an equerry with him, nor the Queen any lady to attend her when she goes her airings." Under such circumstances, George was at his happiest. The marriage was not a discontented one. Miss Burney described a typically warm scene when the queen playfully tried to kiss the king's hand. "He would not let her, but made an effort, with a countenance of the highest satisfaction, to kiss her. I saw instantly in her eyes a forgetfulness at the moment that anyone was present, while drawing away her hand, she presented him her cheek. He accepted her kindness with the same frank affection that she offered it . . . I could not but see with pleasure that the Queen had received some favour with which she was sensibly delighted, and that the King, in her acknowledgments, was happily and amply paid."

Meanwhile, as their firstborn squalled in the royal cot, fresh storm clouds rumbled outside the palaces.

Part II

THE TIDES OF REALITY

CHAPTER 11

Wilkes and Liberty

On the evening of Saturday, April 9, 1763, the day after
George Grenville succeeded Bute as first minister, James
Boswell amused himself by strutting beneath the windows
of the rooms of his first London mistress, in Southampton
Street, off the Strand. Later, he went to the park, where
he "performed concubinage with a strong, plump, good-
humoured girl called Nanny Baker. I then went to Drury
Lane gallery and saw the entertainment of *Thomas and
Sally*, in which Mrs Love appeared for the first time, with
pretty good applause." After the play, he met some friends
at the Piazza coffeehouse, "where we had some negus and
solaced our existences."

It was a fairly conventional night for Boswell and the
bloods, but scarcely one the king's new minister would have
approved. Grenville was, and looked, a hard-boiled lawyer;
not unhandsome, but somehow impassive and cold. While
the contemporaries of his youth had gathered at White's,
the Cocoa Tree or Newmarket, Grenville had applied himself single-mindedly to work in the dismal chambers of one
of the Inns of Court. It had given him a good grounding for
his professional life, but had left him suspicious, dogmatic,
lacking in human warmth. He was a wearisome talker and

a poor listener. Moreover, it was said to be impossible to
convince him that he was wrong. His views were expressed
clinically, without embroidery or eloquence; he was minutely
versed in the business of the state, with which he could
deal from dawn to dusk without tiring; like the king, he
was obsessed with the virtues of economy, and he seemed to
have few enthusiasms outside the House of Commons. Once,
when he fainted at work and M.P.s called for smelling
salts, a wit exclaimed: "Why don't you let him sniff the
journals?"

Grenville's personal conduct was unimpeachable and he
was held a devout man. "Mr Grenville," declared Bishop
Newton, "was not only an able Minister, but was likewise
a religious good man, and regularly attended the Service
of the Church every Sunday morning, even when he was in
the highest offices." In many ways, he seemed suited to serve
the demanding George. As one historian has pointed out:
"His official connection with Bute, his separation from the
great Whig families, his unblemished private character,
his eminent business faculties, his industry, his methodical
habits, his economy, his freedom alike from the fire and
vagaries of genius, his contempt for popularity, were all
points of affinity." And in no single way were George and
Grenville more in unison than in their aversion for one man,
the incorrigible John Wilkes, who now buzzed about them
like a hungry horsefly around two fastidious thoroughbreds.

Wilkes was in his thirties when he attained the height
of his fame as editor of the *North Briton,* a journal vehement
in its attacks on the court party. Facially, he was ugly to the
point of fascination, with squint eyes, poor teeth and a
boxer's nose, but his personality was sharp and engaging.
"He was a delightful and instructive companion," testified
a friend, "but too often offensive in his freedom of speech
when religion or sex was mentioned. In his manner and
habits, he was an elegant epicurean." So relentless was

Wilkes's wit, according to the same authority, that wagers were laid on the number of people who would laugh at his comments during the walk from his house in Great George Street to the Guildhall. Declared Edward Gibbon, the historian: "I scarcely ever met with a better companion. He has inexhaustible spirits, infinite wit and humour, and a great deal of knowledge. He told us himself that in this time of public dissension he was resolved to make his fortune."

Wilkes had already gone through one fortune. Born the son of a Clerkenwell distiller and educated by strict Presbyterian tutors, he had married a wealthy woman ten years his senior and rapidly squandered her money on pleasure. From an early age he had pursued what an acquaintance termed a "debauched" life. He drank a lot. After one party, he consumed a bottle of claret in bed. "In private society," wrote Wraxall, "Wilkes was pre-eminently agreeable, abounding in anecdote, ever gay and convivial, converting his very defects of person, manner and enunciation to purposes of merriment and entertainment. If any man ever was pleasing who squinted, who had lost his teeth and lisped, Wilkes might be so esteemed." He belonged to the notorious Hell Fire Club, organized by the easy-going Sir Francis Dashwood, which held secret meetings at Medmenham Abbey, near Marlow, to celebrate the pleasures of Bacchus and Venus in a style Rabelaisian enough to scandalize even the fast-living society of the day. Other members of the club included Lord Sandwich, Charles Churchill, poet friend of the high-living journalist, and Thomas Potter, son of an Archbishop of Canterbury. At Medmenham, bizarre humor and carnal appetites mingled in colorful rituals. At one meeting, Communion was administered to an ape.

Having exhausted the assets of his long-suffering spouse, Wilkes turned to Parliament, becoming an M.P. in 1757, and seeking profit as a political journalist. His hallmark was wit and acrimony; his stock-in-trade, patriotism—"The last refuge," as Johnson described it, "of a scoundrel." His publication, the *North Briton,* to which he and Charles Churchill were the principal contributors, was so audacious that it quickly overwhelmed its competitors. It was said that two Bute-sponsored papers died of the sheer fright of it. Other publications might timidly hint at celebrities by their initials —Wilkes published names in full, reveling in scandal and personalities. Bute and Augusta were particularly held up as targets. Rebuked by their defenders, Wilkes talked righteously of free speech and "the liberty of the subject." George was appalled by such insolence. When the forty-fifth edition of the *North Briton* directly attacked the king's speech following the appointment of Grenville—a speech dealing, among other things, with the peace and the cider tax—both George and Grenville decided they had had enough.

"Every friend of his country," the *North Briton* had blared, "must lament that a prince of so many great and admirable qualities, whom England truly reveres, can be brought to give the sanction of his sacred name to the most odious measures and to the most unjustifiable declarations from a throne renowned for truth, honour and unsullied virtue." George was mollified neither by Wilkes's note of patronization, nor by the fact that Number 45 clearly stated that "the King's Speech has always been considered by the legislature, and by the public at large, as the Speech of the Minister." The sovereign considered himself nobody's mouthpiece. Grenville, on the other hand, was incensed at the emphasis on his own responsibility for the "odious" and the "unjustifiable."

A less inflexible and arbitrary man might have dealt with the problem tactfully. It was certain that Wilkes had his price. He had actually intimated to Bute on one occasion that an appointment to the government of Canada would render him a loyal servant of the Crown. But Grenville was a lawyer, and, now invoking the full weight of the law against the editor, he mistakenly wielded a sledgehammer at a small, if pestiferous, political insect. His action was rendered the more ridiculous by lack of evidence that Wilkes was the actual perpetrator of the offensive item—or, indeed, of any of the writings in the journal—for nothing in the *North Briton* was signed. Furthermore, as a member of the House of Commons, Wilkes could claim certain priviliges of expression. Still, it was resolved to proceed against him on a charge of treason, and Lord Halifax, one of the Secretaries of State, was ordered to take the necessary action. With George and Grenville panting at his shoulder, Halifax panicked. Instead of a specific warrant of arrest, he issued a general warrant authorizing his agents to apprehend any number of suspected persons and their papers without specifying names or the crimes with which they were charged. Such a process was not only illegal, but, in the words of one peer, "a daring public attack on the liberty of the subject and in violation of the 29th Chapter of Magna Carta."

On the night of April 29, Wilkes's house in Great George Street was rudely entered by three messengers from the Secretary of State's office, who began to seize his papers. At the same time, Halifax's agents swooped and arrested no fewer than forty-nine people allegedly connected with the *North Briton*. Wilkes was not, at this moment, among them. Next morning, he was approached in the street outside his home by a messenger who showed him a general warrant of arrest, declaring that he had instructions to apprehend the journalist. Wilkes invited the man to enter his house and talk the matter over. If there was to be any attempt to take him in the street, he warned, he would not be responsible for the messenger's safety. Inside, Wilkes asserted that the warrant was without validity, "a ridiculous warrant against the whole English nation." It might just as well be served, he exclaimed, on Halifax himself, Lord Bute, or his next-door neighbor. The messenger listened patiently. "I am to arrest Mr. Wilkes," he insisted.

There followed an impasse. More officials arrived, demanding that Wilkes accompany them to Lord Halifax. When the boss-eyed editor declined to co-operate, the government switched tactics, Halifax sending a number of diplomatic invitations that Wilkes should drop by and see him. Wilkes replied politely that the honor was somewhat diminished by the "rude and ungentlemanlike" method of its original delivery. At this stage, his colleague on the *North Briton*, Charles Churchill, walked into the room. Realizing that Churchill would be arrested if the messengers recognized him, Wilkes observed glibly: "Good morning, Mr Thomson. How is Mrs Thomson today? Does she dine in the *country?*" Churchill took the hint, excused himself on the grounds that his wife awaited him, and promptly fled from London to safety. Next, a constable arrived to remove Wilkes by force. Wilkes responded by demanding that the entire Halifax posse should leave at once: "I know and shall support the rights of an Englishman in the sanctuary of his own house." The constable retorted that a regiment of guards would be sent to effect the arrest if necessary. At last, Wilkes yielded his sword and prepared to meet Halifax.

On the afternoon of the thirtieth, George wrote of the examination of the prisoners that both the publisher and printer of the *North Briton* declared Wilkes and Churchill the sole authors of the paper, and that Number 45 had been written in Wilkes's hand. If so, the imperturbable Wilkes was unabashed. Face to face with Halifax, he proclaimed his loyalty to the king but added coolly that His Majesty was ill served by insolent and despotic ministers. "Your lordship," he told the earl, "is very ready to issue orders which you have neither the courage to sign, nor, I believe, to justify." Halifax ordered Wilkes to be confined in the Tower of London "until he shall be delivered by due course of law."

At the same time, the editor's house was thoroughly ransacked by Crown agents for incriminating evidence, which failed to materialize. On May 6, under a writ of *habeas corpus* obtained by his friends, Wilkes appeared before the Court of the King's Bench, where his counsel applied for a discharge on the ground that the commitment was invalid. To the fury of George and Grenville, the judge, Sir Charles Pratt, found in favor of the prisoner, declaring that general warrants were illegal and that the charge was insufficient to overrule Wilkes's privileges as a member of Parliament. The crowd gathered outside the court received the verdict with a roar of exultation that was to echo through the country. To many, it seemed that the press had taken over the duty abused by Parliament of representing the people. Wilkes had become a symbol of popular freedom; the affair a grave embarrassment to court and government. George was horrified. The mood of street patriotism engendered was anathema to the king. The fault must be rectified, he ordered, or the mob would be governing *him* next.

At the end of the summer, Grenville reopened his campaign against Wilkes and the press. Fortuitously for the minister, Wilkes and his fellow Hell Fire member Thomas Potter had composed an indiscreet parody of Pope's *Essay on Man* entitled *Essay on Woman*. Whereas Pope had inscribed his poem to Lord Bolingbroke, commencing the dedication "Awake, my St John!" the Wilkes version was inscribed to Fanny Murray, a fashionable courtesan, and began "Awake, my Fanny!" It also parodied Bishop Warburton's commentaries on the original with a series of blasphemous observations professing to be from the pen of the prelate. According to an outraged contemporary who was familiar with the text: "The natural abilities of the ass are made the subject of an unclean description . . . The sense of Pope's Universal Prayer is perverted to serve the vilest purpose of unchastity . . . Next follows an inimitably profane paraphrase of Veni Creator, which he ludicrously affects to call the *Maid's Prayer*. The Blessed Spirit of God is ludicrously insulted by a repetition of the grossest obscenity . . ." etc.

Grenville proceeded methodically. His first objective was to obtain a copy of the parody. This raised a difficulty, for Wilkes had restricted the circulation of the offending piece to some twelve or thirteen copies, most of them distributed among members of the Hell Fire Club. It transpired, however, that a copy of the poem had been kept by one of the printers. The printer was eventually bribed by a certain John Kidgell, chaplain to the Earl of March, to part with it. Kidgell promptly placed it in the hands of the Solicitor of the Treasury.

On November 15, the Earl of Sandwich rose on behalf of the government and slapped the *Essay on Woman* on the table of the House of Lords. The choice of Sandwich as government spokesman was a shrewd one, for his own association with the Hell Fire Club was well known. If Sandwich professed shock at the publication, the House might be expected to infer, it must be a matter of utmost gravity. In fact, Sandwich was nursing a grudge against Wilkes arising from an extravagant drinking session. In a drunken stupor, his lordship had invoked the devil, whereupon Wilkes, with a flash of mischief, had released a pet monkey at the bemused earl, almost frightening him out of his wits. Sandwich now inveighed at length against the poem, reading some of its most offensive passages, and denouncing it as a highly blasphemous, obscene and "abominable libel." It was the first time, commented another Hell Fire member, that he had ever heard the devil preach.

One consequence was that the edge between Wilkes and Sandwich became razor-sharp. Soon afterwards, they bumped into each other at a drinking club. Sandwich is reputed to have asked sneeringly whether Wilkes expected his career to be ended by the pox or the hangman's noose, to which the journalist made his celebrated riposte: "My Lord, that might depend upon whether I embraced your lordship's mistress or your principles." Public opinion against Sandwich was violent. When, at a Covent Garden performance of *The Beggar's Opera,* Macheath exclaimed, "That Jemmy Twitcher should peach me I own surprised me. 'Tis proof that the world is all alike, and that even our gang can no more trust each other than other people," there were shouts from the audience of "Sandwich! Sandwich!" For the rest of his life he was known as Jemmy Twitcher.

For the moment, however, a large body of peers was genuinely offended by Wilkes's lines, and their disgust was plain in the House of Lords. Bishop Warburton displayed his anger in a most irreverent manner. Purple with rage, he ranted that the blackest fiends in hell would not keep company with the author, adding that he begged the pardon of Satan for linking their names together. When the outcry subdued, the Lords voted the *Essay* a "scandalous, obscene and impious libel," found the author guilty of a breach of privilege against the bishop and presented an address to the king demanding Wilkes's prosecution for blasphemy. In the House of Commons, a further attack on Wilkes was to take place.

In an earlier edition of the *North Briton,* a certain Samuel Martin, M.P. for Camelford and a former Secretary of the Treasury under Bute, had been described as a "low fellow and dirty tool of power." When Parliament reassembled, he jumped to his feet bristling with rage, appraised the House of the insult, and denounced Wilkes as a cowardly and malignant scoundrel. In an exchange of letters afterwards, Wilkes admitted his authorship of the attack on Martin, while the latter demanded to meet Wilkes at pistol point in Hyde Park.

Wilkes was in an unenviable position. On the one hand, it was not unknown that Martin had been occupying himself in the country with some assiduous target practice with his pistols. On the other, should the writer by luck out-shoot his opponent, he could expect little mercy from the government. In order to be prepared for a hasty flight, Wilkes drove to Hyde Park in a post chaise. For all Martin's practice, his first shot went wide. Wilkes's pistol misfired. He was on the point of attempting his second shot when Martin winged him, causing his weapon to drop from his hand and a wound to open in his side. Having assured Martin that he would not betray him to the authorities, Wilkes was carried home and confined indoors as an invalid.

His future looked ominous. Despite a petition that no further steps should be taken against him before his recovery, Grenville and the king had scented blood and were preparing to close on their victim. Wilkes did not wait for them. During the Christmas recess, he slipped out of the country to France, from where, in due course, he sent a doctor's certificate claiming that he was unable to return to England without endangering his health. In Paris, Madame de Pompadour is supposed to have asked him how far a writer in England could with impunity abuse the royal family. "Madam," he replied, "that is exactly what I am trying to find out." There was not long to wait. On January 19, 1764, he was expelled from the House of Commons for scandalous and seditious libel, and, on February 21, the Court of the King's Bench found him guilty of seditious libel and blasphemy for having reprinted Number

45 and for printing the *Essay on Woman*. Having failed to appear before court, he was outlawed for contumacy.

At last rid of the object of his abhorrence, George wreaked vengeance on those who had failed to uphold his view of the journalist. "Firmness and resolution must now be shown, and no one's friend saved," he wrote Grenville in February. "Those who have deserted may feel that I am not to be neglected unpunished." One Wilkes sympathizer, Temple, was struck from the list of Privy Councillors. Another, General Henry Conway, was removed from his office of groom of the bedchamber and from command of his regiment. Other officers and government officials who had wavered in their loyalty were dismissed. Yet Wilkes *in absentia* proved as potent a symbol to many as Wilkes present—perhaps more so, for it was now easier to forget his excesses and remember his connotation with freedom and unbridled comment. Lord Chesterfield described him as "an intrepid defender of our rights and liberties." Another wrote of the "sons of Wilkes and Liberty, who hate despotic sway," upholding Wilkes as "an injured martyr" to the cause of personal freedom.

Lord Temple paid most of Wilkes's legal expenses, and, subsequently, the Rockingham Whigs made him an allowance of £1,000 a year. To the masses, he was a hero—those who opposed him, villainous. When Number 45 of the *North Briton* was ordered to be burned at the Royal Exchange by the public hangman, a huge crowd gathered at the venue chanting "Wilkes and liberty!" The law officers at the scene were put to flight, a window of the sheriff's coach was smashed and the sheriff burned on the face by a flaming brand. Singed pages of the journal were seized from the hangman and waved aloft in triumph, while, in their lieu, a jackboot and petticoat were hurled into the flames amid roars of approval from the multitude. Later, when a printer named Williams was placed in the pillory in Old Palace

Yard for daring to republish the *North Briton,* the crowd collected £200 for his benefit and escorted him boisterously away in a hackney coach bearing the numerals 45.

Well-known supporters of Wilkes gained public approbation. Chief Justice Pratt, who had found in favor of the editor at the first court hearing, was granted the freedom of the cities of London, Dublin, Bath, Exeter and Norwich, and honored by having his portrait by Reynolds hung in the Guildhall above the inscription, "in honour of so eminent a man, the assertor by the law of English liberty." Tradesmen cashed in on Wilkes's popularity by marking their goods 45. The king, by contrast, plunged to new depths in public disfavor. On one occasion, a placard was hurled into his coach bearing the words: "If you do not keep the laws, the laws will not keep you. Kings have lost their heads for their disobedience to the laws." For years, the mention of the name Wilkes brought anguish and gloom to George.

Once, to his horror, when he had punished the young Prince of Wales for unseemly behavior, the boy turned on him and screeched:

"Wilkes and Number 45 forever!"

CHAPTER 12

The King's First Illness

For a while, the attributes George and Grenville shared had made for a harmonious relationship, but, as Grenville gained confidence, their very similarities led to new tensions. Tactless, stubborn and overbearing in his own right, the king soon recognized the same qualities in his first minister and resented them. "When I have anything proposed to me, it is no longer as counsel, but what I am to obey," he sulked after long sessions with Grenville. "When he has wearied me for two hours, he looks at his watch to see if he may not tire me for an hour more." Grenville particularly upset George by refusing to buy for the Crown a plot of land overlooking Green Park, where the royal family took its private walks from Buckingham House. The king wished to guarantee his privacy by preventing development on the land. Grenville insisted that the asking price, £20,000, was too much.

By the midsummer following Grenville's appointment, George was already asking Bute for advice about changing the government. Grenville was furious. At a meeting fraught with emotion, he accused the king of treason to his ministers and demanded that Bute should forthwith cease to enjoy the royal confidence. When George countered by demanding a pause for reflection, Grenville retired to the country in deep dudgeon. "I have heard that Mr Grenville is at Wotton," declared a contemporary, "relieving his vast mind from the fatigue of his omnipotent situation . . . Atlas has left the globe to turn upon its own axis."

In August, Bute, with the king's blessing, called at Pitt's house in Jermyn Street to sound its occupant's reactions to current affairs. Pitt declared himself ready to meet the king if so commanded, and the next day received a summons to attend at St. James's. At the appointed hour, Grenville happened to call at the palace on business, when, to his astonishment, he saw a sedan chair carried toward the king's chambers with the conspicuous gouty foot of Mr. Pitt protruding from it. For two hours, the irate minister was kept waiting, and, when finally he saw George, the king was "confused and flustered." No mention was made by either man of Pitt's visit. "My reception," Grenville told Halifax, "was a cold one; and no proposition was made, or seemed likely to be made, either relative to you or myself."

Three days later, a second interview took place between George and Pitt. At the first, the veteran statesman had exchanged views with the king on the need for reshaping the government, and had promised to come back with positive proposals. Whatever they were—and the details are not known—Pitt would have wanted to bring in a largely Whig government. Walpole reported that "one party asked too much, and the other would grant too little," while, according to another source, "the style of a dictator was assumed by Pitt; terms were no longer proposed but prescribed, and conditions exacted that nothing but the most abject meanness or most absolute despondency could assent to. A total *bouleversement* of the Government was demanded; an universal proscription of all who had served it boldly threatened, with a few invidious exceptions."

George is said to have terminated the discussion with an abrupt: "I fear, Mr Pitt, this will not do."

The king was now in the humiliating position of having to ask Grenville to stay in office. Grenville agreed, but only after subjecting George to a severe lecture on his duty, in future, to remain loyal to his government. It was a severe strain on the king's self-esteem. Worse was to follow, for the indignant minister was determined to put an end to Bute's influence. In concert with his henchmen Halifax and Sandwich, Grenville demanded that Bute should relinquish his post as Keeper of the Privy Purse and put at least thirty miles between himself and the palace. The king was dumbfounded. Without avail, he promised Grenville to "take his advice and his alone" if the demands were dropped. Without avail Bute promised to "retire absolutely from business." Nothing would satisfy the minister but that Bute should remove his wife and family from their home in South Audley Street to the country, where the king's old favorite settled at Luton in Bedfordshire.

The departure of Bute, the rudeness of Grenville and the upsetting Wilkes affair, each brought fresh turmoil to the series of emotional upheavals which had become the king's life, including his struggle of conscience over his love for Sarah Lennox and the bitterness of having to sell out his ideals of political integrity to gain a court majority in Parliament—especially of having to employ the corrupting Fox. In the second week of January 1765, he developed an illness which, though announced by his physician, Sir William Duncan, as a severe cold, appears to have been a harbinger of the mental disorders which would mar his later life. Hints of significant ups and downs in the king's disposition during the months of illness—consistent with attacks of depressive behavior—are to be found in Grenville's diary of the period:

Sunday, January 13th. Sir William Duncan came to let Mr Grenville know that he had been with the King, who had a violent cold, had passed a restless night, and complained of stitches in his breast. His Majesty was blooded 14 ounces.

Monday, January 14th. The King is better, but saw none of his Ministers.

Tuesday, January 15th. Mr Grenville went to the King, and found him perfectly cheerful and good-humoured and full of conversation.

Monday, February 25th. The King was blooded and kept his bed with a feverish cold.

Sunday, March 3rd. The King had a good night, but waked in the morning with a return of fever and pain upon his breast; he was blooded in the foot.

Tuesday, March 5th. The King sees nobody whatever, not even his brothers. Lord Bute saw him on Monday for a quarter of an hour, for the first time, though he had desired and pressed to see him before.

Wednesday, March 6th. The King was not so well as he had been; his pulse rose in the morning, but sunk again at night, and he was much better and quite cheerful in the evening.

Sunday, March 17th. The King sent a note to Mr Grenville (differently worded from what they usually were) to appoint him at two o'clock the next day. Mr Grenville went to the Drawing Room, where the Queen told him she was afraid he would not agree with her in wishing that the King would not see his servants so often, nor talk so much upon business. Mr Grenville told her Majesty that for his part he never wished to break in upon his Majesty. She again repeated that she thought he had better not speak much upon business.

Monday, March 18th. Mr Grenville found the King's countenance and manner a good deal estranged, but he was civil, and talked upon several difficult subjects.

Friday, March 22nd. Mr Grenville went to the Queen's House to carry a written note for his Majesty, in case he did not see him. The page told him the King was not so well as he had been, and that the physicians had seen him in the morning and desired him to keep quiet. Mr Grenville sent up the note and received the answer in writing. The King was cupped the night before.

Monday, March 25th. The King sent Mr Grenville a note to appoint him at two o'clock; he found his Majesty well to all appearance; he had been out to take the air.

Wednesday, April 23rd. Mr Grenville received notice from Lord Sandwich that the King was to have a levee. Mr Grenville went to it: the King spoke civilly to him, and took notice of his having a very bad cold.

There is no indication that Grenville suspected anything but a physical disorder in the king—the cold and fever diagnosis put out by the physicians—but it is interesting that Charlotte's wifely intuition and common sense warned her that George needed a break from the worries of business. Had more attention been paid to her, less to those who allowed him to remain in touch with duties, his recovery might well have been a quicker one. Not everyone was convinced by the medical bulletins. Wraxall wrote of the illness that "though many conjectures and assertions have been hazarded in conversation, and even in print, no satisfactory information has ever been given to the world." The public, quick to jump to conclusions, for the most part jumped the wrong way. The favorite theory was that George was consumptive. Suddenly, it dawned on the populace that no provision had been made for a regent should the king die.

In consequence, the question of regency became an urgent one. "My late indisposition," George told the nation upon his apparent recovery in April, "though not attended with danger, has led me to consider the situation in which my kingdoms and my family might be left if it should please God to put a period to my life while my successor is of tender years."

There followed a remarkable wrangle between palace and government. To "prevent faction," as it was put to Grenville, the king sought the power to nominate a regent by will and to keep his choice secret, thus avoiding the displeasure, for instance, of his mother should he appoint his wife, or of his wife should he appoint the princess dowager. Secrecy could hardly be acceptable to the government, but a compromise was reached whereby George *would* be allowed to nominate by will, his ministers restricting the choice to the queen "or any other person of the royal family usually residing in Great Britain." The vagueness of the limitation was strangely at odds with the legalistic mind of George Grenville. Grenville's primary concern was to exclude Augusta, and hence Bute, from inheriting power, but he balked at a direct confrontation with the king on the subject. Instead, he left it to Parliament, prompted by the strong antipathy to the princess dowager in the country, to do his dirty work. The House of Lords was quick to accept the invitation. After a long, and sometimes absurd discussion on who was or was not a member of the royal family, the Lords gravely decided the king's mother was not!

The Commons had still to make its wishes felt. On May 3, Halifax and Sandwich presented themselves at the palace and were admitted to an unsuspecting sovereign. Audaciously, they now announced that the House of Commons would unquestionably demand Augusta's exclusion from the regency bill, forcefully suggesting to George that the only way to save his mother from humiliation would be to forestall the parliamentary action by eliminating her candidacy himself. Public opinion, they impressed upon him, would applaud his sensitivity. Taken by surprise, and in some confusion, George yielded to his ministers. "I consent," he told Halifax, "if it will satisfy my people."

The news of the king's decision elated the government as much as it dismayed Augusta's following. "The astonishment of the world is not to be described," reported one observer. "Lord Bute's friends are thunderstruck; the Duke of Bedford [a Whig politician who particularly disliked Bute] almost danced around the House for joy." But George had been tricked, and he knew it. On May 6, furious at the insult to his mother, and for having been made a part of it, he asked his uncle, the Duke of Cumberland, to undertake fresh overtures to William Pitt. This time, he was ready to be rid of Grenville's government even if it meant recalling the Whig families *en bloc*. "The Regency Bill has shown such a want of concert and want of capacity in the Ministers," wrote a contemporary, "such an inattention to the honour of the Crown, if not such a design against it; such imposition and surprise upon the King; and such a misrepresentation of the disposition of the Parliament to the sovereign that there is no doubt that there is a fixed resolution to get rid of them all . . .

"Nothing but an intractable temper in Pitt can prevent a most admirable and lasting system being put together, and this crisis will show whether pride or patriotism be predominant in his character; for you may be assured he has it in his power to come into service of his country upon any plan of politics he may choose to dictate, with great and honourable terms to himself and to every friend he has in the world, and with such a stretch of power as will be equal to everything but an absolute despotism over the King and kingdom. A few days will show whether he will take his part . . ."

The aged "Butcher of Culloden" and the veteran statesman met at the latter's residence at Hayes on May 12. Everything in Cumberland's hot-blooded temperament led him to dislike the calculating Grenville, and he approached his mission with relish. "There is no animal on the face of the earth that the Duke has a more thorough contempt for, or a greater aversion to, than Grenville," observed one reporter. On the other hand, as an old soldier, Cumberland found points to admire in the lofty Pitt. "I represented to him the manner in which this Administration used his Majesty, and that no time was to be lost as Parliament must soon be up—that this country looked up to him as the man who had been the author of the great successes during the war—that they almost universally wished him at the head of public affairs." For all that, the approach was ill fated. Cumberland found Pitt "verbose and pompous" but not unco-operative. The stumbling block was Grenville's brother, Temple. Temple refused to join a ministry formed to displace the minister. Pitt refused to take office without Temple. Discussion dragged on unproductively. Cumberland eventually left Hayes bearing, in his own words, "nothing but compliments and doubts in answer to his Majesty's gracious offers."

Once again, George allowed an obsessive distaste to prompt premature action. Without waiting for Pitt's final verdict, he made it clear he was finished with Grenville. When the minister called to discuss the royal speech for closing the parliamentary session, George growled: "There is no hurry. I'll have Parliament adjourned, not prorogued."

Grenville eyed him coldly. "Has your Majesty any thought of making a change in your administration?"

"Certainly. I cannot bear it as it is."

"I hope your Majesty will not order me to cut my own throat."

"Then who must adjourn the Parliament?"

"Whoever your Majesty shall appoint my successor."

George had effectively dismissed his ministers with no one to replace them. "This is neither Administration or

Government," it would be written soon after. "The King is out of town; and this is the crisis in which Mr Pitt, who could stop every evil, chooses to be more unreasonable than ever." Indeed, Pitt was adamant in his stand beside Temple. Unhopefully, Cumberland searched the land for a replacement. "Offended in the highest degree with the insolence offered him by his Ministers," it was reported of the frustrated George, he "would have put any mortal in their place that could have carried on business." But to his eyes there were none, and Cumberland reluctantly advised his nephew to recall the old government.

Now there was no holding Grenville. "The King is reduced to the mortification—and it is extreme—of taking his old Ministers again. They are insolent enough you may believe," declared an observer. Grenville, treating the king in the most impertinent manner, lectured him endlessly on his failings. The Cabinet discussed the terms they might impose on the captive monarch. George II, who had more than once surrendered to a cabal, had never done so in circumstances of such insult and humiliation. Grenville's remonstrances droned on without mercy. Once, after listening to his chilling rebukes for a full hour, George reflected: "If I had not broken out into the most profuse sweat, I should have been suffocated with indignation." On the evidence of the Earl of Albemarle, the king's ministers lacked elementary decency in dealings with their master. Cumberland was outraged. Angrily, he protested "the *déboires* and indignities with which *these gentlemen in power* insulted his Majesty each day, instead of applying themselves to the good of the public in general."

Among others of the king's friends now forced from office by Grenville's vengeful government was Bute's brother, Stuart Mackenzie, who had been Keeper of the Privy Seal of Scotland. Apart from his relationship with Bute, there was nothing to justify Mackenzie's sacking, but the ministers were determined that he should go. Their decision was particularly painful for George, since he had personally promised Mackenzie his post for life, and the king went so far as to shed tears in pleading with Grenville. According to the minister, George "fell into great agitation," exclaiming that he would be disgraced if he broke his word. "I informed him," Grenville recorded unemotionally, "that Mr Mackenzie's absolute removal was considered as too essential an object to be waived; a circumstance which evidently appeared to pain and distress him. He then asked me if I concurred with those gentlemen who thought the removal indispensably necessary; to which I answered he should do me the justice to suppose I never would offer to him any proposition of which I did not approve. Upon this, he told me, but with the greatest seeming reluctance, that he would give way to it."

"I have said I will do it, can you expect more?" exclaimed George dejectedly. "I will not throw my kingdom into confusion. You force me to break my word, and must be responsible for the consequences."

Wrote his former beloved, Lady Sarah: "The poor man has been obliged to swallow the pill, but his anger is turned to sulkiness and he never says a word more than is necessary . . . I think he ought to have been violent and steady at first, but since he once submitted he had better not behave like a child now." In fact the king's "sulkiness" was more ominous than mere childishness. His mental health was endangered by a relapse. A reception at court was suddenly canceled, the sovereign was absent from Sunday church, and, on May 24, was observed to be "very gloomy with an air of great dissatisfaction." That night, the royal physicians were called in.

The doctors waited a considerable time while the dukes of York and Gloucester were with the king. Eventually, George opened the door himself, and bade them enter.

Giving Sir William Duncan his hand to feel the pulse, which was quick, he explained that he had been hurried for some days past, had eaten very little, and had not slept above two hours for several nights. His agitation was manifest.

That May, the capital was rocked by the so-called Weavers' Riots, an outbreak of sufficient violence and disorder to cause one Londoner to speak of "such a general spirit of mutiny and dissatisfaction in the lower people, that I think we are in danger of a rebellion in the heart of the capital in a week." For some time, the weavers of the Spitalfields area had been seriously distressed by an influx of cheap foreign silks which threatened their livelihood. Large numbers of the workers had been turned out of employment, and many families were faced with starvation. When a bill to restrict imports by raising the tariff was rejected by the House of Lords, largely due to the efforts of the Duke of Bedford, about four thousand "pale and emaciated" weavers set out to appeal to the king, who was then in residence at Richmond.

The queen, strolling in the grounds of Richmond Lodge, was appalled to be confronted, suddenly, by the drawn, hungry faces of a poor, scarecrow mob. But its progress was orderly—"rather like a parcel of recruits going to their regiments than a populace following the dictates of rage and passion," as a witness had it—and the pathetic marchers redirected their steps peacefully to Wimbledon on learning that George had gone there to review some troops. Touched by the plight of the weavers, the king promised to look into their complaints, only to be informed by Grenville that nothing more could be done about the matter.

At length, patience exhausted, the crowds grew hostile, surrounding the Houses of Parliament and abusing the peers as they came and went. When Bedford left, at about five in the afternoon, the protesters followed him, hooting and hurling missiles. One stone cut his upthrown hand and struck him a heavy blow on the forehead. At his mansion in Bloomsbury Square, the duke discovered more men at his gates. Hailing them from his coach, he invited two to enter his home and discuss their grievances with him. The offer was accepted, but the weavers appear to have been less impressed by his arguments than his hospitality, and the demonstrations continued. Arms stores were broken into and weapons stolen, shops selling foreign silks had their windows smashed and an improvised weavers' flag was raised at the House of Lords beside the royal standard.

But the brunt of the storm was directed at Bedford House. So alarmed was the duchess that her doctors promptly bled her. On the evening of May 17, Halifax wrote a report to the king on the troubles: "Lord Halifax dutifully begs leave to inform his Majesty of the many disagreeable scenes in which he has this day engaged . . . he was at dinner at Bedford House when the Company was informed by the Servants that the Mob was in Sight; and very soon they appeared in thousands in Bloomsbury Square. Had it not been for a small party of soldiers which were providentially lodged within the Walls of Bedford House, Lord Halifax makes no Doubt but that his Grace's House would have very soon been levell'd with the Ground; and most probably his Grace and Company murdered. Upon the Gates being almost forced, the Party was ordered to prime and charge, and being drawn up in a Line opposite to ye Gate, it was ordered to be open'd. Upon ye appearance, the Mob for some Time drew back; but very soon afterwards were more outrageous than ever. Every Method was tried to appease them, but to no Purpose. By this Time the Horse Guards were come, but their Appearance had no Effect but that of Insults, Stones and Brick bats."

When the crowd began to demolish the walls of Bedford

House and force its way into the garden, the situation was reckoned grave enough to justify the reading of the riot act. The formality, performed by a Justice Winch, had no effect, and it took a cavalry charge to clear Bloomsbury Square. It was not until reinforcements of horse and foot troops arrived that the demonstrators dispersed, and then only temporarily.

At this moment of crisis, George seems to have discovered a new lease of resolution. Ever fearful of being charged with the weakness he dreaded within himself, and heartily sick of being coerced, the king rounded on the weavers with a vehemence expressive of his long frustration by the government. Among other repressive measures, he instructed a regiment to move toward London from Chatham, ordered "Butcher" Cumberland to be ready at a moment's notice to assume command as captain general, and threatened to place himself at the head of an army against the demonstrators. It was the sudden, overstated reaction of a depressed man, and it was lucky for London that nothing came of it. After a few days, the riots subsided, the weavers placated by a large public subscription on their behalf and promises from their employers to outlaw foreign silks.

Bolstered by his renewed sense of decisiveness, George turned like a resentful lion on his ringmaster, Grenville. Characteristically, the minister refused to believe his own danger. Public disorder had helped to discredit him, but his final downfall was the conviction that he was indispensable. "The fool said, 'The King cannot do without me,'" wrote Lord Holland, and, at last, the king proved otherwise. Galvanized to new efforts, George threw off his depression and once more commissioned Cumberland to seek a new government. This time, the old man fell back on a young and relatively inexperienced politician, the Whig Marquis of Rockingham. Rockingham agreed to take office.

On July 10, 1765, Grenville received a laconic note from

the Lord Chancellor intimating his dismissal: "Dear Sir—
I have this moment received His Majesty's commands to
signify to you his pleasure that you attend His Majesty
at St James's this day, at twelve o'clock, with the seal
of your office. I am very unhappy to convey so unpleasing
commands, as I have the honour to be with great respect,
etc." Grenville was staggered. When he demanded an explanation, George informed him loftily that too much "con-
straint" had been placed on the monarch. This was a new
king. It was no part of the monarch's duty, proclaimed
George, to "obey" his ministers. Grenville heard him frigidly,
issuing one final and lengthy harangue before departing.

For once, it was said, George heard him out with equanimity.

CHAPTER 13

A *Loyal American*

Looking back from the twentieth-century shadow of America's greatness, it is hard for an Englishman to visualize the time when his forefathers regarded the western colonies as lands of no special consequence. Yet few colonials, even, in the seventeen-sixties dreamed of the scope of their country's future. For most Englishmen, the colonies in America were a quaintly Puritan collection of plantations and trading posts, of no greater commercial significance than the West Indies, and certainly of less importance in world affairs than, say, Ireland.

A few Englishmen, some vociferous, spoke up for the admirable qualities which, they pointed out, had enabled their western cousins to thrive under pioneer conditions. But what these champions of the New World saw as rugged independence, the majority saw as obstinacy and cussedness.

Were not the Americans, they asked, totally dependent on Britain? Had not English lives and English money saved them from being overrun by the French? Did their economy not depend upon English credit? Should not these remote people who depended for their very survival on the mother country, be grateful for her sacrifice? And yet how did they repay their protectors and creditors? By flouting navigation laws, smuggling and invading trade areas Britain considered to be her own. On top of which, hotheads stood up in their plantations, flourished their spades and hoes, and made ridiculous speeches about independence and rebellion. It was all very disgruntling, emotionally provocative, but scarcely to be regarded as serious.

The hard facts of life were against the Americans. The infant might bawl and throw its tantrums, but one could ignore these. In the end, all infants were obliged to accept the parent-child relationship.

That was how Britons, with a few exceptions, saw it. For the Americans themselves it was different. For them, British control and economic dominance were not features of benevolence, but obstacles in their quest for increasing wealth. This they sought by expanding their foreign trade. Already, they had a profitable connection with the West Indies, and promising European dealings. They saw their merchant fleet as potentially the pride of the shipping lanes. But they were fettered by what they regarded as out-dated and one-sided British regulations which they had to overcome by lawbreaking in order to flourish.

That was only part of their bitterness. Increasingly, they resented their dependence on English currency. Credit from London, which had placed the tobacco traders in a position of heavy debt, was regarded as a form of exploitation, hardly made more bearable by Britain's pose as a protector. To Americans, British protection was a pretense to enable the merchants of the mother country to operate with an unfair advantage.

There were other disaffections. Among military men it rankled that provincial officers of whatever rank were held subordinate by the British War Office to any officer holding the king's commission. One who particularly resented this was George Washington, the son of a Virginia plantation owner. A sturdy six-footer who reveled in wrestling, horse breaking and other physical activities, Washington had hankered after the military life. "My inclinations," he once wrote, "are strongly bent to arms."

In 1752, at the age of twenty, Washington had been made adjutant of one of Virginia's four military districts, and, two years later, dispatched by Governor Dinwiddie against the French who were then encroaching on the Ohio. In this early engagement of the French and Indian War, he had shown valor but no outstanding brilliance. After a brief success against a small French detachment, his force of 350 men had been besieged at Great Meadows by a French force of 700, and eventually allowed to retain the honors of war on condition that it return to Virginia. Washington had not allowed the episode to subdue his military ambitions. "I have heard the bullets whistle, and believe me, there is something charming in the sound," he had observed in a letter to his brother.

In October of that year, 1754, he had resigned his commission in protest against the insulting treatment and underpayment of colonial officers, but, in 1755, agreed to join the British general Edward Braddock as an aide-de-camp with the courtesy title of colonel. Braddock, a former Coldstream Guardsman with forty-five years of service, was an old-school officer of the drill-book variety, and a favorite of Cumberland's. As personalities, the old man and the young one clashed violently, Braddock abusing the colonials as inefficient and dishonest while Washington staunchly defended them. But as men of action there was a vein of mutual respect in the relationship which held it together.

Braddock and his army, including Washington's Virginians, had been assigned to march on Fort Duquesne. They were still nine miles from their destination when they were ambushed and routed by a numerically inferior force of French and Indians. Braddock displayed great personal courage. Five horses were shot under him before he fell, mortally injured. But his formal tactical concepts, proving disastrous, did nothing to increase American confidence in British protection. It was left to Washington and his Virginians to salvage what little glory accrued from the action by covering the escape of the British force. Still only twenty-three years of age, Washington had been rewarded by being appointed overall commander of the Virginian forces.

In Braddock's camp, Washington's path had crossed that of an American of a very different disposition, Benjamin Franklin. Franklin detested war and violence. "Men," he once wrote with a distaste barely concealed by his customary humor, "have more pride and even pleasure in killing than in begetting one another, for without a blush they assemble in great armies at noonday to destroy, and when they have killed as many as they can they exaggerate the number to augment the fancied glory; but they creep into corners and cover themselves with the darkness of night when they mean to beget, as being ashamed of virtuous action."

Nevertheless, as Franklin had put it, "The King's business must be done," and he had used his influence with American farmers to provide Braddock with wagons and pack-horses for his campaign, even using his own money as surety. Franklin personified the wide range of moderate opinion in the colonies which stood for a reasoned accommodation with the British, a basic loyalty to the Crown. Indeed, perhaps more than that of any individual, his patience and goodwill in the face of transatlantic differences was to highlight the intransigence of George and his ministers, and renders him worthy of closer attention.

Both Franklin's and Washington's families hailed from the English country of Northamptonshire, where the Franklins—unlike the Washingtons, who were lords of a manor—

had earned their living for generations as blacksmiths. Among the first to break this tradition had been Josiah Franklin. Settled in Milk Street, Boston, Josiah had traded the anvil for the tools of a candlemaker, commencing to produce, as well as night lights, no less than seventeen children. Among his favorites was Benjamin, a lad of studious and practical attributes.

Benjamin Franklin was born in January 1706, concluded his formal education at the age of ten, and, two years later, was apprenticed to his older brother James, as a printer, a job which gave some scope to his passion for reading. Characteristically, the favorite works of his early days included Defoe's *Essay on Projects*, concerned with such matter-of-fact subjects as road systems and banking, and Dr. Cotton Mather's *Essays to do Good*, which treated of benevolence as a social blessing.

At seventeen, Franklin left Boston to seek his fortune in New York, from where, out of luck and reduced to his last coppers, he moved on to Philadelphia. Here, his pleasing manner and common sense commended him to the governor, Sir William Keith, who offered to set him up as a printer, sending him to London to purchase equipment. On arriving in London, Franklin was shocked to discover that Keith's credit was worthless. The young American was obliged to seek work in the city's printing houses. It did not dismay him. Life in the capital was stimulating. The printing trade buzzed with unprecedented activity as the age of reason, inquiry and controversy gained impetus. Supping at such "literary" taverns as The Horns in Cheapside, attending the theaters, meeting authors and celebrities, Franklin began to absorb radical ideas, and was soon putting them into words on his own account. Among his first essays into dialectic, *A Dissertation on Liberty and Necessity, Pleasure and Pain,* impressed his city friends and lent him some influence.

Eighteen months later, he returned to Philadelphia, at

once a budding intellectual and a man of the world. Practical as ever, Franklin spent some time studying accountancy and marketing before, in his twenty-third year, he established his own business as a printer. Quiet, though assured of manner, with the large, soulful eyes of an amiable spaniel, he had a fetching sense of humor and mixed well with most men.

Growing interests in science and philosophy were allied in his make-up with that absorption in morality that was found among many colonists. At about this time, he drew up a chart of virtues and set himself to practice a different one each week. Among these, silence, order and resolution, ranked with frugality, temperance and cleanliness. He also drew up a form of worship, which concluded with thanksgiving for peace and liberty, also "for the common benefits of air and light; for useful fire and delicious water; for knowledge and literature and very useful art; for friends and their prosperity, for the fewness of his enemies; for life and reason and the use of speech; for health and joy and every pleasant hour."

Franklin's creed was a mixture of simplicity, humanity, utility and tolerance. Just where in his philosophy he placed the birth, at this period, of his first child, an illegitimate son, is uncertain. But since "chastity" was one of his listed virtues, perhaps it had been tempered by his urge to moderation.

The business grew rapidly. Concerned with the furtherance of his workers' interests, as well as his profits, Franklin formed a discussion club for them known as the Junto. Its subjects, reflecting the typically Franklin-esque blend of philosophy and practicality, varied from "Is self-interest the rudder which steers mankind?" to "How may smoky chimneys best be cured?" In 1730, he acquired in the *Pennsylvania Gazette* a tool for influencing opinion on a wider scale than his works club. Zealous in his defense of the governed against government abuses, he did not, however, identify the latter in principle with Crown rule. Indeed, Franklin saw Americans and Britons as inseparable, observing that the colonists could count among their blessings the retention of that "ardent spirit of liberty and undaunted courage which has in every age so gloriously distinguished Britons and Englishmen from the rest of mankind."

Franklin believed that all men of goodwill should come together. "There seems to me at present," he wrote, "to be great occasion for raising a United Party of Virtue, by joining the virtuous and good men of all nations in a regular body, to be governed by suitable and wise rules, which good and wise men may probably be more unanimous in their obedience to than common people are to common law."

Yet, when danger threatened, he was no pacifist. In 1747, now married and surrounded by admiring friends, he used his eloquence in a pamphlet entitled *Plain Truth* to persuade peaceful and Quaker-influenced Pennsylvania to take arms against the threatening forces of France and Spain. The pamphlet helped to raise a militia of more than 10,000 men, in which Franklin, though elected its colonel, chose to serve as a common soldier. In *Plain Truth* he made the point that the government owed the people protection, as well as the people obedience to the government. "Should we remind them that Public Money raised from all belongs to all?" he asked. The *Truth* earned him a bad reputation in some quarters of London, where he was described as "a dangerous man of uneasy spirit."

Certainly, he spoke out against disreputable ideas from the capital. When London conceived the notion of shipping convicts and felons to America, he proposed, as a fair exchange, sending rattlesnakes to St. James's. Yet he still belonged steadfastly to that body of American opinion which saw no overriding incompatibility between Britain and

America—nothing which could not be put right by men of reason and "virtue." Indeed, he saw the peoples of the two lands as natural partners in an empire of expanding possibilities, a political edifice of greater potential, he maintained, than the world had ever seen.

In 1748, Franklin sold his business and embarked on a scientific interlude. On both sides of the Atlantic learned men were absorbed investigating the powers of electricity. Franklin joined them with a questing zest which was to carry his name throughout Europe. His letters linking electricity and lightning were read to scientific bodies in London and Paris, and earned him congratulations from Louis XV. Five years later, the Royal Society distinguished him with a medal and made him a member. Yale and Harvard universities conferred degrees on him. Meanwhile, in the field of good works, he had raised money for a new academy, for a hospital and for poor immigrants. He was tireless and remarkably successful in his efforts. In 1750 he had been elected to the General Assembly of Pennsylvania, and, in 1753, was distinguished with the Crown appointment of deputy postmaster general of America, an office he held jointly with William Hunter of Virginia. Within five years he had wiped out a chronic deficit and the service began to make a profit for the British Government.

In 1754 he experienced his first major failure. With the commencement of the Seven Years War, London issued orders for a colonial congress to meet at Albany to look into measures of defense. Franklin proposed a scheme, duly adopted by the congress, whereby a military governor-general should preside over a grand council representing the provincial assemblies. The governor would be in charge of overall defense; the council would be responsible for dealing with the Indians in its territories, the forming of militia, and other local matters. In this way, the colonies would retain their independence in the business closest to them while providing a central body under the Crown to deal with wider emergencies.

Franklin's plan proved abortive. "Its fate," he bemoaned, "was singular. The assemblies did not adopt it, as they all thought there was too much *prerogative* in it, and in England it was judged to have too much of the *democratic*. The Board of Trade therefore did not approve of it, nor recommend it for the approbation of his Majesty."

When an alternative plan arrived from London denying the electors of the colonies a say in selecting the council, yet proposing to tax them for English purposes, Franklin touched on an issue which was to have far-reaching consequences. "It is supposed," he pointed out, "an undoubted right of Englishmen not to be taxed but by their own consent . . . the frontiers of an empire are properly defended at the joint expense of the people in such an empire." It was unfair on the colonists, Franklin added, "that by hazarding their lives and fortunes in subduing and settling new countries, extending the dominion and increasing the commerce of the mother nation, they have forfeited the native rights of Britons, which they think ought rather to be given to them, as due merit, if they had been before in a state of slavery."

In another letter, he expressed the hope that "the people of Great Britain and the people of the colonies would learn to consider themselves as not belonging to a different community with different interests, but to one community with one interest, which I imagine would greatly lessen the danger of future separations. And if there be any difference, those who have most contributed to enlarge Britain's empire and commerce, to increase her strength, her wealth and the number of her people at the risk of their own lives and private fortunes, ought rather to expect some preference."

Franklin was closely involved in tax matters. In Pennsylvania an angry controversy about taxes centered on the descendants of one William Penn, who, in 1681, had been granted the province by Charles II. These descendants, Thomas and Richard Penn, were absentee landlords of the worst kind. They lived in London, yet ruled the province, through their appointed governor, like feudal barons. From the Penns, the governor had received orders not to pass any acts for the defense of Pennsylvania unless their huge estates there were exempt from taxation. At last, in its frustration, the Assembly decided to send the diplomatic Mr. Franklin to London to raise the matter of the Penns and taxation with the government.

The prospect of returning to the old capital delighted him. Back in London, he revisited the haunts of his youth, the taverns and theaters, the printing shops and lodgings of humbler days. This time, his fame had preceded him and he was besieged by friends of influence, clamoring in particular to see and hear more of his electrical experiments. Franklin was flattered, and at home in the sophisticated circle which surrounded him. "Of all the enviable things England has," he wrote a British friend, "I envy most its people—its sensible, virtuous and elegant minds." But he did not lose sight of his mission. For five years he pursued his political objective, and, in the end, after much wrangling with the government, he won the day for Pennsylvania.

The Penn estates were no longer exempt from taxation, though Franklin had to agree they would not be "too highly taxed." The affair brought him a considerable diplomatic reputation both at home and in London, a city which had by now so won his heart that he considered sending for his family and settling there. In the interests of a home-loving wife, however, he returned at last to Philadelphia, not suspecting that, two years later, he would be back in London on a mission of even greater portent, and facing the most signal failure of his whole life.

CHAPTER 14

A Matter of Taxes

Charles Watson-Wentworth, Second Marquis of Rockingham, thirty-five years of age on becoming the king's minister,
was a likable fellow, exceptionally fond of horse racing,
with a pointed nose, sloping forehead and receding chin,
which gave his profile a curious wedge shape. His father,
originally a country gentleman named Watson, had risen
so spectacularly in the service of Robert Walpole, that it
had once been joked of him: "We shall soon see our friend
in opposition, for he has had no promotion in the peerage
for a fortnight." According to Edmund Burke, who was
indebted to Rockingham's patronage, the new minister possessed sound principles and unbroken fortitude. "If ever
there lived a truly good man," wrote one who knew him
well, "the Marquis of Rockingham was such." No one, on
the other hand, protested his brilliance, and even his intimates had to admit that the Duke of Cumberland had
perceived greater talents in their friend than they had been
able to discover.

"I thought," said the king on one occasion, "that I had
not two men in my Bedchamber of less parts than Lord
Rockingham." So great was his dread of public speaking

that one peer dubbed him "the poor dumb thing," and George was constrained to suggest that the premier should hear more of his own voice. Rockingham could truly swear he had never sought office.

The government formed around him was liberal, but inexperienced and lightweight. As Secretaries of State, he had the Duke of Grafton, then thirty, and Henry Seymour Conway, forty-four. Grafton's family had colonial connections—a grandfather had been governor of New York and the Jerseys—and he supported the cause of human rights. But he was pleasure-seeking and indolent. Conway had been deprived of his army commission by the king for his stand on the Wilkes affair, and was also a friend of the colonies. Edmund Burke, who at thirty-six became private secretary to Rockingham, was a newcomer to practical politics. "It was," declared one, "a mere lute-string administration—pretty summer wear, but it would never stand the winter." Averred Chesterfield: "It is an heterogeneous jumble of youth and caducity, which cannot be efficient." In fact, the record of its short life was not bad.

The group headed by Rockingham was part of a wider reform movement which stretched beyond formal politics, expressing itself in the progressive attitudes of successful men in many different walks of life. Josiah Wedgwood was typical of this type. The youngest son of a potter from Burslem, Staffordshire, he came of a family of potters and, in due course, set up in business on his own account in his hometown. Thanks in part to the patronage of Queen Charlotte, his cream-colored earthenware, soon known as "queen's ware," became a standard domestic pottery and achieved in time a world market. His success was based on a tireless search for new methods—of deploying labor, of organizing business, of overcoming transport problems and in his exhaustive experiments in materials and techniques.

"All things," wrote Wedgwood, "yield to experiment." With a growing number of men of his period, he attributed his success to the employment of rational principles, and the eschewal of traditional attitudes and prejudice.

Some were little-known outside their own areas; others—the Watts, the Boultons, the Strutts and the Arkwrights—became famous, to prove that logical ideas and methods paid dividends. Among these men, devoted to such prophets of a new age as Erasmus Darwin, the botanist, Joseph Priestley, the chemist, and Richard Price, the philosopher, the like of George and his followers were dinosaurs, outmoded reactionaries, their principles and systems of government obsolete. The new school, flourishing in business and science, looked upon Parliament as in dire need of a shake-up, the Crown as an urgent candidate for curtailment.

Rockingham himself, though scarcely immoderate, was too radical by half to last long in the prevailing climate of Westminster. Moreover, his administration faced formidable inherited problems. In October 1765, a few weeks after its inception, it suffered a dramatic setback. On the evening of the thirtieth, Cumberland was playing piquet with General Hodgson, another veteran of Culloden, when he underwent a mild stroke. The following evening, he complained of suffocation, collapsing at his Grosvenor Street residence. As a servant opened a vein to bleed him, the old soldier croaked, "It's too late; it's all over," and lost consciousness. He was dead before a doctor could get to him. Rockingham had been robbed of the maker of his ministry—the one link that might have reconciled its views with the palace. As it was, the new government's rude disposal of old policies startled George and his ex-ministers. The cider tax was repealed, an end put to general warrants, and a momentous issue faced in the question of colonial taxation. There was to be scant rapport in the stormy

months that followed between George and his pleasant
young premier.

George, Grenville and Bute were each obsessed in varying
degrees with economy, and not without reason. Pitt's wars
had been as costly as they were successful; his victories
bought at the price of enormous loans. At the time of the
Treaty of Paris, the government had owed a hundred and
forty million pounds. Among Bute's first considerations on
the signing of peace, therefore, had been that of dealing
with such obligations, and, since these had been incurred
partly in defense of the American colonies, it was decided
that America should bear a share in repaying them. In this,
as in most things at the time, George and Bute had been in
agreement.

Bute's plans for America had included an internal stamp
tax, a vigorous enforcement of the Navigation Acts, by
which a monopoly of colonial trade was secured to Great
Britain, and a general policy toward the colonists based on
their theoretical dependence on Westminster. These plans
had been carried forward by Grenville on the Scotsman's
retirement. Among Grenville's first steps had been the sup-
pression, by strong law enforcement, of the thriving contra-
band trade which had grown between America and the
Spanish West Indies. As usual, Grenville had shown a nicer
understanding of legalities than of human feelings, and
resentment in the colonies was widespread. When Grenville
next announced his intention of pushing through the Stamp
Tax, the resentment swelled into a profound change in
relations between Britain and America. Benjamin Franklin
put the American case in London: No taxation without
representation—and the colonists had no representatives in
Parliament. Like many before him, he found Grenville inflexible.

Grenville's agrument was that since Britain defended the

colonies, they should contribute to the cost; moreover, that since the money thus raised in America was to be spent there, there could be no valid objection to the tax. He had no mind to change his plans without an assurance, which Franklin could not give, that the colonists would devise a method to tax themselves. George was in the early throes of depression when the Stamp Act was put before Parliament, but, in a previous speech, had declared unequivocally: "The wise regulations which have been established to augment the public revenues, to unite the interests of the most distant possessions of my Crown, and to encourage and secure their commerce with Great Britain, call for my hearty approbation." Pitt, stricken with gout, was absent from the Commons, and it was left to Colonel Isaac Barré, a member of no great influence, to make the most stirring speech of opposition.

"Children planted by your care?" he exclaimed of the colonists. "No, your oppressions planted them in America! They fled from your tyranny to a then uncultivated and inhospitable country. Nourished by your indulgence? They grew by your neglect of them! Protected by your arms? They have nobly taken up arms in your defence!" The colonists, Barré declared hotly, were "sons of liberty." But the mood of Parliament was apathetic. A mere forty members agreed with him, and the Stamp Act passed through both Houses "with less opposition than a turnpike bill."

All America was galvanized to protest. As one English writer put it:

Sad news in the papers—God knows who's to blame!
The Colonies seem to be all in a flame,
This Stamp Act, no doubt, might be good for the Crown,
But I fear 'tis a pill that will never go down.

Grenville's fall was welcomed with delight in America, and news of Conway's appointment in the new administration received with optimism. Conway had been among the few to oppose the Stamp Act. Still, indifference to colonial troubles was a feature of the English summer scene, and Rockingham's procrastination, despite warnings from British commercial interests, a sign of his ministry's weakness. By the end of the year, with America withholding some four million pounds owed to British manufacturers and merchants, pressure on the government had mounted, and George himself was growing anxious. "I am more and more grieved at the accounts of America," he wrote Conway in December. "Where this spirit will end is not to be said. It is undoubtedly the most serious matter that ever came before Parliament; it requires more deliberation, candour and temper than I fear it will meet with." The king's attitude was itself ambivalent. He recoiled from the weakness and muddled leadership implicit in repealing the Stamp Act, yet shuddered at the alternative of risking war to maintain the tax. His doubts were of no help to a weak and harassed government.

In other quarters, there was less hesitancy. Pitt had not shown himself in Parliament for many months, but the resistance of the American people had aroused a fiery sympathy in his breast and he was determined at all costs to be present after the Christmas recess. "My resolution is taken," he told a friend on January 9, 1766, "and, if I can crawl or be carried, I will deliver my mind and heart upon the state of America." News that Pitt had chosen the American question on which to make his comeback swept the webs of apathy from the subject and the people waited eagerly for his exposition. They were not disappointed. Though still lame and suffering, his performance on the day was electric. In withering terms, he dismissed the Grenville government's performance before turning to the present ministers. "Their characters are fair," he said sweetly, "and I am always glad when men of fair character engage in his Majesty's service.

But, notwithstanding, I love to be explicit. I cannot give them my confidence . . . confidence is a plant of slow growth in an aged bosom; youth is the season of credulity."

The House listened avidly. "It is a long time, Mr Speaker," Pitt continued, "since I have attended Parliament. When the resolution was taken in the House to tax America, I was ill in bed." He wished, he said, that he could then have been carried to Westminster to speak against the measure, but, since that had not been possible, he was present to say now that Great Britain had no right to tax a people who were not represented in Parliament. "They are subjects of this kingdom, equally entitled with yourselves to all the natural rights of mankind, and the peculiar privileges of Englishmen; equally bound by its laws, and equally participating in the constitution of this free country. The Americans are the sons, not the bastards, of England.

"Taxation," said Pitt, expanding his argument, "is no part of the governing or legislative power. Taxes are the voluntary gift and grant of the Commons alone. In legislation, the three estates of the realm are alike concerned, but the concurrence of the peers and the Crown to a tax is only necessary to clothe it with the form of a law; the gift and grant is of the Commons alone. In ancient days, the Crown, the barons and the clergy possessed the lands. In those days, the barons and clergy granted to the Crown—they gave and granted what was their own. At present, since the discovery of America, the Commons are become the proprietors of the land; the Church has but a pittance; the property of the Lords, compared with that of the Commons, is as a drop of water in the ocean. And this House represents those Commons, the proprietors of the lands. And those proprietors virtually represent the rest of the inhabitants. When, therefore, in this House we give a grant, we give and grant what is our own. But, in an American tax, what do we do? We, your Majesty's Commons for Great Britain, give a grant to your Majesty of what? Our own property? No. We give a grant to your Majesty of the property of your Majesty's Commons of America. It is an absurdity in terms.

"The distinction between legislation and taxation is essentially necessary to liberty. The Crown, the peers, are equally legislative powers with the Commons. If taxation be a part of simple legislation, the Crown and the peers have rights in taxation as well as yourselves—rights which they will claim, which they will exercise when the principle can be supported by power . . . The commoners of America, represented in their several assemblies, have ever been in possession in the exercise of this, their constitutional right, of giving and granting their own money. They would have been slaves if they had not enjoyed it. At the same time, this kingdom, as the supreme governing and legislative power, has always bound the colonies by her laws, by her regulations and restrictions in trade, in navigation, in manufactures—in everything *except* that of taking their money out of their pockets, without their consent. Here I would draw the line."

Grenville, sitting one seat removed from William Pitt, was quick to reply.

Taxation, he insisted in his precise and monotonous manner, was a part of the sovereign power. It had been exercised over chartered companies, the proprietors of stock and many manufacturing towns—over Chester and Durham, for instance, long before they had been allowed to send representatives to Parliament. When he had introduced the Stamp Act, no one had questioned the *right* to tax America. Protection implied the obedience of the protected, and Great Britain was entitled to expect as much from her colonies in return for protecting them. England, he declared, had incurred a vast debt in protecting America, and, now that the colonists were required to make a small contribution, what was the consequence? "They renounce your authority, insult your officers, and break out, I might almost say, into open rebellion."

Pitt again thrust himself painfully to his feet.

"The *gentleman*," he exclaimed angrily, "tells us that America is obstinate; that America is almost in open rebellion. Sir, I rejoice that America has resisted. Three millions of people so dead to all the feelings of liberty as voluntarily to submit to be slaves would have been fit instruments to make slaves of all the rest. I come not here armed at all points with law-cases and Acts of Parliament," he shot at Grenville, "with the statute book doubled down in dog's ears, to defend the cause of liberty. If I had, I myself would have cited the cases of Chester and Durham. I would have cited them to show that, even under arbitrary reigns, Parliaments were ashamed of taxing a people without their consent, and allowed them representatives. The gentleman asks when were the colonies emancipated. But I desire to know when were they made slaves."

Was American opinion to be crushed by armed force? In a good cause, Pitt asserted, British troops might crush America; but, in a bad one, success would be hazardous. "America, if she fall, will fall like the strong man. She will embrace the pillars of the state and will pull down the constitution along with her. Is this your boasted peace? Not to sheathe the sword in its scabbard, but to sheathe it in the bowels of your fellow-countrymen!"

While there was argument among those who opposed the Stamp Act on the legal right of Parliament to tax America, Pitt's oration brought fire to the general cause. In the Lords, Chief Justice Pratt, now Lord Camden, took a similar stand. "My position," said the celebrated judge of the Wilkes case, "is this. I repeat it. I will maintain it to my last hour. Taxation and representation are inseparable. This position is founded on the laws of nature. It is more. It is itself an eternal law of nature, for whatever is a man's own is absolutely his own. No man has a right to take it from him without his consent, either expressed by himself or his representatives. Whoever attempts to do it, attempts an injury. Whoever does it, commits a robbery. He throws down and destroys the distinction between liberty and slavery."

Both Rockingham and Grenville now sought the king's ear, the former to seek advice, the latter to persuade the monarch to stand firm on taxation. So anxious was Grenville to impress George with his own view that he went as far as to swallow his pride and beg an interview with Bute, in the hope that his old enemy could exert influence at the palace. Bute agreed to meet Grenville and Bedford, but only, it seems, for the purpose of gaining malicious satisfaction. "The Favourite," wrote Walpole, "had the triumph of beholding the Duke of Bedford and George Grenville prostrate before him, suing for pardon, reconciliation and support. After enjoying this spectacle for some minutes, the lofty Earl, scarcely deigning to bestow upon them half a score of monosyllables, stiffly refused to enter into connection with them."

George, still between the devil and the deep in his own mind, gave Rockingham little help. Asked frankly whether he was "for enforcing the Act by the sword, or for the repeal," the king veered toward repeal, but, as Rockingham understood it, "most certainly preferred modification to either." Wrote George on February 11: "From the first conversations on the best mode of restoring order and obedience in the American Colonys, I thought the modifying the Stamp Act the wisest and most efficacious manner of proceeding . . . but if the unhappy factions that divide this country would not permit this . . . I thought repealing infinitely more eligible than enforcing, which could only tend to widen the breach between this country and America; my language to all ever continu'd pointing out my wish for modification." When repeal seemed inevitable, George marked his equivocation by telling his court friends that they were at liberty to vote against his ministry "and keep their places."

Characteristically, Rockingham tried to please everyone. His method was to propose the repeal of the Stamp Act, but to qualify the measure with the so-called Declaratory Bill, asserting the supreme sovereignty of Parliament over the colonies. This anomalous procedure—insisting on an abstract right while admitting a reluctance to sustain it —was in line with the king's confused thinking, and was put to Parliament on February 21. For the moment, the compromise proved digestible. At half-past one next morning, wearied by many long speeches, the House divided to carry the government proposals. "The joy in the lobby of the House of Commons, which was full of considerable merchants both of London and from different manufacturing parts of the country, was extreme," Rockingham informed the king.

Grenville, who had continued to harangue to the last— "It was," declared a humorist, "too much that he should give up his favourite Bill and his favourite occupation, talking, both at once"—flounced away to proclaim disgustedly: "England and America are now governed by the mob." In the lamplight outside the Commons, a party of rejoicing merchants upset him so violently that he grasped one man by the throat and shook him. Conway, by contrast, emerged wreathed in smiles, his countenance, as Burke observed it, "the face of an angel." But it was Pitt the crowd wanted. Cheering and shouting congratulations, they surged round his sedan chair, many following him through the darkened roads as far as Bond Street.

On March 4, the Repeal Bill was carried by the House of Lords, and, later that month, received the royal assent. From this moment, Rockingham's ministry was overwhelmed by a general feeling that Pitt was the country's natural leader, and, at length, George was compelled to call him to office. Wrote the king reluctantly, July 1766: "Mr Pitt, your very dutiful and handsome conduct last summer makes me desirous of having your thoughts how an able and dignified ministry may be formed. I desire, therefore, you will come for this salutary purpose, to town." Pitt judged the time right. Temple had deserted him over the Stamp Act, and he no longer felt bound by his relative. The people were with him. "Penetrated with the deepest sense of your Majesty's goodness to me," he replied fulsomely, "and with a heart overflowing with duty and zeal for the honour and happiness of the most gracious and benign sovereign, I shall hasten to London as fast as I possibly can, wishing that I could change infirmity into wings of expedition."

But while Pitt had immense popularity in the country, and might sway the Commons with his eloquence, the ageing and testy cripple had retained few friends of ministerial caliber. His government, comprising such of these as he could muster, together with a number of Rockingham men and even some king's friends, was described by Burke as a mosaic ministry, "a chequered and speckled administration; a piece of joinery so crossly indented and whimsically dovetailed; a cabinet so variously inlaid; here a bit of black stone and there a bit of white; patriots and courtiers; King's friends and republicans; Whigs and Tories; treacherous friends and open enemies—that it was indeed a very curious show . . . unsafe to touch and unsure to stand on."

Initially, it was sustained by public enthusiasm for its leader, especially in the City of London, where Pitt was a hero. To mark his new office, the Corporation planned to present him with a loyal address, to banquet him at the Guildhall and to illuminate the Monument and other sights of the capital. Then, overnight, the festive mood changed. On July 30, Pitt, the Great Commoner, accepted an earl-

dom. That he had earned a peerage could hardly be questioned. Perhaps an awareness of failing health made him
look to the Lords as a future haven from the storms of the
Commons. But, to the nation, he seemed to have sold his
soul to the court, and, as one writer put it, "that fatal title
blasted all the affection which his country had borne him."
Orders for the public address, the banquet and the illuminations were canceled. "The City have brought in their verdict,"
wrote a Londoner of the fickleness of public opinion. The
man who had soared as a commoner had crashed as the Earl
of Chatham, the title he adopted, and with him plunged all
hopes for his ministry. Within months, the new premier was
exhibiting the signs, as familiar to George as to any, of a
nervous breakdown. At first, he retired to Bath, the popular
health resort, then to the country town of Marlborough,
where he shut himself in the Castle Inn and declined to
see visitors. "It is by no means practicable for me to enter
into the discussion of business," he admitted in February
1767.

When Chatham felt able to receive again, his visitors were
shocked by his condition. "So childish and agitated was his
whole frame," reported one, "that if a word of business was
mentioned to him, tears and tremblings immediately succeeded to cheerful, indifferent conversation." Exclaimed another: "He sits all day leaning on his hands, which he
supports on the table; does not permit any person to remain
in the room; knocks when he wants anything, and, having
made his wants known, gives a signal without speaking to
the person who answered his call to return." Much as George
disliked Chatham, he was touched to see his own affliction of
two years past echoed in the frame of the once formidable
statesman. Offering to visit the sick man, the king promised
to avoid talking of business. He only wanted to demonstrate
his sympathy.

Meanwhile, the government had been led, to use the term

rather loosely, by the pleasure-loving former Rockingham minister Augustus, Duke of Grafton. Boyishly good-looking, with a greater affection for his dogs, it was said, than for politics, Grafton's main claim to the public eye was his remarkable attachment to his mistress, Nancy Parsons. Though Nancy was by this time a somewhat wilted beauty—an acquaintance called her "one of the commonest creatures in London"—the sporting duke was inordinately proud of her. "He brings everyone to dine with him," declared Lady Temple. "His female friend sits at the upper end of his table; some do like it, and some do not. She is very pious, a constant Church-woman, and reproves his Grace for swearing and being angry, which he owns is very wrong and, with great submission, begs her pardon for being so ill-bred before her."

Grafton not only displayed his "female friend" at Ascot, but flaunted her at the opera in the presence of a shocked George and Charlotte—a violation of public decorum which, in the opinion of one journalist, could never be forgiven. "It is not that he kept a mistress at home, but that he constantly attended her abroad. It is not the private indulgence, but the public insult of which I complain. The name of Miss Parsons would scarcely have been known if the First Lord of the Treasury had not led her in triumph through the Opera House, even in the presence of the Queen. When we see a man act in this manner we may admit the shameless depravity of his heart, but what are we to think of his understanding?"

Whatever people thought, Grafton was clearly not the man to infuse the government with vigor or union. Chatham's plans for the future were allowed to drop. He had dreamed of improving the administration of Ireland, of transferring power in India from the merchants to the Crown and of cementing an alliance with Prussia and Russia to balance the

Bourbon compact. When the sick man emerged sufficiently from his illness to take stock, he found that not only were his plans unrealized, but that, against all his known sentiments, the ministry had carried through Parliament a bill to tax American imports. "During your absence," he was informed by the *Public Advertiser* writer Junius (supposed by many to have been the politician and pamphleteer Sir Philip Francis), "it is well known that not one of the ministers has either adhered to you with firmness, or supported with any degree of steadiness those principles on which you engaged in the King's service."

At the same time, through the disintegration of the parties, especially the Whig families, into hostile segments—and the progressive weakening of governments—George had been moving, slowly but effectively, toward his undiminished ambition, the personal rule of the sovereign. Already, he had used court favorites in Parliament both to promote his own policies and to confuse governments of which he disapproved. Now, with the last great independent leader, Chatham, a spent force, the king's men were gathering, insinuating a really potent influence. Protested the outspoken and highly partisan Junius: "Ministers are no longer the public servants of the state, but the private domestics of the sovereign. One particular class of men are permitted to call themselves *the King's Favourites,* as if the body of the people were the King's enemies: or as if his Majesty looked for a few favourites against the general contempt and detestation of his subjects. Edward and Richard the Second made the same distinction between the collective body of the people and a contemptible party who surrounded the throne."

Bolingbroke might sing the praises of the patriot king omnipotent, but most Englishmen instinctively rejected the idea as inconsistent with their traditions of government.

When the next general elections proved more corrupt than any yet witnessed, the people demonstrated indignation by their fresh backing for an absent but unforgotten agitator. In February 1768, there returned to England, and a hero's welcome, the compelling, squint-eyed person of the incorrigible John Wilkes.

CHAPTER 15

The People Demonstrate

Since his conviction and outlawry following the publication of Number 45 of the *North Briton,* and the *Essay on Woman,* Wilkes had twice visited England without trouble from the government. The Rockingham administration had even taken up a collection among its members and raised a few hundred pounds to help pay his debts in France. But if the exiled journalist now deduced correctly that neither the ministry nor the Commons had any particular desire to reopen the Wilkes affair, he reckoned without George and the increased hold of the monarch on Parliament. With the constitutional forces paralyzed, the only opposition the king still feared was from public discontent, and this he intended to deal with most firmly. When, that February, Wilkes had the audacity to send a man to the door of Buckingham House with a letter requesting the king's pardon, George was amused neither by its contents, nor the method of delivery. Few things could have been more calculated to raise his wrath than the thought of that blasphemous insulter of his family once more rousing the city mob.

"The expulsion of Mr Wilkes must be effected!" the king cried.

The ordinary people of London thought otherwise. So

alive was Wilkes's popularity that, with customary opportun-
ism, the former editor promptly announced his participation
in the ensuring elections as a candidate for the county of
Middlesex—a constituency adjacent to, and in some places
overlapping metropolitan London.

The election was attended by scenes of wild excitement.
Crowds of Wilkes supporters took over the main roads of the
area, refusing passage to anyone who failed to sport the
appropriate colors or produce a ticket marked "Wilkes and
No. 45." Carriages were stopped, the numbers 45 scratched
on their panels and the occupants forced to get out and shout
for the popular candidate. A rival contestant, Sir William
Beauchamp Proctor, had his coach smashed to pieces. The
London constabulary proved totally inadequate to the task
of keeping order. Wealthy people were roused from their
mansions and compelled to produce liquor and drink the
health of Wilkes; others were told to light up their
windows or have them smashed. The Austrian ambassador,
a somewhat pompous gentleman, was stopped in the street
and subjected to the indignity of having "45" chalked on
the soles of his expensive shoes.

If some found it a good joke, the king was not one of
them. He would like, he rumbled threateningly, the crowds
to attack the queen's house, "in order that he might have an
opportunity of dispersing them at the head of his Guards."
When the result of the Middlesex election proved Wilkes
victorious, George clamored for his arrest on his previous
convictions. The government hastily drew up a warrant,
but the sheriff's officers were apprehensive of using it.
"I cannot conclude," George wrote the Secretary of State
on April 25, 1768, "without expressing my sorrow that so
mean a set of men as the Sheriff's Officers can, either from
timidity or interestedness, frustrate a due exertion of the law.
If he is not soon secured, I wish you would inquire whether

there is no legal method of quickening the zeal of the Sheriffs themselves."

Two days later, the new member for Middlesex allowed himself to be apprehended by the harassed law officers, and brought to court, where bail was refused and his committal ordered to the King's Bench Prison. Once again, the authorities were bent on making a martyr of John Wilkes. "In my own opinion," declared an onlooker with some pertinence, "the House of Commons is the place where he can do the least hurt, for he is a wretched speaker and will sink to contempt." By the time the government reached the same opinion it was too late. A free pardon was suggested, but George was enraged beyond clemency. Meanwhile, the hackney coach in which the marshal of the King's Bench was escorting Wilkes to prison got as far as Westminster Bridge when it was surrounded by shouting Wilkites. Turning loose the horses, they hauled their idol manually to a beerhouse on Cornhill. Wilkes enjoyed himself a while at the tavern, then slipped away to surrender himself magnanimously at the prison.

With Wilkes inside, the crowds became menacing. Each day, a mob converged on the prison, where, wrenching slats from the footways and fences, it stoked huge bonfires to brighten its vigil. The scene at dusk was vividly portrayed in one journal. Lean, resentful men, underpaid or unemployed; wrathful hags; abusive, hollow-eyed harlots, and hordes of scraggy, barefoot urchins cast angry shadows in the fire glow. "If these tumultuous assemblies continue before the King's Bench Prison," wrote George grimly, "it is worthy of consideration whether the Attorney-General ought not to move the Court that Mr Wilkes be removed to the Tower, where the like illegal concourse will be effectually prevented, without harassing the troops. If a due firmness is shown with regard to this audacious criminal, this affair will prove a fortunate one, by restoring a due obedience to the laws. But if this is not the case, I fear anarchy will continue till what every temperate man must dread, *I mean an effusion of blood,* has vanquished."

While George prepared for a showdown, a number of the king's ministers suddenly discovered urgent appointments out of town. Grafton bundled Nancy Parsons into a coach and left the angry city for what Junius described as "a rural retirement in the arms of faded beauty." Others declared business duties in the provinces. In London, public demonstration was contagious. If the people could protest over the imprisonment of Wilkes, it seemed, they could as well protest over the inadequacy of wages, the expensiveness of food, the general impoverishment of the masses in the face of the affluence of the few. "We have independent mobs that have nothing to do with Wilkes," it was reported, "and who only take advantage of so favorable a season. The dearness of provisions incites—the hope of increased wages allures— and drink puts them in motion. The coal-heavers began; and it is well it is not a hard frost, for they have stopped all coals coming to town. The Sawyers [timbermen] rose, too, and at last the sailors, who have committed great outrages in merchant-ships and prevented their sailing."

With the precedent of the weavers to inspire them, four thousand seamen, banners and ensigns flying, marched on the king at Richmond Lodge. This time, he was not sympathetic. "I find they have just passed Kew Bridge," he wrote the Home Secretary, "and have in consequence ordered the gates to be shut, and the Guards to keep everything quiet. I have ordered the servants to say that I am out, not liking, by giving any answers, to encourage these acts of licentiousness." Three days later, Parliament reopened and large crowds assembled between the prison and Westminster in the hope that Wilkes would be allowed to take his seat in the Commons. George was prepared for their disappointment. He was ready, he declared, to take action at the shortest notice and at any hour. Justices and troops, he warned, would "show that vigour which alone makes them respected."

When Wilkes failed to materialize, the people decided to fetch him. Converging on the prison gates, they roared for their hero to be brought out. In vain, the magistrates told them to disperse. The riot act was read. The magistrates were jeered and pelted. Troops, racing to the rescue, became in turn the targets for stones and other missiles. At this point, a young man whose accuracy of aim particularly irritated the red-coated soldiers was chased by an ensign and three troopers, one of whom, attempting to stop the fugitive, mistakenly shot a bystander. Immediately, the mood of the crowd changed from frustration to fury. The troops opened general fire. Some twenty people fell, half a dozen injured mortally. The dead were snatched up and paraded through the streets by the angry mob.

At the same time, another demonstration was taking place outside Westminster, where thousands swarmed into the yards with the avowed intention of breaking into the Commons and disrupting what was widely held a corrupt and unrepresentative Parliament. George resolved to leave Richmond immediately for London. "This continuation of collections of the populace has a greater appearance of plan than any I remember," he asserted. "I therefore, in the most earnest manner, require that the Justices be told to show the vigour in Westminster that has been this day at the King's Bench Prison. Bloodshed is not what I delight in, but it seems to me the only way of restoring due obedience."

True to his patriarchal instinct, George refused to believe that the discontent of his subjects could be genuine. It was all a plan, he concluded, hatched and pursued by his political enemies. And, indeed, the activity of opposition agents was unquestionable—aristocratic young men in tat-

tered clothes could be seen encouraging outrage. But the
king confused exploitation with origination. The causes
were basic. The people were sick of the government.

On June 18, the Court of the King's Bench sentenced
Wilkes to two years imprisonment and fines amounting to
a thousand pounds. Wilkes immediately submitted his case
to the House of Commons. He did not help it, however, by
accusing the Secretary of State of deliberately projecting
bloodshed. "Were I permitted," he told the Commons, "I
could bring such evidence as would induce this honourable
House not only to entertain the same sentiments as myself, but also to forward an impeachment on the noble
lord . . ." There followed perhaps the most extraordinary
series of events ever to befall a member of Parliament. By
eighty-three votes, the Commons expelled Wilkes. In the
consequent election for the vacant seat, Middlesex returned
him again to the House, which again declared him ineligible. There followed a further election. Once more, Wilkes
was elected and rejected by Parliament. Once more, the
freeholders of Middlesex placed him in nomination.

This time, an established member of the House, Colonel
Henry Louis Luttrell, gave up his seat to contest the election.
So ardent was the support for Wilkes—a public subscription
to pay his debts raised twenty thousand pounds—that Luttrell's life was prudently insured at Lloyd's coffeehouse.
Large private wagers were made on his safety or otherwise.
Luckily for Luttrell, Wilkes's victory was so overwhelming
that the vanquished candidate was allowed to leave the
district by a delighted crowd. Thousands of freeholders,
accompanied by banners and a blaring band, marched to the
King's Bench Prison to congratulate the victor. With astonishing logic, the ministry now persuaded the House that,
since Wilkes was ineligible, Luttrell should be regarded as
the duly elected member for Middlesex.

"Thus," as Burke had it, "ended the fifth act of this

tragi-comedy—a tragi-comedy acted by his Majesty's Servants, at the desire of several persons of quality, for the benefit of Mr Wilkes and at the expense of the Constitution!"

At this point, a number of wealthy city merchants, enraged by the disaffection of the urban labor force, unadvisedly resolved to stage a counter-demonstration in favor of the sovereign and his government. Donning their finest costumes, and armed with a loyal address to the monarch, they set out, in company with a body of the "King's Friends," in a large procession of carriages for St. James's Palace. Such provocation brought the people back to the streets in renewed strength. Out of their hovels, the alehouses and sweatshops they poured, determined on battle. At many stages of its journey, the loyalist cavalcade was ambushed by violent crowds slinging mud and excrement. Closing the gates of Temple Bar, the rioters forced the procession to alter course onto their chosen fighting grounds. Some of the merchants turned their horses through back streets and fled for home. Others, including the chairman of the demonstration, struggled bespattered and torn from their vehicles and sought refuge in buildings along the way. About a third eventually reached the palace, still hounded by angry pedestrians.

"Everybody," reported the Duke of Chandos, "was covered with dirt, and several gentlemen were pulled out of their coaches by neck and heels at the palace gate. The Dukes of Kingston and Northumberland had their chariots broken to pieces, and their own and servants' clothes spoiled; and some had the impudence to sing—*God save great Wilkes, our King.* The troops beat to arms, and the Guards were trebled. Many were greatly insulted, the mob coming up to the muzzles of their firelocks, but it was thought proper for them not to fire."

If George's adrenaline pumped fast as he watched from the palace windows, his determination to remain calm and resist panic prevailed. The same day, he held his customary levee, and "one could not find out," maintained a witness, "either in his countenance or his conversation, that everything was not as quiet as usual." Earl Talbot, the pugilistic Lord Steward of the Household, was less restrained. As the crowd attempted to force the palace gates with a hearse bearing a painting of the recent shootings, he charged into the melee, grabbed two of the ringleaders in his sizable hands and dragged them into arrest. At that moment, a strong force of law officers turned up and the crowd became more restrained.

In South Audley Street, a violent attack on Bute's house lent speed to a developing resolve in the mind of the former favorite to seek refuge overseas. His diminished influence in royal affairs had not been matched by a corresponding increase in popularity, and the ailing Scot despaired of ever escaping his tormentors in England. "Whatever advantage to my health this odious journey may be," he wrote a friend before setting off, "I know too well the turn of Faction to suppose my absence is to diminish the violence I have for so many years experienced—a violence and abuse that no fear has made me too sensible to; and perhaps the more, that I may think I merit a distinguished treatment of a very opposite nature from a people I have served at the risk of my head. I have tried philosophy in vain . . . I cannot acquire callosity." Bute added that he would in many ways prefer a life of "bare necessities" in Scotland, France, Italy or Holland "to fifty-thousand pounds a year within the atmosphere of this vile place."

Royal George, controller of governments and the nation's destiny, was too preoccupied to care much about the departure of his former mentor and Dearest Friend.

At the height of the tumults, the Earl of Chatham recovered his health sufficiently to arrive unexpectedly at a royal levee one morning and roundly denounce the king for his policy toward Wilkes and America, and for the dishonesty of Parliament. Like a ghost from the past, Chatham rolled a critical eye around the political scene and saw honesty only in the Rockingham group, those liberals he had once attacked for their inexperience. "For my part," he said, "I am grown old and unable to fill any business; but this I am resolved on, that I will not even sit at Council but to meet Lord Rockingham. He, and he alone, has a knot of spotless friends, such as ought to govern this kingdom."

On January 22, 1770, Rockingham reviewed the state of the nation in a speech to the House of Lords which showed equally scant respect for the king's role in politics. Since George's accession, he declared, the condition of public affairs had grown increasingly deplorable, the discontent of the people correspondingly formidable. The new trend of government, he insisted, meant the extension of the royal prerogative and threatened the liberties of the subject. It had been encouraged by the current crop of ministers. Their policy, he exclaimed, was monstrous. Their abuse of the constitution had inflamed the whole country. It was the duty of the Lords to guide the Crown in correcting its errors; to press for a government "more in harmony with the genius and interests of the people."

Aye, growled Chatham, respect the constitution and the people would return to tranquillity; ignore it and—"may discord prevail for ever!"

George continued obstinately in his policy of treating public disquiet with contempt. In a speech to Parliament that month, he made more of a cattle disease than of the unrest in the capital. "While the whole kingdom was agitated with anxious expectation upon one great point," thundered Junius, "you meanly evaded the question, and instead of the explicit firmness and decision of a king, gave us nothing but the misery of a ruined grazier and the whining piety of a Methodist." Grafton evaded the issue more effectively. Six days after Rockingham's attack, he resigned the cares of the ministry to devote his full time to the more pleasurable demands of Nancy Parsons and Newmarket races. George was faced, suddenly, with a new embarrassment. His opponents called for a general election, but to have dissolved Parliament and appealed to the country at this of all times would have opened the gates to a flood of opposition such as no amount of bribery and manipulation could have offset. From somewhere he had to produce a minister who would both follow the court line and prove strong enough to pull the government together. He went to the Exchequer and called for the Chancellor, Lord North. "If *you* don't accept," he said plaintively, "I have no one else."

Frederick, Lord North, eldest son of the first Earl of Guildford, was thirty-seven when he became premier. Thickset and corpulent, his bloated, drowsy features hunched into his shoulders, he was, on face value, a distinctly bizarre choice. "Nothing could be more coarse, or clumsy, or ungracious than his outside," declared one critic. "Two large prominent eyes that rolled about to no purpose—for he was utterly short-sighted—a wide mouth, thick lips, and inflated visage, gave him the air of a blind trumpeter." Others likened him to a stranded fish or a fat frog. But North was shrewd, honest, quick-witted and, for all their insults, amiable. Recorded his daughter, Lady Charlotte Lindsay: "I never saw my father really out of humour. He had a drunken, stupid groom, who used to provoke him, and who, from this uncommon circumstance, was called by the children 'the man who puts Papa in a passion' . . . I think he continued all his life putting Papa in a passion and being forgiven, for I believe he died in his service."

When a member of Parliament once spoke of North as "that thing called a Minister," the "thing" grinned owlishly and patted his plump sides. "Well," he responded, "to be

sure I am a thing . . . I could not be angry at that. But when
he added 'that thing called a Minister,' he called me that
thing which of all things he himself most wished to be, and
therefore I took it as a compliment." If North's equability
disconcerted his enemies, nothing infuriated them more
than his habit of sleeping peacefully in Parliament through
their most violent attacks on him. "Even now," protested an
opponent on one such occasion, "the noble lord is slumber-
ing over the ruin of the country!" North stirred impercep-
tibly. "I wish to heaven I was," he yawned.

Wrote Burke of Frederick North: "He was a man of
admirable parts, of general knowledge, of a versatile understanding, fitted for every sort of business, of infinite wit
and pleasantry, of a delightful temper, and with a mind
most perfectly disinterested; but it would be only to degrade
myself by a weak adulation, and not to honour the memory
of a great man, to deny that he wanted something of the
vigilance and spirit of command that the time required."
For George, the new premier had several special virtues,
including an unblemished private life and a convenient lack
of connection, by blood or otherwise, with the great Whig
families. Above all, North was unimpressed by Wilkes and
the popularity of causes. "In all my memory," he once
asserted, "I do not recollect a single popular measure I
ever voted for . . . I state this to prove I am not an ambitious
man. Men may be popular without being ambitious, but
there is rarely an ambitious man who does not try to be
popular." George and Lord North were well matched.

By this time, the king had a firm grip on the "business"
side of the House of Commons and no longer needed a jobbing premier in the style of Fox. He knew the voting figures
for all the constituencies, the financial status of likely candi-
dates and their asking prices for standing as "King's Friends."
Distasteful as such matters might be to the pious sovereign,
he had become, like most autocrats, reconciled to the opinion

that ends justify means, and he had a flair for the details of management. He had studied the family histories and genealogies of his gentry. He was conversant with the army list. He was familiar with the personnel of the universities —what doctors were inclined to Socinianism, and who were sound Churchmen. He understood court etiquette to a nicety, and could recite the smallest particulars regarding the routine of ministers, secretaries, embassies and audiences. From his ministers of state to the smallest page in the anteroom or the humblest kitchen maid in the palace, Geroge knew their characters. He knew who could be bullied and who should be bribed, and he wrote quite frankly of dispensing his "golden pills."

Against the combined front of George's stubborn reaction and North's bland eschewal of popularity, the immediate riots and demonstrations were to blow out. A more effective agent of public opinion was growing to take their place. Already, journalists of such influence and vigor as Junius had risen from the "squibs" and "squeakers" of the original news sheets. Since the accession of the Georges, political journals, notably *The Senate of Lilliput,* had contrived to give approximate reports of the more important debates at Westminster. But the secrecy of parliamentary proceedings forced inaccuracies on the papers, and their inaccuracies provided ammunition for their enemies. In 1771, the Commons forbade the publication in any form of its discussions, and six printers who defied the House were called to account. Once more, public opinion was outraged, and, when the magistrates of London stepped in to exonerate the printers, the attempt to interfere with the press was quietly dropped.

A situation of momentous dimensions was developing. Not only were the electors at last to be effectively informed of the performance of their representatives, but the views of the nation itself would be stridently conveyed to government by a free press. From this era of public frustration and unrest dated the first great English newspapers, gathering and disseminating public opinion of all shades, influencing the course of debates, illuminating ministerial actions, generally becoming a force in practical statesmanship.

Meanwhile, Wilkes had opted out of turmoil for a new life. In April 1769, he had been released from prison and elected an alderman of London. No longer impoverished, the opportunist emerged proudly as a man of the establishment, seeking comfort for his middle age. When the county of Middlesex again returned him as its member of Parliament, the Commons raised no objection, and the one-time agitator happily became not only lord mayor, and later chamberlain of the city of London, but even a respectful courtier. Time healed the king's bitterness. Once, when they met at a royal reception, George asked the new, mellow Wilkes what had become of an old friend of his rebel days. "*Friend,* Sir!" exclaimed Wilkes. "He is no friend of mine! He was a Wilkite, Sir . . . I never was."

CHAPTER 16

The Storm Breaks

If there is a form of courage to be found in the bold actions of naturally fearful men which transcends that of men who are by nature fearless, George was indeed brave. From the moment he accepted the destiny of greatness expounded by his father and others—a destiny shunned by the earlier Georges—his predominant fear had been of his own incapacity to live with it. Sensitive, introverted, temperamentally vulnerable, the king struggled to eliminate his inherent weaknesses by overcompensating, by acting the stubborn, inflexible strong man. Especially was this true of his attitude to the colonies. The repeal of the Stamp Act, the "fatal compliance" as he came to regard it, jangled on George's nerves like a bad tooth. A bolder, more assured leader would have cursed the circumstance and forgotten it. George nursed the memory of his impotence, his imagined humiliation, with characteristic obsession. When the opportunity arose, he returned, still smarting, to the battlefield.

His chance came during Chatham's illness. While Pitt had been at the helm of the state, George had been powerless to interfere in America. But when ill health removed the premier, George was quick to bring pressure to bear on the Chancellor of the Exchequer, then Charles Townshend.

Townshend was induced to reopen the matter of American taxes. As Burke said: "The whole body of courtiers drove him onward. They always talked as if the King stood in a sort of humiliated state until something of the kind should be done." Townshend was acting against the wishes of his leader and knew it. But Chatham was not pursuing him, George was. The ambitious Chancellor was flattered. "I will not use so strong an expression as to say that Townshend was treacherous to this administration," wrote an observer, "but he certainly saw that the Earl of Chatham's greatness was on the decline; and that he should most readily increase his own importance by acquiescing in the wishes of the King. He therefore brought forward measures tending to revive the question of the right of the British Parliament to tax the American colonies."

Townshend's bill—to impose a tax on tea, and a few other items imported into the colonies—was not in detail significant. The entire revenue involved was less than £40,000 a year, while the actual tax on tea, threepence a pound, was a fourth of the tax on tea in England. What was important to Townshend was that George should be gratified by the principle. More important to the world, the colonists were mortified. Injury led to anger; anger to violence. When the first blood was shed in the Boston riot of 1770, George was able to strengthen his own views in the Cabinet by the inclusion, among others, of the rabidly anti-American Sandwich, who openly alluded to the colonists as rebels and cowards, loudly exclaiming that three battalions and a few frigates would bring them to their senses.

On the subject of America, George was both stubborn and ignorant. He might spend hours talking to the men on his farms, inquiring of their lives and their welfare, but his interest in the problems of his overseas subjects was marred by a blind spot. "George shared the opinion of most of his people [in England] that the colonists could safely be

despised, and that if firmness were used they would submit,"
one historian has written. Like precocious children, as the
king saw it, they should be taught to be seen and not heard;
to obey their royal father. This, of all times, his attitude
suggested, was the time to "be a king," to trust in God and
an untroubled conscience. "No one," he wrote later, "must
suppose the Americans poor mild persons who after unheard
of grievances had no choice . . . the truth is that the too
great leniency of this country increased their pride and
encouraged them." His distrust of those who differed with
him on the matter, even in the smallest way, became chronic.
"I wish nothing but good," he asserted, "therefore everyone
who does not agree with me is a traitor and a scoundrel." In
one terse statement he had branded not only his enemies,
but such loyal and reasonable men as Franklin and the
moderation they represented.

A bold, if singularly respectful address from American
delegates, now met in a Congress, did nothing to placate
the king. "As your Majesty enjoys the signal distinction of
reigning over free men," ran the message, "the language of
freedom cannot be displeasing. We ask for peace, liberty
and safety. We wish not a diminution of the prerogative,
nor do we solicit the grant of any new right in our favour.
In the magnanimity and justice of your Majesty and Parliament, we confide for a redress of our grievances, trusting
that when the causes of our apprehensions are removed, our
future conduct will prove us not unworthy of the regard we
have been accustomed, in our happier days, to enjoy. We
implore, therefore, your Majesty, as the loving father of all
your people, connected by the same bonds of law, loyalty,
faith and blood, not to suffer the transcendant relation,
formed by these ties, to be further violated in uncertain
expectation of effects which, if attained, never can compensate for the calamities through which they must be
gained. So may your Majesty enjoy every temporal felicity,

through a long and glorious reign, and your descendants inherit your prosperity and dominions, till time shall be no more."

To this, George replied coldly, without compromise: "It is with the utmost astonishment that I find any of my subjects capable of encouraging the rebellious disposition which unhappily exists in some of my colonies in North America. Having entire confidence in the wisdom of my Parliament, the great council of the nation, I will steadily pursue those measures which they have recommended for the support of the constitutional rights of Great Britain and the protection of the commercial interests of my kingdom."

In December 1773, an incident at Boston provided the monarch with a chance to display the full weight of his righteous indignation. According to a report received at the Admiralty, London, from the Commander in Chief, North Coast of America: "Last evening between 6 and 7 o'clock, a large mob assembled with axes, etc., encouraged by Mr John Hancock, Samuel Adams, and others, and marched in a body to the wharf where the tea-ships lay, and there destroyed the whole by starting it into the sea. During the whole of this transaction neither the Governor, Magistrates, owner, or Revenue Officers of this place, ever called for my assistance. If they had, I could easily have prevented the execution of this plan, but must have endangered the lives of innocent people by firing upon the town."

The so-called Boston Tea Party, though not an event of the gravest category, was deplored both by America's friends in England and by her own leading statesmen. Washington and Chatham alike were prepared to back North's government in seeking redress. But for George, redress was not enough. Through repression, the king sought to demonstrate the weight of his authority. In this, as in most of his American policies, he carried the more conciliatory premier with him. North was by nature and training a loyal man, and

George quickly learned to exploit his allegiance. At the beginning of 1774, a bill was introduced to Parliament closing the port of Boston to all commerce. Another punished Massachusetts by withdrawing the liberties it had enjoyed ever since the Pilgrim Fathers landed there. Its charter was altered. The choice of its council was transferred from the people to the Crown, and the nomination of its judges was transferred to the governor.

Massachusetts responded angrily. Into the Crown offices, London, during the ensuing months, flowed news of mounting unrest. One report, from the naval officer in charge of the station, stated ominously: "Disguised mobs have lately in the night-time surrounded the houses of the newly-made Councillors of this Province, and endeavoured, by threatening their lives and properties, to compel them to resign the King's appointment. One of those Councillors called on me this morning, who is obliged to quit his house and for safety come with his family to Boston. There are more in the same situation, and there is great reason to apprehend every extravagance from these misled, violent people." Again, some days later: "Since I closed my last letter, affairs have suddenly taken a more serious turn than I believe was generally apprehended. The mob yesterday assembled in great numbers at Cambridge, a place eight miles from Boston, some with arms, others with clubs. They seized the High Sheriff of the County and obliged him, to save his life, to sign an obligation to desist entirely from any execution of his duties under the new laws. They pursued a Commissioner of the Customs within sight of the piquet of the Guard at the Town Neck, and it was with the utmost difficulty he got safe to Boston, now become the only place of safety for people in employment of the Crown. Their infatuation seems to be such that an effectual interposition of the military power is, I am afraid, the only means left to restore these deluded people to a right use of their reason."

Meanwhile, if Chatham had deplored the Tea Party, he was outraged by a punishment which deprived the townspeople indiscriminately of their livelihoods. "Reparation," he wrote, "ought first to be demanded in a solemn manner and refused by the town and magistracy of Boston before such a bill of pains and penalties can be called just." In Parliament, Thomas Pownall, one of the members best informed on America, sounded a prophetic warning. "I tell you that the Americans will oppose the measures now proposed by you in a more vigorous way than before . . . Should recourse be had to arms, you will hear of other officers than those appointed by your governor. Should matters once come to that, it will be, as it was in the late civil wars of this country, of little consequence to dispute who were the aggressors. That will be merely a matter of opinion."

North was not to be shaken from the king's purpose. "The Americans have tarred and feathered your subjects, have plundered your merchants, burned your ships, denied all obedience to your laws and authorities; yet so clement and so long-forbearing has our conduct been that it is incumbent on us now to take a different course. Whatever may be the consequence," North told the House, "we must risk something. If we do not, all is over." Not only both Houses of Parliament agreed with him, but much of the country. According to North, the average taxpayer in Great Britain contributed twenty-five shillings a year to the revenues, the average American only sixpence. "Is this equitable?" he demanded. The country gentlemen of England saw no reason to be sorry for the colonists.

As the preparations for military action got under way, the nation's commercial interests joined the middle classes behind George. "The merchants began to sniff the cadaverous *haut goût* of lucrative war," declared Burke; "the freighting business never was so lively, on account of the prodigious taking up for transport service: great orders for provisions of all kinds, new clothing for the troops, puts life into the woollen manufactures."

For the first time in his life, George had a popular following. The die was cast, he wrote excitedly to Lord North. The colonies must either prove themselves or submit, and they would remain lions, he asserted, only so long as the government were lambs. Four regiments would be enough to frighten the Americans. "If we take the resolute part, they will undoubtedly be very meek." Such was not the opinion of others. Warned the French minister, the Duc de Choiseul: "Let England but attempt to establish taxes in her colonies and those countries, greater than England in extent, and perhaps becoming more populous—having fisheries, forests, shipping, corn, iron and the like—will easily and fearlessly separate from the mother-country." Pownall stressed the economic strength of the colonies. "The only sacrifice they have to make," he told the government, "is that of a few follies and a few luxuries. Necessity is not the ground of their commerce with you. It is merely the affectation of your modes and customs, the love for home, as they call England, that makes them like everything that comes from thence. But passion may be conquered by passion. They will abominate, as sincerely as they now love you; and if they do, they have within themselves everything requisite to the food, raiment, or the dwelling of mankind, and have no need of your commerce."

On December 24, 1774, the Secretary for War, William Lord Barrington, sent to the Secretary for the Colonies, then William Lord Dartmouth, an objective and carefully reasoned argument against embarking on a war with the colonies. Some of the points he listed were as follows: That the contest would cost Britain more than she could possibly gain. That the dispute was merely a point of honor, since no ministry of the future would try to impose internal taxes on America. That success in such a conflict was extremely problematical due to the vast extent of the colonies and the fact that the population was practiced in the use of firearms. That even overwhelming success would be at the expense of the horrors and sufferings of civil war, and that the cost of maintaining the country in subjection would be enormous. "It is true," said Barrington of the Americans, "they have not hitherto been thought brave; but enthusiasm gives vigour of mind and body unknown before."

Still George was stubbornly unimpressed. It was precisely the "point of honor" which concerned him. Moreover, he refused to believe that British armies, which had defeated the flower of the French forces from Canada to India, would be worried by raw colonial militiamen.

In January 1775, Chatham echoed Barrington's arguments in the House of Lords, adding that war with America would inevitably involve France and Spain and threaten the whole empire. Chatham was now influenced by Benjamin Franklin, with whom he had spent many hours discussing American affairs. Following his previous stay in London, Franklin had paid visits to Scotland, Ireland, France and Germany, in each of which he had been well received. But his most important business had been in England. In 1768, Georgia had appointed him her agent in London, and, in 1770, Massachusetts had followed suit. Franklin had fought tirelessly against British methods of taxing America. He had tried humor, publishing the so-called *Edict of the King of Prussia,* a popular skit in which England was settled by German colonists claiming the same kind of duties from England as England claimed from America. He had tried to offer the British government a way out by blaming some of their policies on the Tories of America. His efforts had brought him ministerial insults and his removal from the deputy postmaster generalship of America. Increasingly, Franklin turned to Chatham.

"If his Lordship, with the other great and wise men of his nation, would unite and exert themselves, it might yet be rescued out of the mangling hands of the present set of blundering ministers," Franklin said. Every day, his dual role as ardent American and loyal subject of the king was becoming less tenable. Shortly before Chatham's speech in the House of Lords, Franklin had impressed on him the need to reduce the heat from the situation by withdrawing the British forces in Boston. Their presence, he said, was both futile and provocative. A casual squabble might spark the flames of a civil war. Chatham accordingly moved an address to the throne for the removal of the king's forces from the American port. Having recommended what he called the "decent, manly and properly expressed" petition of Congress to the monarch, the decrepit but still fiery statesman told the House: "I trust it is obvious to your Lordships that all attempts to impose servitude upon such men [the American leaders], to establish despotism over such a mighty continental nation, must be vain, must be fatal. We shall be forced ultimately to retract. Let us retract while we can, not when we must."

Unfortunately for the friends of America, while the court party was stirred to extremes of loyalty by the king's tenacity—as a contemporary wrote, "The war was considered as the war of the King personally. Those who supported it were called the King's friends, while those who wished the country to pause and reconsider were branded as disloyal"—the opposition was weakened by the dogmatism of Chatham and Rockingham. The former refused to budge from the view that Britain had no right to impose taxes of any kind on America. The latter clung obstinately, even smugly, to his brainchild, the Declaratory Act. "I look back with very great satisfaction and content," wrote Rockingham, "to the line which I—indeed, emphatically I—took in the year 1766. The Stamp Act was repealed, and the doubt of the right of this country was fairly fixed." Such differences helped to confuse the doves of Parliament.

When the Lords rejected the motion to withdraw troops from Boston, Chatham conferred further with Franklin, then, in February, limped back to the House with a positive plan of conciliation. In short, he proposed that Britain should renounce the Declaratory Act while America would acknowledge her allegiance to the British Crown in all matters relating to the general interests of the empire. Thus, the two countries would return to the harmonious relationship which had existed prior to the Stamp Act, and "true reconcilement avert impending calamities."

Chatham's speech was received appreciatively by Franklin and many American merchants gathered at Westminster to witness the proceedings. Sandwich, replying for the government, was heated and abusive. He found it hard to believe, he exclaimed, that a proposal so favorable to the hostile and traitorous American people could be the work of any British peer. It seemed to him rather the product of some colonist. Glowering at Franklin, he continued: "I fancy I have my eye on the person who drew it up; one of the bitterest and most mischievous enemies this country has ever known." Retorted Chatham with alacrity: "The plan is my own. Yet I make no scruple to declare that, were I the first minister of this country and had the care of settling this momentous business, I should not be ashamed of publicly calling to my assistance a person so perfectly acquainted with the whole of American affairs as the gentleman alluded to, and so injuriously reflected on—one whom all Europe holds in high estimation."

With the virulence and overwhelming weight of the king's friends against him, Chatham lost his temper. Turning to the ministers present, he shouted: "I am not much astonished, not much surprised that men who hate liberty should detest those who prize it, or that those who want virtue themselves should endeavour to persecute those who possess it. Were I disposed, I could demonstrate that the whole of your political conduct has been one continued series of weakness, temerity, despotism, ignorance, futility, negligence, blundering and the most notorious servility, incapacity and corruption. On re-consideration, I must allow you one merit—a strict attention to your own interests . . . Who can wonder that you should put a negative on any measure which must annihilate your power, deprive you of emoluments, and at once reduce you to that state of insignificance for which God and nature designed you?"

This attack on the monarch's hirelings demoted Chatham to a new low in George's estimation. The old man's brain, he wrote the premier later, "contains nothing but specious words and malevolence." Nevertheless, George and North were stung into a conciliatory gesture of their own, albeit a halfhearted one, by way of restoring appearances. If the colonists would promise to contribute an unspecified sum toward the defense of the empire, the maintenance of civil government in America and the administration of justice, offered North, Britain would impose no more taxes upon them, unless for the regulation of commerce. Chatham described the proposal as "mere verbiage; a most puerile mockery that will be spurned in America, as well as laughed at here by the friends of America and by the unrelenting enemies of that noble country." It left the amount of money required for defense to be decided not by the colonial assemblies but by the Crown. It did not provide for the repeal of the Declaratory Act. Nor did North combine the proposal with any steps to postpone the punitive measures already voted. As Franklin saw it, the government was offering an olive branch in one hand, a sword in the other.

After a last unsuccessful attempt to influence George

through the king's friend Earl Howe, Treasurer of the Navy, Franklin finally left England under threat of arrest. In his opinion, there were no "clashing interests." Settlement was "rather a matter of punctilio, which two or three sensible people might settle in half an hour." If so, sensible people were notably lacking in government. The day before departing, Franklin confided to Burke that America had enjoyed happier days under British rule than possibly she might ever enjoy again. Now, he said, must come the separation. Burke was moved. A few days later, he made an eloquent speech for settlement in the House of Commons, but the government's support was too strong for him. "A great empire and little minds go but ill together," he flung at the ministers. Wrote Walpole: "Pacification with America is not the measure adopted. More regiments are ordered thither. They are bold Ministers, methinks, who do not hesitate on a civil war."

"I am not sorry that the line of conduct seems now chalked out," George had already written to Lord North.

In the spring of 1775, George received news of the clashes at Lexington and Concord. The reports of the British officers, biased in support of the behavior of their own troops, and sometimes distorted by personal animosity toward colonists, did nothing to soothe the king's feelings toward America. Lieutenant-General Thomas Gage, the amiable but less than dynamic British commander at Boston, had obtained intelligence of a rebel munitions store at Concord, about twenty miles from the seaport. Accordingly, as George duly learned, Gage had detached Colonel Francis Smith of the 10th Foot, and some nine hundred grenadiers and light infantrymen, with orders to destroy the magazine. At five o'clock in the morning, a section of the force under a Major Pitcairn entered Lexington to find the militia of the place assembled on the green.

"I understand," ran Smith's official account of the incident, "from the report of Major Pitcairn, and from many officers, that they found on a green, close to the road, a body of the country-people drawn up in military order, with arms and accoutrements, and, as appeared after, loaded; and that they had posted some men in a dwelling and meeting house. Our troops advanced towards them, without any intention of injuring them, further to inquire the reason of their being thus assembled, and, if not satisfactory, to have secured their arms. But they in confusion went off, principally to the left; only one of them fired before he went off, and three or four more jumped over a wall and fired from behind it among the soldiers, on which the troops returned it and killed several of them. They likewise fired on the soldiers from the meeting and dwelling house. We had one man wounded, and Major Pitcairn's horse shot in two places." On arriving at Concord, "We had opportunities of convincing them [the Americans] of our good intentions, but they were sulky, and one of them even struck Major Pitcairn."

Having destroyed the ordnance at Concord, and engaged in a further skirmish, Smith's companies proceeded to withdraw toward Boston, when, according to British reports, they were assailed in an exceedingly ungentlemanly fashion by the people of the country, who fired upon them "in the most wanton manner, from behind trees, houses and hedges." When a relief force from Boston formed a hollow square with textbook precision to receive the harassed column, the American response was beyond the bounds of military etiquette. The colonists simply remained in cover and picked off the pride of the British infantry with relative impunity. If this was not enough to scandalize king and court, there were gruesome details of colonial behavior. "The rebels fought like savages," reported one officer, "and treated some who had the misfortune to fall like savages, for they scalped them and cut off their ears with the most unmanly brutality. This has irritated the troops to a very high degree; and if in future contests they should meet with some severities from us, they may thank themselves. We got to Boston in the evening, fatigued with the march and duty of the day."

Gage was now blockaded in Boston by the rebels. British journals carried harrowing accounts of the plight of the city. "Perhaps this is the last letter you will ever receive from me," wrote a Boston merchant whose correspondence appeared in the *Edinburgh Weekly*, "for before the return of Captain Brown I may be buried in the ashes of Boston, should not a pitying Providence interfere and save it from destruction. I have a sick mother, a lying-in wife, and five children, all completely wretched. It would soften the most brutal nature to behold children crying to their parents and mothers weeping over their starving children." George urged hasty action on the government, and reinforcements were sent to the besieged town under Sir William Howe, colonel of the Welsh Fusiliers. Though still outnumbered, Gage had the advantage of crack regiments against militiamen, and should not have been insecure. Incredibly, however, he had failed to occupy the heights on the outskirts, and, at daybreak of June 17, the captain of the British ship *Lively* reported them occupied by the enemy.

The subsequent contest for the vital eminence—the Battle of Bunker Hill—was a public spectacle. Wrote one who was present: "Far on the left, across the waters of the Charles, the American camp had poured forth its thousands to the hills, and the whole population of the country inland for many miles had gathered to witness a struggle charged with the fate of their nation. Beacon Hill rose from out the appalling silence of the town of Boston like a pyramid of living faces, with every eye fixed on the fatal point; and men hung along the yards of the shipping, or were suspended on cornices, cupolas, and steeples in thoughtless security, while every other sense was lost in the absorbing interest of the sight."

They saw the renowned British infantry in their square-skirted coats, their pipe-clayed breeches, long queues and Kevenhuller hats, wading uphill through the long grass, bayonets flashing. They saw them fall, waver, reassemble and advance again on the American redoubt. They saw the inexperienced militiamen opposing them fight like veterans under the steadying influence of Israel Putnam. And, like John Burgoyne, who witnessed the scene from the batteries, they saw the suburb of Charlestown aflame from incendiaries, "a large and noble town in one great blaze. The church-steeples, being timber, were great pyramids of fire above the rest . . . The roar of cannon, mortars and musketry; the crash of churches, ships upon the stocks, and whole streets falling together . . . made the whole a picture, and a compilation of horror and importance, beyond anything that ever came my lot to be witness to."

George was getting his showdown.

CHAPTER 17

O Brothers! O Sisters!

As the grim rumblings from America crossed the Atlantic, George's desk was stacked high with trouble from elsewhere in the empire. America, in the end, proved George's obsession, but there were times when other problems seemed equally pressing. The defeat of the French in India had raised the poorly paid merchant-clerks of the East India Company into rulers whose quick exploitation of the situation by tyranny and corruption threatened the ruination of Britain's interests and vast areas of the country. In two years, one sixth of the population of Bengal died of starvation. Robert Clive, the victorious officer who had profited more than most by the spoils of his Indian enterprise, at last realized that private gain must give way to a new attitude of responsibility. From 1765, Clive embarked on a struggle to eliminate private dealings by the company's officials, and to prevent their accepting gifts from the natives. For his trouble, he was rewarded with the opposition of the great majority of the clerks in India, and with mutiny in the ranks of the Army. On top of this, the intrigues of Madras officials to enlist the fighting Mahrattas against the military adventurer Haidar Ali of Mysore failed, and Haidar

Ali's saber-wielding horsemen poured onto the plains of the Carnatic.

In the spring of 1766, George learned that the invading tribesmen had reached Madras and Fort St. George, while the French, it was said, were preparing to re-enter the eastern theater of war. In the event, Haidar Ali was temporarily pacified, but company affairs had dropped to a low ebb. Shares plummeted; prominent investors were ruined. As more native princes proved intransigent, military expenses rose by over £160,000, while revenues declined in the same period by £400,000. By 1771, the company was in the position of needing three years in which to pay outstanding bills, and, a year later, was looking for loans from the government. With Clive now crying the misgovernment of India, George and North were faced with acting or witnessing the collapse of the eastern enterprise.

The solution decided upon was a typical North compromise. Shy of actually taking over Bengal, Madras and Bombay—the company's bases in India—the government opted for a loan of £1,400,000 linked with measures of reform which would give the Crown some control of the administration in India. The so-called Regulating Act of 1773 established a governor-general and a supreme court of judicature for all British possessions in India, "prohibited judges and members of Council from trading, forbade any receipt of presents from the natives, and ordered that every act of the Directors should be signified to the Government to be approved or disallowed."

Meanwhile, a committee set up by Parliament to investigate the activities of the company provoked the angry remonstrance from Clive that he had been arraigned like a common sheep-stealer. Resolutions were passed censuring "the corruption and treachery" of the early days of British rule in India, but a censure of Clive himself was defeated, the Commons voting unaminously "That Robert Lord Clive did at the same time render great and meritorious services to his country."

Warren Hastings, who had accepted a writership (clerk's office) in the company's service while still a boy, was named the first governor-general of Bengal and did much through his administrative and humanitarian attributes to raise Britain's interest in India above mere commercial considerations. Hastings pensioned off many of the native princes who had hitherto hindered effective government, organized the basis of a civil service which later became the pride of British India, and stamped on corruption with due severity. Familiar with Indian languages, he was both sympathetic with, and enjoyed the sympathies of, many of the indigenous people and their leaders. Nevertheless, the Regulating Act was still a half measure, and many troubles lay ahead. Hastings, frequently hamstrung by the company, beset by the blunders of subordinates and undermined by French conspiracies, was to endure many failures in military campaigns until at last, London learned once more that the feared Haidar Ali was on the march.

Nearer home, Ireland posed problems of the most depressing kind. The great majority of the people of Ireland, the native Catholics, were impoverished, little better than serfs to their Protestant masters, who boasted their foreign extraction and regarded the appellation "Irishman" an insult. Not even all the Protestants were well off. The Presbyterians, the bulk of the Ulster settlers, were prohibited by law from holding civil, military and municipal offices. Administration and justice remained in the power of the Established Church (about a twelfth of Ireland's population), while the government was monopolized by a handful of absentee landowners who left their affairs in the hands of the so-called parliamentary undertakers, a small group who undertook to "manage" Parliament on their own terms. For these men, Irish politics meant pensions, preferment, bribery and plunder. True, the Irish Parliament was subordinate to the English Privy Council, but the undertakers, when united, were a very powerful body. Not only could they block business in their own Parliament, but they were skilled at provoking the discontented and bewildered peasants to riot.

A repeated Irish demand was for free trade. Ireland was a grazing country, yet to protect the interests of English graziers, the Irish were forbidden to export cattle to England. To protect English wool-producers, the export of Irish wool was prohibited, while other manufactures were loaded with duties. The advent of the American war, bringing further prohibitions on commerce, saw the free-trade movement gather strength, and its English opponents rally to counter it. When the Irish emulated the colonies by forming non-importation agreements against English goods, the similarity between the situation there and in America was too striking for George's comfort. That there would be dire trouble in Ireland if something were not done to relieve the position was obvious. That there would be trouble at home if something *were* done, was equally patent. The king and North could scarcely shift for their problems. When they turned from one crisis, another was facing them.

If George received headaches from afar, he suffered more personally from heartaches at close hand. Looking back to his childhood, he must have reflected on the determination with which his mother had isolated his brothers and sisters from the society whose morals she so deplored, and wondered what good it had done most of them. Augusta had enforced her rule firmly in the early days. George's lively brother Henry had once complained that, while other children were confined by colds and epidemics, he was confined permanently. When one of her sons had offended her, Augusta would instruct the others: "Laugh at the fool! Just laugh at him!" Even the drowsiest of her children, William, had been provoked to protest. "I was wondering," he had told his mother one day, "what I should feel if I had a son as unhappy as you made me."

For all her nursery strictures, Augusta had proved no match in the end against the erotic, pleasure-seeking Hanoverian blood which had beguiled most of her children at an early age. George alone conformed approximately to the pattern she had planned for him. Those of the others who survived adolescence, quickly kicked over the maternal traces to plunge into the life of indulgence Augusta denounced. Like their paternal ancestors, they were destined to take to the beds of their lovers with more enthusiasm than they took to the duties of their station, and the inhibited, rigidly moralistic George watched their exploits with mounting anxiety and disgust.

Frederick, the king's youngest brother, had died at fifteen of consumption, a disease which also claimed a sister, Louisa Anne, in her late teens. By some accounts, they had been the most promising of Augusta's brood. There remained, apart from George, the dukes of York, Gloucester and Cumberland, and the princesses Augusta and Caroline. Of these, Edward, Duke of York, was the first to show his paces. A generous but foppish young man with defective eyesight, Edward was soon on sufficiently close terms with, among others, the Duchess of Richmond, Lady Stanhope and the Countess of Tyrconnel, perhaps to compensate for the weakness of his vision. It may not have been that poor: at least one of his favorites, Lady Mary Coke, was a celebrated beauty. So assured was her ladyship of his intention to marry her that, it was said, she took to signing her name in the fashion of royalty.

To add to the displeasure occasioned George by his brother's amorous merry-go-round, Edward quickly threw in his lot with the political opposition. It was not a consid-

eration for too long, since he died in Monaco in 1767, his
health seemingly weakened by a chill caught at one of the
balls to which he was addicted. According to one report:
"His immoderate pursuit of pleasure and unremitted fatigues
in travelling . . . succeeded without interuption by balls
and entertainments, had thrown his blood, naturally distempered and full of humours, into a state that brought on
a putrid and irresistible fever."

William, Duke of Gloucester, less flighty than Edward,
but equally passionate, was the closest in temperament of
Augusta's brood to his brother George. Walpole described
him with uncustomary respect as "reserved, serious, pious,
of the most decent and sober deportment, and possessing a
plain understanding, though no brilliance." William also
resembled the king in his large nose and flaccid mouth.
Where he diverged sharply from his senior brother was in
his determination to be diverted neither by duty nor propriety from youthful infatuation. William was scarcely out
of boyhood when he fell in love with Lady Maria Waldegrave, the illegitimate daughter of a milliner, and the
widow of a first husband old enough to be her father.
Maria was beautiful, ambitious, engaging and dignified,
with a striking and statuesque elegance. She was also several
years older than her royal lover, and already possessed
three children.

George tried to put an end to the scandal. "The report
of this week," gossiped his old sweetheart, Lady Sarah,
"is that the King has forbid the Duke of Gloucester to speak
to his pretty widow; the truth is that she has gone out of
town, but more 'tis difficult to know. He has given her five
pearl bracelets that cost £500—that's not for nothing,
surely?"

For a brief fortnight, the couple remained apart, but William's infatuation was persistent and their intimacy soon
resumed. In 1766 they were secretly married, although it

was not until 1772 that the fact was made public. During the intervening years, George, no less than his subjects, assumed Maria to be his brother's mistress. News of the marriage did little to console him. The *"mésalliance,"* he insisted, was "a highly disgraceful step." He could not receive such a woman at court "without affronting all the sovereigns of Europe." To Lord North, he wrote dejectedly: "I cannot deny that on the subject of this Duke my heart is wounded: I have ever loved him with the fondness one bears to a child." Later, George told the premier that his sister-in-law "must always be odious to me." Nevertheless, time and the Duchess of Gloucester's irreproachable domesticity softened the king's heart, and he showed her, eventually, both kindness and generosity. William, himself, was less gracious. Before long, he had formed an attachment to a Lady Almeria Carpenter. Maria obtained an informal separation.

Henry, Duke of Cumberland, the youngest brother, was a fellow of very different mettle. The handsome one of the bunch, he had good, firm features, but a weak and frivolous character which impelled him, on release from his mother's supervision, immediately to the brothels and drinking pads of London. While this placed him at no great variance to many well-bred contemporaries, his involvement with the wife of Lord Grosvenor, a notorious libertine and opportunist, was singularly incautious. Grosvenor brought a court action for damages in which letters from the duke to Lady Henrietta Grosvenor quickly settled the issue. Samples produced in court were so appalling in spelling, style and syntax that the proceedings were repeatedly held up by gusts of laughter from the public. "His royal highness's diction and learning," it appears, "scarce exceeded that of a cabin boy." Of his relationship with Lady Henrietta, his "ever dearest little angel," however, there could be no doubt.

As a result of the action, Henry was ordered to pay

£10,000 damages to Lord Grosvenor and a further £3,000 in legal costs. Not possessing such money, he begged the aid of his older brother William, and the two of them pleaded with George for assistance. The king, already shocked by the publicity, was now doubly horrified. "A subject of the most private and delicate kind," he confided to North, "obliges me to lose no time in acquainting you that my two brothers have this day applied to me on the difficulty that the folly of the younger has drawn him into; the affair is too public for you to doubt but that it regards the lawsuit; the time will expire this day seven-night, when he must pay the damages and the other expenses attending it. He has taken no one step to raise the money, and now has applied to me as the only means by which he can obtain it, promising to repay it in a year and a half.

"I therefore promised to write to you, though I saw great difficulty in your finding so large a sum as thirteen thousand pounds in so short a time; but their pointing out to me that the prosecutor would certainly force the house, which would at this licentious time occasion disagreeable reflections on the rest of the family as well as on him. I shall speak more fully to you on this subject on Wednesday, but the time is so short that I did not choose to delay opening this affair until then; besides, I am not fond of taking persons on delicate affairs unprepared; whatever can be done ought to be done; and I ought as little as possible to appear in so very improper a business."

The money was found, and Henry received a weighty royal lecture. "I cannot express how much I feel at being in the least concerned in an affair that my way of thinking has ever taught me to behold as highly improper," wrote the outraged George. "But I flatter myself the truths I have thought it incumbent to utter may be of some use in his future conduct." The king was an optimist. The case was hardly settled when the wayward Duke of Cumberland, abandoning Henrietta Grosvenor, embarked on a similar intrigue with the wife of a wealthy timber merchant. Fortunately for the royal family, this time the husband was a sufficiently obsequious devotee of royalty to be flattered by the dubious connection. He allowed his wife to parade openly with her lover. This latest scandal was still common currency when Henry announced his marriage to a pert widow named Anne Horton. Mr. Horton had been a country gentleman of Catton in Derbyshire.

Of all types, Anne was the type Henry found hardest to resist. Lithe and slender, with a girlishly pretty face, her talents, as Wraxall put it, "were more specious than solid—better calculated for show than for use, for captivating admiration than for exciting esteem." Her eyes were so flirtatious, her coquetry so habitual, that, according to those who knew her, one was simultaneously undeceived and impressed. "The new Princess of the Blood," exclaimed Walpole, "is a young widow of twenty-four, extremely pretty, not handsome, very well made, with the most amorous eyes in the world, and eyelashes a yard long; coquette beyond measure, artful as Cleopatra, and completely mistress of all her passions and projects. Indeed, eyelashes three-quarters of a yard shorter would have served to conquer such a head as she has turned."

George summed up his brother's betrothal in two weary expletives: "You fool! You blockhead!"

His distress was not diminished by the fact that Augusta was by this time dying of cancer, and could scarcely draw comfort from her youngest son's recklessness. The king immediately let it be known that those who chose to associate with the Cumberlands would be unwelcome at St. James's. He also pressed upon Parliament the Royal Marriage Act, a measure to prevent any further descendants of George II, except foreigners, marrying without the sovereign's consent. The bill provoked much private opposition in the government, one school of thought asserting that it was a sop to the queen's pride—a device to protect her from undesirable sisters-in-law—while another claimed it would merely encourage irregular relationships in the royal family. "It was well said of some persons," wrote a contemporary, "that the title of the Bill should be 'An Act to encourage Fornication and Adultery in the descendants of George II.'"

But George was resolute. "I do expect every nerve to be strained to carry the bill through both Houses with becoming firmness, for it is not a question that immediately relates to administration, but personally to myself, and therefore I have a right to expect a hearty support from every one in my service, and shall remember defaulters." Westminster did his bidding.

Meanwhile, George could find little comfort in the rest of his family. His eldest sister, Princess Augusta, who looked remarkably like him, had been an admirer of Pitt, and, to the chagrin of both the king and his mother, "inveighed openly and boldly against the policy of the Court." She was married off to Charles, Prince of Brunswick, who took her abroad but reserved his fondest attentions for another woman. "My father," wrote his daughter by the Princess Augusta many years later, "was most entirely attached to a lady for thirty years who, in fact, was his mistress. She was the beautifullest creature and the cleverest; but though my father continued to pay my poor mother all possible respect, my poor mother could not suffer this attachment. The consequence was that I did not know what to do between them: when I was civil to the one I was scolded by the other; and I was very tired of being shuttlecock between them."

There remained the youngest and most charming of all the princess dowager's surviving children, Caroline—clever, athletic and comely, yet, for all her advantages, bound by the curse of the family. At fifteen, Caroline was tragically married to Christian of Denmark, a king whose perverting influence was anticipated by many, perhaps even by Caroline herself. "The poor Queen of Denmark," bemoaned a lady of the time, "is gone out alone into the wide world; not a creature she knows to attend her any further than Altona. It is worse than dying; for die she must to all she has ever seen or known; but then it is only dying out of one bad world into another just like it, and where she is to have cares and fears, and dangers and sorrows, that will all yet be new to her. May it please God to protect, and instruct and comfort her, poor child as she is! They have just been telling me how bitterly she cried in the coach, as far as anybody saw her." Reynolds, who painted Caroline before her departure, reported that she sobbed every time she sat for him.

Marriage to the debauched and futile Christian was a traumatic experience for the English princess. Taking the lead from her husband, Caroline quickly decided that if she were not to enjoy a normal married existence, she would have to make a life for herself. The change in her style was dramatic. Affecting a black slouched hat and masculine riding habit, she scandalized the ladies of the Danish court by riding astride like a man, meddling like a man in the country's politics, and involving herself in scandal with John Struensee, the young Prime Minister. She made an implacable enemy of the king's mother, Juliana, who planned to seize the throne for her younger son, Frederick.

When Juliana's officers, bursting into the palace one night at the end of a royal ball, found Struensee's white bearskin cloak in Caroline's bedroom, the young queen's days of desperate gaiety were over. The premier was executed and his alleged mistress imprisoned in a fortress near Copenhagen. Caroline was eventually released when George sent warships into the Baltic, but her health was poor and she died, aged twenty-three, a few years later. "I am going to appear before God," she said on her deathbed. "I now protest I am innocent of the guilt imputed to me, and that I was never unfaithful to my husband." Struensee, on the other hand, had not denied their intimacy.

The year 1772 opened brutally for George III. Hard on the news of his sister's arrest, and the attendant scandal, the king learned that his mother was dying. For one whose bluster and obstinacy had never exorcised his essential sensitivity, it was a profoundly emotional period in his life. Few women had attracted more public opprobrium, or been more openly insulted in their day, than Augusta. It was typical of her tough, autocratic character that while her resented activities—the intriguing with Bute and encouragement of George's absolutism—were little concealed, she had kept her more likable traits to herself. Installment by installment, she had contrived to repay out of income the large debts left by her husband, while anonymously contributing substantial donations to a number of charitable causes. She was particularly concerned with the welfare of retired royal servants, and rented a rest home for them on Kew Green.

Augusta faced the final stages of her illness dispossessed of private fortune but possessed of great fortitude. Walpole, who, in his time, had attacked her with the rest, described her fight against pain with admiration. "She could swallow," he wrote, "but with great difficulty, and not enough to maintain life long. At times her sufferings, and her struggles to hide them, were so much beyond her strength that she frequently fainted and was thought dead: yet she would not allow she was ill, even to her children; nor would she suffer a single physician or surgeon to inspect her throat, trusting herself solely to a German page who had some medical knowledge; and going out to take the air long after it was expected that she would die in her coach." For all his other problems and duties, George visited his mother daily in her illness, usually at eight o'clock in the evening, when he took the queen with him.

The dramatic events in Denmark struck the dowager a hard blow. "She existed on cordials alone for ten days," it was reported, "from the time she received the fatal news from Denmark . . ." Nevertheless, on the king's and queen's final visit, Augusta rose and dressed to receive them, keeping them talking with her for four hours. It was her last bid to defy the inevitable. She did not survive the night. Shortly before she died, she told an attendant: "I have nothing to say, nothing to do, and nothing to leave." The king's mother expired without complaint.

Wrote one who knew her, Sir Robert Keith, then British minister at Copenhagen: "You all know how much I thought myself honoured by the good opinion of the Princess, who I am firmly persuaded possessed as many intrinsic good qualities, and as much affability of temper, as any lady in Europe. The distresses of our worthy sovereign are indeed manifold; and if ever a King deserved the tender affections of his subjects, as well as their obedience, we may safely say without flattery he is that King."

CHAPTER 18

Westminster and America

Lord North's ministry saw the peculiar energies and interests of George III stretched perilously near breaking point. Not merely was the king's domination of governmental structure at the peak of its intensity, he seemed scarcely able to delegate the smallest item of administrative detail. It has been said that if he could personally have ordered the lives of every one of his subjects from Montreal to Madras, it would not have drained his reserves of solicitude. Whether the matter was the design of a button, the husbandry of a farmstead or the formation of a military unit, George had a view on it—and it was hard to persuade him that his view was second-best. Like Philip II of Spain, he ruled his empire with pen and paper, and, as his copious letters attest, nothing was too large or too small for his interest. One historian spoke of "the microscopic attention which he paid to every detail of public business." George's ministers were deluged with royal advice and homilies. The dispatch of trappings for an investiture in India, the handling of a disturbance in Suffolk, the appointment of a second master at Eton, the execution of a forger, the repair of a broken marriage, the habits of the Lord Lieutenant of Ireland, the promotion of a junior officer—George had instructions for each case, and countless more, many of less importance. He even had advice for the Duchess of Aylesford in one of her pregnancies. She can scarcely have needed much, in her twentieth confinement.

When North jibbed at the constant, almost neurotic pressure of the king's attentions, George treated him like a temperamental woman, chiding and flattering him by turn. "The week has elapsed without your producing it," he nagged of a ministerial statement, "and your aversion to decide would lead you to postpone it till too late, unless forced by me . . . yet with activity, decision and zeal, things may soon wear a very different appearance." Again: "It has been a certain position with me that firmness is the characteristic of an Englishman, that consequently when a Minister will show a resolution boldly to advance that he will meet with support."

More cajolingly, when North talked in desperation of retiring (a frequent occurrence), the king wrote: "I never can think that he, who so handsomely stood forward on the desertion of the Duke of Grafton, would lose all that merit by following so undignified an example." And, generously, combining temptation and affection: "I have understood by your hints that you have been in debt ever since you settled in life. I must therefore insist that you allow me to assist you with ten thousand, fifteen thousand, or even twenty thousand pounds . . . I want no return but you being convinced that I love you as well as a man of worth as I esteem you as a Minister."

In his handling of the American war, George showed his customary concern with minutiae, behaving more like an inexperienced chief of staff than an emperor. Though the first military actions shocked him, he awaited complacently an early surrender of the rebels. "May my deluded subjects on the other side of the Atlantic behold their impending destruction with half the horror that I feel on the occasion," he said, surveying the casualty lists of Long Island, "then I think I shall soon hear of their throwing off the yoke of republicanism and, like loyal subjects, returning to that duty they owe to an indulgent sovereign." In August, he issued "A Proclamation for Suppressing Rebellion and Sedition." This, charging that the revolt had been instigated by "dangerous and ill-designing men," appealed to loyal subjects to become informers. It was their duty, George announced, to "disclose and make known all treasons and traitorous conspiracies which they shall know to be against us, our Crown and dignity [an important element for the touchy George]; and for that purpose that they transmit to one of our principal Secretaries of State, or other proper officer, due and full information of all persons who shall be found carrying on correspondence with or in any other manner or degree aiding or abetting the persons now in open arms and rebellion . . . in order to bring to condign punishment the authors, perpetrators, and abettors of such traitorous designs." Such blustering could only make matters worse.

The so-called "Olive Branch" petition—America's last attempt to avert the war—arrived in London on September 1, addressed to the "King's Most Excellent Majesty." George did not deign to reply to it. Instead, he went to Parliament to castigate the freedom-seeking colonists as "an unhappy, misled and deluded multitude," and, with remarkably feeble insight, planned to fight them with German troops. "He informed me that a large body of German troops was to join our forces," wrote Grafton, "and appeared astonished when I answered earnestly that his Majesty would find, too late, that twice that number would only increase the disgrace, and never effect his purpose."

The measure brought wide condemnation. Frederick the Great declared that he would "make all the Hessian troops, marching through his dominions to America, pay the usual cattle tax, because, although human beings, they had been sold as beasts." Chatham complained to the king's ministers of "the traffic and barter driven with every pitiful German prince that sells his subjects to the shambles of a foreign country. This mercenary aid on which you rely irritates to an incurable resentment the minds of your enemies. To overrun them with the mercenary sons of rapine and plunder, devoting them and their possessions to the rapacity of hireling cruelty! If I were an American, as I am an Englishman, while there was a foreign troop in my country, I never would lay down my arms, never! never! never!"

The persistent and eloquent opposition of Chatham, Rockingham and Burke was unavailing. So, too, was that of the Duke of Richmond and Charles James Fox, both of whom had family reasons for resenting George. Fox, the irrepressible son of the former minister, was an admiring nephew of the ill-used and beautiful Lady Sarah Lennox. Richmond was her brother. Ranged beside them were such lesser lights as Wilkes, Barré and others, who, along with the more perceptive sections of the populace, appreciated that liberty was no less at stake at home than in America.

Unfortunately for the opposition, the bulk of the middle classes of British society, burdened by heavier taxes than the Americans, and instinctively averse to disorder, backed the king and his ministers. Loyal and unsolicited addresses poured in from all parts of the kingdom. According to the historian Gibbon, Lord North was "as much surprised" by this spontaneous demonstration of support as anyone. In November, he confidently submitted his "Prohibitory Bill" to Parliament, outlawing trade with the United Colonies. The measure, carried in the Commons by 112 to sixteen votes, authorized the seizure of all ships laden with American property, and contained a provision, branded by its opponents as a "refinement in tyranny," allowing captured American sailors to be impressed for service on British warships engaged against their own countrymen. Observed Dr. Richard Price, a well-known British advocate of American rights, Britain would now be execrated throughout the globe. She had left the colonists no alternative but "to declare themselves independent and fight to the death."

For the first time, in a Declaration of Independence finally signed by all thirteen colonies in July 1776, the American leaders laid the responsibility for their actions unequivocally at the feet of the sovereign. George's history, they claimed, was one of repeated injuries and usurpations. In the face of his plain intention to establish an absolute despotism, it had become their right, indeed their duty, to secure themselves against further aggressions. "In every stage of these oppressions we have petitioned for redress in the most humble terms. Our petitions have been answered only by repeated injuries. A Prince, whose character is thus marked by every act which may define a tyrant, is unfit to be the ruler of a free people. We, therefore, the representatives of the United States of America, in General Congress Assembled, appealing to the supreme Judge of the World for the rectitude of our intentions, do, in the name and by the authority of the good people of these Colonies, solemnly publish and declare that these United Colonies are, and of right ought to be, 'FREE AND INDEPENDENT STATES.'"

Following the capture of New York by the British, and their victory at the battle of White Plains, George returned to Parliament to inveigh once more against those he termed the selfish and desperate rebels of America. Against the charges of his own tyranny, he spoke of the tyranny of the American leaders who had exchanged the blessings of law and order for the calamities of war. Victory, he believed, was in sight, and ministers learned that "another campaign" could bring the war to a successful close. Even some American sympathizers in the Commons were apprehensive that such might indeed be the case. "We should look with the utmost shame and horror," declared one, "on any events tending to break the spirit of any large part of the British nation; to bow them to an abject unconditional submission to any power whatsoever; to annihilate their liberties, and to subdue them to servile principles and passive habits by the mere force of foreign mercenaries."

"The evil," cried Wilkes, "grows more desperate. Last year only twelve colonies humbly petitioned the throne. This year, by the accession of Georgia, we have seen a federal union of thirteen free and powerful provinces asserting their independency as high and mighty states, and setting our power at defiance. This was done with circumstances of spirit and courage to which posterity will do justice. It was done directly after the safe landing of your whole force." Barré warned the government of the mounting danger of an attack from France. "The attack will shortly be made, and made within the hearing of those who now sit in this House. Gentlemen may laugh; but I dare aver that those who laugh now will, in the moment of danger, be lying in tears on their backs, like cowards." Asserted Rockingham forcibly: "There is no man who has access to his Majesty, who has integrity and magnanimity of mind sufficient to enable him to go and say to his Majesty—'the measures and policy of the Ministers towards America are erroneous.'"

But it was left to Chatham to fire the major opposition salvos. In May 1777, he struggled to his feet in the Lords with the aid of a stick to deliver a speech which his son, William Pitt the younger, who was present, described as "full of all his usual force and vivacity." Exclaimed the old statesman:

> You cannot conquer the Americans. You talk of your numerous friends to annihilate the Congress, and of your power-

ful forces to disperse their army, but I might as well talk
of driving them before me with this crutch . . . You have
been three years teaching them the art of war, and they
are apt scholars. I will venture to tell your lordships that
the American gentry will make officers enough fit to command the troops of all the European powers. What you
have sent there are too many to make peace, too few to
make war. You cannot make them respect you. You cannot
make them wear your cloth. You will plant an invincible
hatred in their breasts against you . . .

My lords, you have been the aggressors from the beginning. I say again, this country has been the aggressor. You
have made descents upon their coasts. You have burnt
their towns, plundered their country, made war upon the
inhabitants, confiscated their property, proscribed and imprisoned their persons . . . The people of America look
upon Parliament as the authors of their miseries. Their
affections are estranged from their sovereign. Let, then, reparation come from the hands that inflicted the injuries. Let
conciliation succeed chastisement, and I do maintain that
Parliament will again recover its authority, that his Majesty
will be once more enthroned in the hearts of his American
subjects, and that your lordships—as contributing to so great,
glorious and benignant a work—will receive the prayers and
benedictions of every part of the British empire.

Like George, Chatham could not bring himself to believe
in an independent America, a condition both men conceived
as the ultimate tragedy. George would prevent it by conquest; Chatham by reconciliation—a suggestion which, by
this time, the king considered downright traitorous. Chatham's speeches, he fumed, were sheer "fuel to the rebels."
That summer, Howe's success at Philadelphia so delighted
the king that he rushed into the queen's room when he
heard it, shouting, "I have beat them! Beat all the Ameri-

cans!" But his high spirits were dashed in December. On the third of that month, rumors of a disastrous British defeat were rife in London, and Barré rose in the Commons to ask the Secretary of State for America, Lord George Germain, himself a former soldier, for clarification. With great reluctance, and a face as dark as thunder, Germain declared that the government had no official intelligence, but admitted that expresses from Quebec corroborated the rumors. In fact, Burgoyne and his army had capitulated at Saratoga on October 16. The whole House was hushed. Then, as the premier's bulging eyes clearly filled with tears, Fox, Barré and Burke rose in quick succession to exploit the opportunities for crushing sarcasm in the situation—the capture of a British army by the "cowardly colonial rabble."

George needed all his courage and stubbornness to survive the shock. According to one report, when the king heard the news he "fell into agonies," concealing his feelings so crudely at a levee the next day that his friends were embarrassed. "To disguise his concern, he affected to laugh and to be so indecently merry that Lord North endeavoured to stop him." Be that as it may, his stoicism prevailed. The crisis, he admitted, was "very serious, but not without remedy." Lord North was more despondent. "My lord," a friend told the premier after the news of the surrender, "you must now see that the whole population of America is hostile to your designs." To which North replied: "I see that as clearly as you do, and the King shall either consent to allow me to assure the House of Commons that some means shall be found to put an end to the war, or I will not continue to be his minister."

As usual, George persuaded North to remain faithful. "I should have been greatly surprised," the king wrote at the beginning of 1778, "at the inclination expressed by you to retire, had I not known that, however you may now and then despond, yet that you have too much personal affection for me, and sense of honour, to allow such a thought to take any hold on your mind." Nevertheless, he was obliged to agree to what proved an abortive mission to America by a number of commissioners empowered to seek an agreement short of independence. George had hardly assented to the measure when it was learned in London that France had recognized the full independence of the United States and had signed a treaty with America. The British ambassador was ordered to quit Paris. The government's position had never looked so black. The king's enemies observed his anguish with sardonic amusement:

> *Thy triumphs, George, the western world resounds,*
> *And Europe scarce thy paper glory bounds . . .*
> *How brave thine admirals! and so discreet*
> *They never risk the honour of the fleet;*
> *Nor trust the dangers of the middle-main,*
> *Where Britain bids her thunder roar in vain . . .*
> *One Revolution rais'd you to the Crown;*
> *Another Revolution may—dethrone.*

In its moment of confusion, the country turned, as before, to Lord Chatham. Though his popular following had been diminished by his elevation to the peerage, and by the restrictions of his illness and old age, influential circles still regarded him as the one man who could rescue the national honor: a man to strike awe in the French, to reach agreement with the Americans—or failing such possibilities, to pursue a successful war against either or both.

Bute regarded the once Great Commoner as the only captain now capable of weathering the storm. Lord Mansfield declared with tears in his eyes that, unless the king sent for Chatham, the ship would surely sink. Asserted Temple of his old colleague: "If there be a man who has served this nation with honour to himself and glory to his country;

if there be a man who was carried the arms of Britain triumphant to every quarter of the globe beyond the most sanguine expectations of the people; if there be a man of whom the house of Bourbon stands more particularly in awe; if there be a man, in this country, who unites the confidence of England and America, is he not the proper person to treat with Americans, and not those who have uniformly deceived and oppressed them? There is not one person present who is ignorant of the person to whom I allude. You all know I mean a noble and near relation, Lord Chatham."

Even North himself, more anxious than ever for a way out, urged the king to send for the veteran statesman. George recoiled in horror from abandoning everything for which he had worked to the old man he saw as a dictator, "a trumpet of sedition." He would tolerate Chatham in the government, he vowed, only so long as North remained first minister. "I declare, in the strongest and most solemn manner," the king wrote the premier in March, "that I do not object to your addressing yourself to Lord Chatham, yet you must acquaint him that I shall never address myself to him but through you, and on a clear explanation that he is to step forth to support an administration wherein you are first Lord of the Treasury; and that I cannot consent to have any conversation with him till the Ministry is formed."

In an extraordinary admission of prejudice George continued: "No advantage to this country, nor personal danger to myself, can make me address myself to Lord Chatham, or to any other branch of Opposition. Honestly, I would rather lose the Crown I now wear than bear the ignominy of possessing it under their shackles. I might write volumes, if I would state the feelings of my mind, but I have honestly, fairly, and affectionately, told you the whole of my mind, and what I will never depart from. Should Lord Chatham wish to see me before he gives an answer, I shall most certainly refuse it. I have had enough of personal negotiation, and neither my dignity nor my feelings will ever let me again submit to it."

But a power greater than George's was working against Chatham's return to government. On April 7, 1778, when the Duke of Richmand moved the independence of America in the House of Lords, few believed that Chatham had the physical strength to appear and oppose him. Lord Camden found the old man resting beforehand in the private apartment of the Lord Chancellor. "Such was the feeble state of his body, and indeed the distempered agitation of his mind, that I did forbode that his strength would certainly fail him before he had finished his speech," said Camden. Chatham tottered into the House supported by his sons and his son-in-law, Lord Mahon. He wore black velvet, against which his face was deathly pale, and his legs were heavily bandaged. "He looked," said one witness, "like a dying man; yet never was seen a figure of more dignity." Spontaneously, the peers rose as he entered, and he bowed to acknowledge the tribute. When he spoke, it was with "sentences broken, and his mind not master of itself," as Camden put it. Yet passages retained the old luster.

> I am old and infirm, with one foot, more than one foot, in the grave [said the veteran]. I am risen from my bed to stand up in the cause of my country, perhaps never again to speak in this House. I have made an effort, almost beyond my strength, to come here this day to express my indignation at an idea which has gone forth of yielding up America. My lords, I rejoice that the grave has not yet closed upon me; that I am still alive to lift up my voice against the dismemberment of this ancient and most noble monarchy. Pressed down, as I am, by the hand of infirmity, I am little able to assist my country in this most perilous

conjuncture; but, my lords, whilst I have sense and memory I will never consent to deprive the royal offspring of the house of Brunswick of their fairest inheritance. Where is the man that will dare to advise such a measure? My lords, his Majesty succeeded to an empire as great in extent as it was unsullied in reputation. Shall we tarnish the lustre of this nation by an ignominious surrender of its rights and fairest possessions? Shall this great kingdom, which has survived whole and entire Danish depredations, the Scottish inroads, and the Norman conquest—that has stood the threatened invasion of the Spanish Armada—now fall prostrate before the house of Bourbon?

My lords, any state is better than despair. Let us at least make an effort, and, if we must fall, let us fall like men. My lords, ill as I am, yet as long as I can crawl down to this House, and have strength to raise myself on my crutches, or lift my hand, I will vote against giving up the dependency of America on the sovereignty of Great Britain, and, if no other lord is of opinion with me I will singly protest against the measure.

By now, Chatham was as out of touch with American sentiments as George himself. At this stage, nothing would have induced the colonists to renounce their newly claimed independence short of military conquest, and, to this extent, Chatham was propounding the king's case. The peers listened in silence. "He made shift with difficulty to declare his opinion," wrote one, "but was not able to enforce it by argument. His words were shreds of unconnected eloquence, and flashes of the same fire which he, Prometheus-like, had stolen from heaven, and were returning to the place from whence they were taken."

Suddenly, Chatham clutched at his heart and fell back on his seat in agony. Reported Camden: "This threw the whole House into confusion. Every person was upon his legs in a moment, hurrying from one place to another; some sending for assistance, others producing salts, and others reviving-spirits; many crowding about the Earl to observe his countenance; all affected; most part really concerned, and even those who might have felt a secret pleasure at the accident yet put on the appearance of distress."

George's integrity allowed no such deceit. When Chatham died, some four weeks later, North, Burke, Fox, Barré and many others of various parties and principles combined to pay tribute to his career. Parliament voted him a public monument and funeral, a discharge of his debts to the tune of £20,000 and an annuity of £4,000 to his title. "I was rather surprised," declared the king, "the House of Commons have unanimously voted an address for a public funeral and monument in Westminster Abbey for Lord Chatham, but I trust it is voted as a testimony of gratitude for his rousing the nation at the beginning of the last war . . . or this compliment, if paid to his general conduct, is rather an offensive measure to me personally."

In the face of mounting pressure for peace, George stated his case explicitly and honestly:

"No man in my dominions desires solid peace more than I do," he wrote in June 1779:

> But no inclination to get out of the present difficulties, which certainly keep my mind very far from a state of ease, can incline me to enter into the destruction of the empire. Lord North frequently says that the advantages to be gained by this contest would never repay the expense. I own that any war, be it ever so successful, if a person will sit down and weigh the expense, they will find, as in this last, that it has impoverished the state . . . but this is only weighing such points in the scale of a tradesman behind his counter. It is necessary for those whom Providence has placed in my station to weigh what expenses, though very

great, are not sometimes necessary to prevent what would
be more ruinous than the loss of money.

The present contests with America I cannot help seeing
as the most serious in which any country was ever engaged.
It contains such a train of consequences that they must be
examined to feel its real weight. Whether the laying a tax
was deserving all the evils that have arisen from it I
suppose no man could allege without being thought fitter
for Bedlam than a seat in the senate; but step by step the
demands of America have risen. Independence is their
object, which every man not willing to sacrifice every
object to a momentary and inglorious peace must concur
with me in thinking this country can never submit to. Should
America succeed in that, the West Indies must follow, not
in independence, but for their own interest they must
become dependent on America. Ireland would soon follow,
and this island reduced to itself, would be a poor island
indeed.

Two centuries later, a United States Government would
argue something like the same "domino" theory to justify
its own overseas military policy. To much of eighteenth-
century England, the argument seemed a valid one.

CHAPTER 19

The Gordon Riots

In June 1780, the webs of anxiety enmeshing George's mind were reinforced by a spidery young man named Lord George Gordon, who precipitated a remarkable furor in London. The background was the mounting tolerance toward Roman Catholics, climaxed by the Catholic Relief Bill of 1778, which had reversed a number of discriminatory laws against the Romanists. Previously, they had been unable to hold or transfer land, to hold religous services, to run parochial schools, or, among other things, to gain promotions in the Army. The ending of such measures reflected both a genuine liberalism in many quarters of Parliament, combined with the graciousness of the king himself, and a certain degree of self-interest from the government. American offers of land and religious freedom to Irish migrants were helping to depopulate their native country, and the absentee landlords, influential in British politics, were threatened with the run-down of their estates in consequence. They supported the counter-inducements. There was also the matter of army recruiting, which had failed lamentably in Ireland, partly due to the restrictions on promotion for Catholics. Predictably, the Relief Act provoked a backlash from militant Protestants. It also provoked Lord George Gordon.

At twenty-nine, Lord George, third son of Cosmo, Duke of Gordon, was an undistinguished if not inconspicuous opposition backbencher. He possessed, in his long, lank hair and pallid face, the popular image of fanaticism—Walpole called him the "lunatic apostle"—yet his motives and ambitions appear to have been vague, even to himself. Eight years earlier, he had left the Navy under the impression that he had deserved a higher rank than lieutenant, and the urge for some kind of recognition seems to have been strong in him. His speeches tended to be wild and eccentric. "Lord George Gordon," it was reported in 1779, "made a speech for which he ought to be shut up . . . He wept several times . . . produced an old print of the Marquis of Huntly; offered to make Lord North a present of it, and called upon twenty members by their names." On one occasion he went so far as to proclaim the time near when he would dictate to the Crown and to Parliament. The king of England, he exclaimed, was held to be a Papist. If the monarch dared depart from his oath to uphold the Protestant religion, his head should fall on the scaffold. That Gordon's fellow politicians refused to take him seriously undoubtedly saved him from trouble, but equally offended his peculiar ego.

For a while, the implications of Catholic freedom caused little stir in England, though Presbyterian Scotland, embracing a more militant Protestantism than the English Church, reacted quickly with riots and violence. In Edinburgh and Glasgow, Roman Catholics were abused and threatened, their homes entered and their property smashed. Prominent at the head of the reactionaries was the intense, gesticulating figure of Lord George. Toward the end of 1779, he was offered, and accepted, the presidency of the Protestant Association of England. His objective was now clear: the repeal of the Catholic Relief Act. At last he could feel he was engaged on something big. But North would not listen to him, or to the Protestant Association, while opposition leaders still failed to regard him as someone of importance. Undismayed, Gordon set to work to collect a petition for the repeal of the Relief Act, advertising his cause in the papers. He accumulated a host of names.

On May 29, 1780, a well-attended meeting of the Protestant Association took place in Coachmaker's Hall, near Foster Lane, Cheapside, where members discussed the best manner of exploiting the anti-Catholic petition. Gordon, the principle speaker, suggested that he should present it to Parliament, backed by a rally of "twenty-thousand citizens." In this seemingly optimistic plan, its proponent revealed a closer feeling for the bigotry and prejudices of the citizenry than the establishment then wished to credit. For, on Friday, June 2, the day publicized for the demonstration, his supporters turned up in greater numbers than even Gordon had expected. At the height of a summer heat wave, the rally assembled in St. George's Fields, Southwark, many participants sporting blue cockades, the emblem of the movement, and waving banners inscribed "No Popery." Here, they sang hymns and listened to Gordon's tactical directions. They should advance by separate routes on Westminster, he advised, and reassemble before the Houses of Parliament.

Though considerably swollen by sightseers, pickpockets, vandals and others, the crowd was by no means the mob of "ragamuffins" some would have had it. At its core were many men of substance, traders aroused by anti-Irish sentiments, and "determined and earnest chapel-going shopkeepers who saw in popery the root of every evil, from adultery in high society to the weakness of the British fleet." According to Gibbon, it was as if "forty-thousand Puritans, such as they might have been in the days of Cromwell, had started out of their graves." The march to Westminster was orderly. By half past two in the afternoon, at about which time ironically the Duke of Richmond was delivering a speech on the rights of the people, Parliament was besieged. From now on, due to a number of factors, not least the oppressive heat and the overwhelming dismissal of Gordon's repeal bid in the House of Commons, tempers became frayed and the crowd grew unruly.

Many peers, on their way to the Lords, suffered violence, while the interior of the House presented an amazing scene. "It is hardly possible to conceive a more grotesque appearance than the chamber exhibited," proceeded one report. "Some of their Lordships with their hair about their shoulders; others smutted with dirt; most of them as pale as the ghost in Hamlet, and all of them standing up in their several places and speaking at the same instant. One Lord proposed to send for the Guards; another for the Justices or Civil Magistrates; many crying out 'Adjourn! Adjourn!' while the skies resounded with the huzzas, shoutings or hootings and hisses in Palace Yard."

Lords Townshend and Hillsborough, mauled as they came through the crowd, arrived with their clothes torn and hair disheveled. Lord Bathurst nursed legs which had been violently kicked. The Archbishop of York, and other clerics, appeared minus the lawn sleeves which had been ripped from their habits. Lord Mountford interrupted the Duke of Richmond in mid-speech to inform the House that Lord Boston had been dragged from his coach and thrown on the ground. Townshend called on the younger peers to draw their swords and sally to his rescue. Meanwhile, the Bishop of Lincoln had fled, fainting, from the multitude into the safety of a nearby house, from which he eventually escaped disguised in woman's clothing. Through it all, Lord Mansfield, presiding as Lord Chancellor, sat on the Woolsack "trembling like an aspen leaf."

At the Commons, Gordon had made his way to an outer gallery to inform his followers that his motion was defeated. The premier, he announced, had described them as a mob, but they should be patient. "His Majesty," he shouted, reversing his earlier testimony, "is a gracious monarch, and when he hears that people ten miles around are collecting, there is no doubt that he will send his ministers private orders to repeal the bill." Gordon had no wish to be arrested for incitement, nor to push his luck too far with fellow M.P.s, whose temper he had already sorely tested. Though he was said to have warned a mildly reproachful North that he could have him torn to pieces by the crowd if he wished, he showed more respect for a number of military gentlemen in the House who were fingering their sword hilts. "My Lord George," snarled an irate colonel as the besieging masses thundered at the doors, "do you intend to bring your rascally adherents into the House of Commons? If you do, I will plunge my sword not into the body of the first man that enters, but into yours!"

That evening, Gordon was seen, worn out by his exertions, drowsing in a chair in the refreshment rooms of the Commons, while the crowd, discouraged by a rescue party of guardsmen and cavalry, had dispersed to vent its wrath on the Catholics of the city. The disturbances now quickly deteriorated from political protest to riot and arson. The king was for firm and exemplary action. "This tumult," he wrote North, "must be got the better of, or it will encourage designing men to use it as a precedent for assembling the people on other occasions. If possible, we must get to the bottom of it, and examples must be made." He was induced to procrastinate, however, by a legal technicality. Troops could not fire on the rioters until magistrates had read the riot act—and the city magistrates were conspicuously absent. Like many other Londoners, they were either fearful of reprisals from a vengeful mob, or shared the same antipathy for the government's policies as did the merchants and traders who now sought an end to North's war-making Cabinet. Prominent among these was the lord mayor of London, a wine dealer named Brackley Kennett. Kennett, who held that "there are very great people at the bottom of the riot," personally congratulated one group of hooligans.

The daylight hours of June 3 and 4 were relatively free of major incidents, which, combined with the fact that the latter date was the sovereign's birthday, may have induced a certain calm in the palace. The king paid regular visits to the guards at St. James's, and even took them food and beverages, but the mob leaders were too shrewd to attack the royal residences. During the next few days, however, they stepped up their efforts until parts of London were a holocaust of fire and anarchy. On June 5 the rioters streamed into the West End, where private houses were attacked, including those owned by Lord George Germain and the Earl of Bute. Burke's home was threatened. On June 6, the major event was the bursting of Newgate prison. Having set fire to points surrounding it, the attackers gained access to the roof via the neighboring house of the prison governor, a man named Ackerman, and broke through the timbers to free the prisoners.

"They broke the roof," reported an eyewitness, "tore away the rafters, and, having got ladders, they descended. Not Orpheus himself had more courage or better luck. Flames all around them, and a body of soldiers expected, they defied and laughed at all opposition. The prisoners escaped. I stood and saw about twelve women and eight men ascend from their confinement to the open air, and they were conducted through the street in their chains. Three of these were to be hanged on Friday. You have no conception of the frenzy of the multitude. This being done, and Ackerman's house now a mere shell of brickwork, they kept a store of flame there for other purposes . . . With some difficulty, they then fired the debtors' prison, broke the doors, and they too all made their escape." Enlarged by the scare-crow figures of the prisoners, the crowd next swept to Bloomsbury Square and the mansion of Lord Mansfield, whose recent support for the Catholic Relief Act had marked him for vengeance.

Nathaniel Wraxall was driving in the vicinity when he was attracted by the commotion. "Quitting the coach, we crossed the square, and had scarcely got under the wall of Bedford House, when we heard the door of Lord Mans-field's house burst open with violence. In a few minutes, all the contents of the apartments being precipitated from the windows, were piled up and wrapped in flames. A file of foot soldiers arriving, drew up near the blazing pile, but without either attempting to quench the fire or to impede the mob, who were indeed far too numerous to admit of being dispersed, or even intimidated, by a small detachment of infantry." That night the rioters, starkly outlined by the light of flaming torches, marched on Lord North's residence, but were dispersed at the last moment by a body of cavalry, which cleared the street at a gallop. A number of city magistrates were less lucky. The houses of three—Sir John Fielding, Justice Cox and Justice Hyde— were attacked and demolished.

Wrote the king to North, with mounting anxiety: "The allowing Lord George Gordon, the avowed head of the tu-mult, to be at large, certainly encourages the continuation of it, to which must be added the great supiness of the civil magistrates. I fear, without more vigour, this will not sub-side." He was proved right. All hope of effective action by the magistrates had now gone, and the Army was impotent under the government's interpretation of constitutional law. June 7 dawned in an atmosphere of rebellion which, for the moment, linked London all too grimly with America. The shops were closed, many windows were boarded up and people of money had armed servants or hired guards to protect their property. Where trouble was expected, the caravanserai of the streets—coaches, vendors, urchins, harlots—mysteriously disappeared. Sympathizers of the revolt had hung blue ribbons in their doorways, and the familiar "No Popery" slogan was everywhere. Germain had barricaded himself in his house in Pall Mall; Downing Street bristled with soldiers; the Secretary of State's servants had discreetly placed blue cockades in their hats, and, when Horace Walpole called on his relative Lord Hertford, he found the earl and his sons briskly loading their muskets. Among predictions which abounded, it was rumored that the inmates were to be turned loose from Bedlam, and the lions from the Tower of London released upon the city.

When the explosion came, it was dramatic. Three more prisons—the Fleet, the Marshalsea and the King's Bench— were broken open and fired, the Bank of England was besieged and a gin distillery in Holborn was sacked and set ablaze. As the streets ran with spirits, pails full of gin were passed through the crowd, while the water supply in the area became alcoholic. Under the huge palls of smoke which hung over the city, men, women and children drank themselves insensible. Many who collapsed were incinerated in the spreading flames. At the height of the rioting, the city council met and passed an urgent resolution once more urging the government to repeal the Catholic Relief Act. "Our disgrace will be lasting," wrote Gibbon, "and the month of June, 1780, will ever be marked by a dark and diabolical fanaticism which I had supposed to be extinct." Exclaimed Dr. Johnson, who surveyed the scene from his study in Bolt Court: "One might see the glare of conflagration fill the sky from many parts: the sight was dreadful."

Meanwhile, the king had decided to procrastinate no longer. Summoning the Attorney General, Alexander Wedderburn, he agreed with him that the need for the reading of the riot act, and other civil procedures, had been rendered unnecessary by the outrages to which the mob had resorted. Once the civil power was ineffective in restraining such activities, allowed Wedderburn, it became the duty of all persons, including soldiers, to employ every possible means to suppress them. This, said the king, was his own opinion, and he invited Wedderburn to affirm it before the Privy Council. "As Attorney-General," demanded George, "is that your declaration of the law?" Wedderburn replied yes. "Then so let it be done!" And, with the assent of an apparently convinced Privy Council, orders were sent to the military commander, Lord Amherst, to disperse the rioters as he thought fit, without warrant from the civil powers.

By this time, Amherst had about ten thousand men under arms, and volunteers were mustering to the defense of the government. When a messenger arrived at the city council to announce the proclamation of martial law, the lord mayor and his colleagues weighed the new odds and changed heart. Wilkes, who had been prominent among them, not only switched sides, but took part in the defense of the Bank of England, boasting afterwards of killing several rioters. Gordon himself, sniffing the fresh resolution of the Cabinet, turned up at the bank to offer his services to the officer commanding, a Captain Holroyd, who declined to be a party to any deal with his lordship. The rank and file of the excited protesters, still raging through the streets, no longer found themselves faced by an inactive and harmless soldiery but by leveled bayonets and musket balls.

Amherst's troops did a thorough job. Around the Bank of England, in Bridge Street and Blackfriars, on the night of the seventh, the carnage was terrible. One witness, present when the soldiers returned to barracks, described their bayonets as literally steeped in blood. Among the crowds trying to escape the military over Blackfriars Bridge, many were crushed to death, or forced over the side to drown in the Thames. According to the Army, nearly three hundred civilians were killed, and a further one hundred and seventy seriously injured. The figures were conservative, taking no account of the dead and wounded carried off by their comrades, or burned, drowned or otherwise lost in the fiery night. Some care was taken by the authorities to conceal the extent of the slaughter. By daybreak, the bloodstained walls of the Bank of England, which opened for normal business of June 8, had been whitewashed, musketry damage had been made good and fresh earth thrown upon the gory stains of Blackfriars Bridge. By a tacit agreement of the parliamentary parties, no tribunal or commission was ever established to investigate the happenings of that eventful night.

June 8 saw sporadic disturbances in the city, but the mob was broken, and, by Friday the ninth, the Army was largely employed removing emblems from buildings and guarding its prisoners, of whom fifty-nine were sentenced to death and twenty-one eventually executed. By the end of the week, the gentlefolk of the city had regained their aplomb. Charlotte Burney, who was in town during the riots, staying with Dr. Johnson's friend Mrs. Thrale, wrote to her sister Fanny:

I am very sorry, my dear Fanny, to hear how much you have suffered from your apprehension about us. Susan will tell you why none of us wrote before Friday; and she says she has told you what dreadful havoc and devastation the mob have made here in all parts of the town. However, we are pretty quiet and tranquil again now. Papa goes on with his business pretty much as usual, and so far from the military keeping people within doors (as you say, in your letter to my father, you suppose to be the case), the streets were never more crowded—everybody is wandering about in order to see the ruins of the places that the mob have destroyed.

There are two camps, one in St James's, and the other in Hyde Park, which, together with the military law, makes almost everyone here think he is safe again. I expect we shall all have 'a passion for a scarlet coat' now. I hardly know what to tell you that won't be stale news. They say that duplicates of the handbill that I have enclosed were distributed all over the town on Wednesday and Thursday; however, thank Heaven, everybody says now that Mrs Thrale's house and brewery are as safe as we can wish them. There was a brewer in Turnstile that had his house gutted and burnt, because, the mob said, 'he was such a *papish,* and sold popish beer.' Did you ever hear of such diabolical ruffians?

To add to the pleasantness of our situation, there have been gangs of women going about to rob and plunder. The Miss Kirwans went on Friday afternoon to walk in the Museum gardens, and were stopped by a set of women, and robbed of all the money they had. The mob had proscribed the mews, for they said, 'the king should not have a horse to ride upon!' They besieged the new Somerset House, with intention to destroy it, but were repulsed by soldiers placed there for the purpose.

Mr Sleepe has been here a day or two, and says the folks at Watford, where he comes from, 'approve very much of having Catholic chapels destroyed, for they say it's a shame the pope should come here!' . . . It sounds almost incredible, but they say that on Wednesday night last, when the mob was more powerful, more numerous, and outrageous than ever, there was, nevertheless, a number of exceedingly genteel people at Ranelagh, though they knew not but their houses might be on fire at the time!

God bless you, my dear Fanny—for Heaven's sake keep your spirits up!

At two o'clock on the afternoon of June 10, the king met his Cabinet, and, after a lengthy discussion, it was decided to detain Gordon for questioning at the War Office. He was arrested at his house in Welbeck Street, Cavendish Square, duly interrogated for some three hours, then transferred to the Tower of London, "escorted by a more imposing military force than had attended Charles the First on his way from St James's Palace to the scaffold." That evening, the Secretaries of State wrote jointly to his lordship's brother, the Duke of Gordon: "We think it a mark of proper respect due to your Grace to give you the earliest intelligence in our power of an event for which we feel the utmost concern. We have been obliged, from the indispensable duty of our office, to commit Lord George Gordon to the Tower for High Treason, of which he stands charged by information upon oath. We beg leave to assure your Grace that it gives us the utmost pain to be under this necessity, and especially as it relates to one so nearly concerned with your Grace."

The duke replied that he would waste no time in appearing before His Majesty "to testify my attachment to his person and Government and to implore his clemency in case my unfortunate brother shall be found guilty."

His pleas were unnecessary. A lesser charge must have gained a conviction, but Gordon, indicted with treason, was acquitted. He displayed a quarto Bible in front of him throughout the trial, and threatened to read four chapters of Zechariah from the witness box. Gordon's partisans were delighted by his release, and most peaceful people relieved to be spared his martyrdom. "Public thanksgivings were returned last Sunday in several churches for the acquittal of Lord George Gordon," it was reported. Dr. Johnson, among others, was glad that Gordon had escaped. But his freedom was temporary. He died in prison later, incarcerated for slander.

The king's standing in the uneasy city was not enviable. "If," wrote Bishop Newton, who had himself fled the disturbances, "the King, of his own notion, had not ordered forth the soldiery, the cities of London and Westminster might have been in ashes." On the other hand, the release of the troops had resulted in massacre, and marshal law still held sway in the capital, where large numbers of criminals were at large and the mass of people was resentful of the establishment. On June 16, when news arrived in London of a substantial victory for Sir Henry Clinton's British forces in America, the government was constrained to suppress its elation for fear that festive gunfire, processions and bonfires would inflame the still smoldering conurbation. George showed his despondency in a letter to North. The situation, he wrote, "obliged me to step forward to save all from confusion . . . The thought was my own . . . I will once more try to set the people right as to my own conduct; if this does not succeed I shall never again attempt to follow any line but that of my duty, and expect no justice or gratitude in return."

Part *III*

DECLINE OF A DESPOT

CHAPTER 20

A Royal Surrender

To a monarch beset by a turbulent India, a rebellious
Ireland, an uneasy capital and the hostility of Holland,
Spain and France, there might have seemed little further
cause for anxiety about a sunny Virginia township of less
than two hundred houses. "Great part of the houses form
one street, on the edge of a cliff which overlooks the river,"
wrote an English visitor to Yorktown at that time. "The
buildings stand within a small compass, and the environs of
the town are intersected by creeks and ravines. Different
roads from Williamsburg enter York in several directions,
and the main route to Hampton passes in front of it."
Looking down on the town and harbor from its heights,
the traveler admired a tranquil scene of higgledy-piggledy
rooftops, interspersed with shady trees and twisting lanes,
the masts of vessels, and, finally, the broad span of water.

Into this peaceful haven, in August 1781, marched the
Earl of Cornwallis and a footsore British army, to be
challenged in a few weeks by Washington and an allied
force of three times as many men. The choice of Washington
as commander-in-chief of the colonial forces, soon after the
first fighting of the rebellion, had resulted from a number
of factors. His reputation from the Braddock campaign had

still been vivid in American minds. Again, Virginia (with Massachusetts) was one of the two most powerful counties, and it was hoped that his appointment would boost the enthusiasm of the Southerners. More directly, New England had been willing to give Virginia the chief command in return for Virginia's support of the New England army. Washington's fortunes in the days ahead had varied. In the early stages of the fighting, in which he had forced the British to evacuate Boston, he had quickly proved himself a firm disciplinarian, imparting order to his army and dealing with squabbling subordinates. The later phases had been more hazardous. In 1776, he had placed his army in dire peril at New York and only revived his reputation, after losing much of his force in the retreat toward the Delaware, by timely blows at Trenton and Princeton. During 1777, he had faced more bitter defeats and had overcome intrigues to replace him. Through the winter he displayed the strength of his character and courage by sustaining a beaten and exhausted army at Valley Forge. At last, with the conclusion of the French alliance a year later, fortunes had changed radically, and now, with the aid of a powerful French fleet, Washington had the British cornered. By September 28, Cornwallis and his troops were completely invested, and, on October 9, the little port shook to the fire of the besieging artillery which now hammered the British defenses.

"Soon after," reported Cornwallis in dispatches, "3,000 French grenadiers, all volunteers, made a vigorous attempt to storm the right advanced redoubt, but were repulsed by only 130 officers and soldiers of the Royal Welsh Fusiliers, and 40 marines. Two other attempts were made by the French to storm the redoubt, which were also unsuccessful." Again cannon roared, reducing the obstinate stronghold to a heap of bloody sand. In an allied charge which followed, Cornwallis' outer positions were overrun and his own guns turned on the British in Yorktown. Their position was critical. The garrison was exposed to constant enfilading fire, while sickness within the encampment was diminishing the number of effective defenders. One group of Fraser Highlanders, expelled from a stronghold in hand-to-hand fighting, petitioned Cornwallis for permission to retake the position and redeem their regimental honor, or die in the attempt. Cornwallis forbade them. Instead, on October 16, a desperate sortie was mounted by the British against the most forward of the French guns.

The assault force, under a Colonel Abercrombie, and comprising detachments of the Guards and the Royal Edinburgh Volunteers, was two hundred strong. Storming forward, it succeeded in spiking eleven pieces of cannon and killing or wounding a hundred Frenchmen. But the attack proved futile. Within a short time, the guns were back in service, and the allies had no less than a hundred artillery pieces in battery. Rather than be pounded to extinction, Cornwallis decided to leave his sick and wounded in Yorktown and try to cut his way through the enemy lines and head for New York and the support of Clinton and his forces there. Unfortunately for the British, a violent storm on the night of September 16/17 upset the first phase of the plan, the crossing of the river, and the project collapsed. Two days later, his defenses in ruins and assailable at many points, Cornwallis surrendered his whole army of more than 7,000 men. George did not yet know it, but his fight for America was virtually lost.

On Sunday, November 25, two days before Parliament reassembled, the news of the surrender reached Lord George Germain in London. Germain hastily dispatched a messenger to the king, then walked from Pall Mall to Downing Street to transmit the fact personally to the premier. "I asked Lord George afterwards," said Wraxall, "how he [North] took the communication when made to him. 'As he would have taken a bullet through his breast,' replied Lord George, 'for he opened his arms, exclaiming wildly as he paced up and down the apartment a few minutes, "Oh God! It is all over!"—words which he repeated many times under emotions of the greatest consternation and distress.'"

Germain was entertaining friends at dinner when he received a reply from the king. Tearing open the seal, he read in George's familiar hand:

"I have received with sentiments of the deepest concern the communication which Lord George Germain has made me of the unfortunate result of the operations in Virginia. I particularly lament it on account of the consequences connected with it, and the difficulties which it may produce in carrying on the public business. But I trust that neither Lord George Germain nor any member of the Cabinet will suppose that it makes the smallest alteration in those principles of my conduct which have directed me in past time, and which will always continue to animate me under every event in the prosecution of the present contest."

Looking up from the message, Germain observed to his dinner guests: "The king writes just as he always does, except that I observe he has omitted to mark the hour and minute of his writing with his usual precision."

Shortly afterwards, George wrote to North: "Many men choose rather to despond on difficulties than see how to get out of them. I have already directed Lord George Germain to put on paper the mode that seems most feasible for conducting the war, that every member of the Cabinet may have his propositions to weigh by themselves, when I shall expect to hear their sentiments separately, that we may adopt a plan and abide by it. Fluctuating counsels, and taking up measures without connecting them with the whole of this complicated war, must make us weak in every part. With the assistance of Parliament I do not doubt, if measures are well connected, a good end may yet be made

of the war. If we despond, certain ruin ensues." The king
would not give up.

In his speech to Parliament on the twenty-seventh, George
called upon the resources of his people, the valor of his
fleets and armies, and upon divine providence, to restore
the position in America. The star of the opposition that day
was Charles Fox. Fox had already demeaned himself in
George's eyes by opposing the Royal Marriage Act and by
his consistent attacks on American policy. The very appearance of the gross, stumpy fellow with the fly-away
hair at his temples and his air of refined dissipation, upset
the king. He loathed Fox's brilliance, his prodigious gambling, his easy liaisons with women. According to an intimate,
Fox's passions were women, play and politics, in that order.
"He never formed a creditable connection with a woman in
his life," and "squandered all his means on the gaming table."
The thought of him holding morning court before his
admirers, as was his custom, clad in a crumpled nightgown,
made George shudder.

"The King," wrote Wraxall, "considered Fox as a man
ruined in fortune, of relaxed morals, and surrounded with
a crowd of followers resembling him in these particulars."
Now Fox weighed in with his usually vivid invective.

Divest the royal speech of its official forms, he asked
the House, and what had the king said? " 'Our losses in
America have been most calamitous. The blood of my
subjects has flowed in copious streams throughout every
part of that continent. The treasures of Great Britain have
been wantonly lavished, while the load of taxes imposed on
an overburdened country is becoming intolerable. Yet I
continue to tax you to the last shilling. When, by Lord
Cornwallis's surrender, hopes of victory are forever extinct,
and a further continuance of hostilities can only accelerate
the ruin of the British empire, I prohibit you from thinking
of peace. My rage for conquest is unquenched and my

revenge unsated; nor can anything except the total subjuga-
tion of my revolted American subjects allay my animosity.'"
As for the king's ministers, added Fox, they were a curse to
their country. They had made Great Britain an object of
scorn and derision to the nations of the earth. "The time will
surely come when an oppressed and irritated people will
firmly call for signal punishment on those whose counsels
have brought the nation so near to the brink of destruction."

While George's hatred intensified, many exulted. "Mr
Fox," wrote one of them, "is the first figure in all the
places I have mentioned, the hero in Parliament, at the
gaming table, at Newmarket." While his views, and those
of the opposition in general, gained favor daily, the king
insisted on fighting. North, with increasing reluctance, supported the sovereign. But the body of national opinion which
had earlier backed the war, had now melted. "A sense
of past error and a conviction that the American war might
terminate in a further destruction of our armies, began from
this time rapidly to insinuate itself into the minds of men,"
wrote a contemporary. "Though majorities in Parliament
were ready to support the American war, all the world was
representing it to be the height of madness and folly."
Declared another: "People now seem by their discourse
to despair more of that cause than ever. There has been
wretched management, disgraceful politics, I am sure; where
the principle blame is the Lord only knows; in many places,
I'm afraid."

On February 22, 1782, a motion for ending the American
war was defeated in the Commons by a single vote. George's
grip on Parliament was crumbling. Despairingly, North again
raised the subject of his resignation and begged the king to
change his government. Still George clung to his principles.
"I shall," he wrote, "never lose an opportunity of declaring
that no consideration shall ever make me in the smallest
degree an instrument in a measure that I am confident would

annihilate the rank in which this British Empire stands among the European States, and would render my situation in this country below continuing an object to me." And again: "The House of Commons seems to be so wild at present, and so runnning on to ruin, that no man can answer for the event of any question. Till driven to the wall I certainly will do what I can to save the Empire; and if I do not succeed, I will at least have the self-approbation of having done my duty, and of not letting myself be a tool in the destruction of the honour of the country."

Loyally, North stuck by his master. As late as March 5, when the government's days clearly were numbered, the premier announced his intention of staying at his post until either the king or the House itself commanded him to leave. It was not for the money, he pointed out. "As to the emoluments of my situation: God knows, were they forty times greater than they are, they would form no adequate compensation for my anxiety and vexations, aggravated by the uncandid treatment that I frequently experience within these walls." Repeatedly, he urged George to consult the opposition. Declared the king stubbornly: "After having yesterday in the most solemn manner assured you that my sentiments of honour will not permit me to send for any of the leaders of Opposition and personally treat with them, I could not but be hurt by your letter of last night. Every man must be the sole judge of his feelings, therefore whatever you or any man can say on the subject has no avail with me . . . if you resign before I have decided what I will do, you will certainly forever forfeit my regard."

Finally, North could take no more. On March 20, in anticipation of a motion that day for his dismissal, the weary premier sent a letter of resignation to the sovereign. George was going hunting when he received it. "Tell him I will be in town to-morrow morning and will then give an answer," he instructed the messenger. Then, turning to his hunting companions: "Lord North has sent in his resignation. I shall not accept it." But this time North was adamant. Commented Wraxall: "The nation, he knew well, was universally weary of war, the misfortunes attending which, though perhaps justly imputable to many other causes or persons, were attributed principally to his errors of management. He beheld himself now engaged in hostilities, direct or indirect, with half Europe in addition to America. Ireland, availing itself of our embarrassments, loudly demanded commercial and political emancipation. On every side, the empire appeared crumbling into ruin. Minorca, long invested, had already surrendered. Gibraltar was closely besieged. In the East Indies, our difficulties, financial as well as military, threatened the total subversion of our wide extended authority in that quarter of the globe, where Haidar Ali, though expelled by Sir Eyre Coote from the vicinity of Madras, still maintained himself in the centre of the Carnatic. If the First Minister looked at the West Indies, the prospect appeared still more big with alarm."

George was possessed alternately with fury and despondency. The former, he took out on North, who, after twelve years of faithful, long-suffering service, the king treated like a traitor. He would have refused him the pension customary to retired premiers, had not the Lord Chancellor, Edward Thurlow, a loyalist, pointed out the likely damage to the royal image. "Lord North is no friend of mine," sulked the king. "That may be so," replied Thurlow, "but the world thinks otherwise, and your Majesty's character requires that Lord North should have the usual pension." The £4,000 a year was granted reluctantly.

In his more despondent moments, George came sufficiently close to retiring himself to draft a notice of abdication:

His Majesty is convinced that the sudden change of sentiments from one branch of the Legislature has totally incapacitated Him from either conducting the War with effect, or from obtaining any peace but on conditions which would prove destructive to the Commerce as well as essential Rights of the British Nation.

His Majesty therefore with much sorrow finds He can be of no further Utility to His Native Country which drives him to the painful step of quitting it for ever.

In consequence of which intention His Majesty resigns the Crown of Great Britain and the Dominions appertaining thereto to His Dearly Beloved Son and lawful Successor, George Prince of Wales, whose endeavours for the Prosperity of the British Empire He hopes may prove more Successful.

Perhaps, on second thoughts, George realized the futility of this last hope. The Prince of Wales had shown little sign of being successful in any fields other than fashion and seduction. At all events, reason prevailed, and the notice was never served. Instead, George nerved himself to the reality of having to surrender, at least partially, the power for which he had struggled tirelessly for more than two decades. At least, he resolved to gain himself the best possible terms. To this end, Thurlow was instructed to sound the individual opposition leaders. The Duke of Richmond did not despise the king's recuperative talents. "For God's sake, your own sake and the country's sake," he warned Rockingham, the most obvious candidate for the premiership, "keep back and be very coy. Nothing but absolute necessity and severe pressure or force will induce the Court to come to you in such a manner as to enable you to do any good. These times are coming, and you must soon see all at your feet in the manner you would wish and with the full means to do what is right. In the meantime they will try all little tricks, and most amply try to flatter your prejudices, if they conceive you have any. If to anything

like this you give way, you ruin yourself and them, and the
kingdom into the bargain, whereas by firmness all will come
right yet, and you will carry the nation with you with such
éclat as to ensure you the means of doing what you wish."

Rockingham took the advice, playing hard to get, while
a despairing George tried unavailingly to find an alternative
premier. On March 27, the king accepted Rockingham, with
Fox as Foreign Minister and William, Earl of Shelburne, a
politician of Chatham's views, as Secretary for Home,
Colonial and Irish Affairs. "At last," moaned George, "the
fatal day is come." The idea of sanctioning Fox's appointment especially sickened him. According to Wraxall: "the
king deprecated as the severest misfortune to himself and
his subjects the necessity of taking such a person, however
eminent for capacity, into his confidence or councils." Rockingham's terms were equally objectionable to the king.
They included the acknowledgment of American independence, the curtailment of Crown influence and the regulation
of sinecures, pensions and royal expenditure generally. When
North was forced to reveal the accounts of the previous
general election, George's humiliation was heightened. Including the expenses of a few by-elections, the cost to the
Crown was a staggering £103,765. 15s 9d.

George fought back where he could, attempting in particular to encourage dissension between Rockingham and
Shelburne at the points where their ideologies were at
variance. In July, Rockingham died and Shelburne was
raised to first minister. The reshuffle excluded Fox and
brought into the Cabinet Chatham's son, William Pitt, a
handsome young man with a sharp intelligence and a
"clean-living" reputation. Whereas Fox in many ways reflected eighteenth-century society, Pitt was closer to the
nineteenth. The two were natural opponents. Burke described Pitt as "not merely a chip off the old block, but the
old block itself." His parliamentary demeanor had been

admired since he had made his maiden speech at the age of
twenty-two. According to Wraxall, his manner was composed, self-assured and dignified. "Formed for a popular assembly, he seemed made to guide its deliberations from
the first moment that he addressed the members composing
it." Another observed of his words that they were "delivered
without any kind of improper assurance, but with the exact
proper self-possession which ought to accompany a speaker.
There was not a word or a look which one would have
wished to correct." When someone remarked that Pitt would
some day be one of the first men of the House of Commons,
Fox admitted generously: "He already is."

Meanwhile, the peace negotiations initiated by Rockingham had been pursued by Shelburne, and, on November
30, preliminary engagements were signed between Britain
and America. In a speech from the throne five days later,
George announced the formal break with the colonies. "In
thus admitting their separation from the Crown of Great
Britain," he said painfully, "I have sacrificed every consideration of my own to the wishes and opinion of my
people. I make it my humble and earnest prayer to Almighty
God that Great Britain may not feel the evils which might
result from so great a dismemberment of the empire, and
that America may be free from those calamities which have
formerly proved in the mother country how essential monarchy is to the enjoyment of constitutional liberty. Religion,
language, interest, affections, may, and I hope will, yet prove
a bond of permanent union between the two countries. To
this end, neither attention nor disposition on my part shall
be wanting." The words took some speaking. "Did I lower
my voice when I came to that part?" George later asked
one who was present.

While the sovereign who had systematically made Parliament the tool of his wishes solemnly declared the monarchy
"essential" to constitutional liberty, North looked back with

curious complacency. "The American war," he told the House of Commons, "has been suggested to have been the war of the Crown, contrary to the wishes of the people. I deny it. It was the war of Parliament. There was not a step taken in it that had not the sanction of Parliament. It was the war of the people, for it was undertaken for the express purpose of maintaining the just rights of Parliament, or, in other words, of the people of Great Britain over the dependencies of the empire. For this reason, it was popular at its commencement, and eagerly embraced by the people and Parliament. Could the influence of the Crown have procured such great majorities within the doors of the House of Commons as went almost to produce equanimity? Or, if the influence of the Crown could have produced those majorities within doors, could it have produced the almost unanimous approbation bestowed without doors which rendered the war the most popular of any that had been carried on for many years? Nor did it ever cease to be popular until a series of the unparalleled disasters and calamities caused the people, wearied out with almost uninterrupted ill-success and misfortune, to call out as loudly for peace as they had formerly done for war."

In seeking to exonerate the king's ministers on grounds of the popularity of their policies, North was not only dealing in half-truths, but tendering an excuse George must have found peculiarly facile. George's criteria had never involved popularity. However mistaken, his motives were worthy. Patriarchal and despotic he might be, but he had sought to control his subjects sincerely for their own good. Like Charles III of Spain, whom he resembled in many ways, George did not expect his "children" to enjoy having their faces washed. Nor did it occur to him that they might have reached the age of self-decision. Indeed, he found their mounting urge to, as it were, leave home and stand on their own feet, profoundly hurtful to him. "George," wrote one historian of a later age, "had at least the satisfaction of reflecting that the motives which had influenced his conduct had been neither those of ambition nor a thirst for empire, but a firm conviction that he was doing no more than his duty in endeavouring to avert by all lawful means in his power a catastrophe which he believed to be alike pregnant with humiliation to his Crown and fatal to the interests of his country."

That the catastrophe had fallen despite every effort, George attributed woefully to the "wickedness" of the age. Four days after the sealing of a general peace on September 3, 1783, the king wrote from Windsor: "I have signed the warrant for the Attendance of the Heralds for the Proclamation of Peace: I have no objection to that ceremony being performed on Tuesday: indeed I am glad it is on a day I am not in Town, as I think this compleats the Downfall of the Lustre of this Empire; but when Religion and Public Spirit are quite absorbed by Vice and Dissipation, what has now occurred is the natural consequence; one comfort I have, that I have also tried to support the Dignity of the Crown and feel I am innocent of the Evils that have occurred, though deeply wounded that it should have happened during my Reign." Having written as much, he dropped his pen, called for a horse and galloped headlong down the avenue leading from the castle—fleeing his thoughts and the loss of half the British empire.

But George was still king, and, on the arrival at St. James's of the first United States ambassador, John Adams, he impressed the American with his customary aura of majesty. Adams eased the meeting with a tactful introduction. "Sir," said the ambassador (as he later remembered it), "the United States have appointed me their minister plenipotentiary to your Majesty, and have directed me to deliver to your Majesty this letter, which contains the evidence of it. It is in obedience to their express commands that I have

the honour to assure your Majesty of their unanimous
disposition to cultivate the most friendly and liberal intercourse between your Majesty's subjects and their citizens,
and of their best wishes for your Majesty's health and
happiness, and for that of your royal family. The appointment of a minister from the United States to your Majesty's
court will form an epoch in the history of England and
America. I think myself more fortunate than all my fellow
citizens in having the distinguished honour to stand in
your Majesty's royal presence in a diplomatic character,
and I shall esteem myself the happiest of men if I can be
instrumental in recommending my country more and more
to your Majesty's royal benevolence, and of restoring an
entire esteem, confidence and affection, or, in better words,
the old good nature and the good old humour, between
people who, though separated by an ocean, and under
different governments, have the same language, a similar
religion, a kindred blood. I beg your Majesty's permission
to add that, although I have sometimes been entrusted
before by my country, it was never in my whole life in a
manner so agreeable to myself."

Replied George, his voice trembling at first, but quickly
growing stronger: "Sir, the circumstances of this audience
are so extraordinary, the language you have now held is
so extremely proper, the feelings you have discovered so
justly adapted for the occasion, that I must say that I not
only receive with pleasure the assurance of the friendly
disposition of the United States, but that I am very glad
the choice has fallen upon you to be their minister. I wish
you, sir, to believe, and that it may be understood in
America, that I have done nothing in the late contest but
what I thought myself indispensably bound to do, by the
duty which I owed to my people. I will be very frank with
you. I was the last to conform to the separation; but the
separation having been made, and having become inevitable,

I have always said, as I say now, that I would be the first to meet the friendship of the United States as an independent power. The moment I see such sentiment and language as yours prevail, and a disposition to give this country the preference, that moment, I shall say, let the circumstance of language, religion and blood have their natural lawful effect."

All the same, George never really reconciled his mind to the loss of America. In disconsolate moments of his old age, he frequently bewailed what he saw as the greatest tragedy of his life. "I that am born a gentleman," he told his friend Thurlow, "shall never rest my head on my last pillow in peace and quiet as long as I remember the loss of my American colonies."

CHAPTER 21

The Pretty Boy

In 1784, the Prince of Wales, who suffered exotically from his passion for women, fell in love with Maria Anne Fitzherbert, a widow several years his elder. When the lady sensibly asked the overheated young man to leave her alone, the prince became almost berserk. For hours on end, he regaled his friends and toadies with his misery, waxing particularly theatrical in the company of Fox, to whom he looked for guidance, and Fox's mistress, Mrs. Armstead. According to Mrs. Armstead, the young man would sit weeping disconsolately and interminably at their Chertsey villa, "testifying the sincerity and violence of his passion and his despair by the most extravagant expressions and actions."

These included "rolling on the floor, striking his forehead, tearing his hair, falling into hysterics, and swearing that he would abandon his country, forego the Crown, sell his jewels and plate, and scrape together a competence to fly with the object of his affections to America." When all this failed, he smeared blood on his body and claimed to have attempted suicide. Far from accompanying the prince to America, Mrs. Fitzherbert fled alone to Holland to escape

his attentions. George III forbade his distraught son to follow.

Peace with America had demolished George's domino
theory. After all the alarms, Britain had lost nothing in
India, she had retained Canada, her West Indian islands
were secure and she had asserted her command of the high
seas. Rodney had devastated the Spanish fleet off Cape St.
Vincent and driven the French fleet from the Atlantic. Howe
had relieved Gibraltar. In the wake of peace with the United
States came treaties with the Bourbon powers, under which
France gained nothing, and Spain gained only Florida and
Minorca. True, the Rockingham ministry established the
legislative independence of Ireland, but this must have
come about, war or no war. Far from being ruined by her
defeat, Britain was developing her industrial energy and
wealth at a brisk pace. In fact, the loss of America actually
increased her commerce with that country.

The industrial future seemed a bright one. There was
adequate capital available, while a shortage of labor encouraged revolutionary mechanical devices. The steam en-
gine was already invented and awaiting exploitation. In
the course of the war, technicians had been experimenting
with the production of bar iron, and the iron industry was
ready for its explosive expansion. A metal bridge had been
built across the Severn in 1776 and the first metal-plated
boat would soon take to British waters. Britain's factories
were growing larger. The cotton industry was booming.
Against three million pounds of raw cotton imported at
George's accession, 32.5 million would be imported by the
end of the eighties, when twenty thousand spinning jen-
nies were working in England. Sir Richard Arkwright's
water-frame spinning mechanism had been patented and
he was employing nearly a thousand workers by the time
the war ended. In 1779, Samuel Crompton had brought out
his "mule," harnessing the jenny to the water-frame to pro-

duce strong, fine thread for the making of muslins superior
to any in the world.

All this was overshadowed for George by the diminution
of his personal empire, and by the mountingly garish exploits of his eldest son. George had doted on his firstborn
since the earliest days of the dimple-cheeked, curly-haired
child, watching over both his secular and spiritual welfare
with the greatest solicitude. The prince repaid him with
marked eccentricity. One of the youth's early acts of self-
expression had been to tear the rod from the hands of his
tutor, Bishop Richard Hurd, and lay it painfully across the
episcopal buttocks. At eighteen, allowed a degree of liberty
by his reluctant parents from the uncongenial tedium of
Kew Palace and Buckingham House, the prince lost little
time before inflicting the deepest anxiety on his father.
His immediate responses to emancipation showed the drift
of his talents. He invented a new shoe buckle, five inches
wide, and seduced one of his mother's maids of honor.
The buckle was an immediate success with the city bucks,
and its creator followed it with other sartorial innovations.
At the first court ball he was allowed to attend, he wore a
coat of pink silk with white cuffs, a waistcoat adorned with
colored foils and pink paste, a hat ornamented with five
thousand metal beads and a frizzed hair style with curls
at the extremities.

The prince's main weapons of persuasion were his abilities to sulk, weep and rave with potent facility. When he
grew tired of living at home, he looked "such a sad, pretty
boy" that his mother was cajoled into promising him his
own establishment. The pretty boy could be charming when
he so wished. His formal manners were exquisite, his taste
florid but intriguing, he was well educated and could talk
brilliantly in sympathetic company. His good looks and
compelling personality tempted many women. In the eyes
of his enemies, he came to have no merits, but Fox, Sheridan,

the Duchess of Devonshire and many other gifted celebrities
of the day found him appealing.

He had a jackdaw's desire for bright objects and an
"amazing quickness in seizing any subject. He seems to
have the particular talent of knowing more about what he
is saying and with less pains than anyone else. His conversation is like a brilliant player at billiards—the strokes
follow one another, piff-paff." From the first, he sided
against his father's politics, once riding through the streets
of London in the buff and blue colors of the American in-
dependents.

Prominent among his early loves was Mrs. Mary Robinson, a young woman who had used her beauty and some
artistic talent to make the best of a hard life. Her father
was a merchant navy captain who had fallen upon financial
difficulties, and subsequently joined the Russian fleet. Mary,
married at fifteen to a profligate attorney who ended in
prison, was obliged to fend for herself, joining the theater,
where, under the patronage of David Garrick, she achieved
a fair reputation. At the age of twenty-three, playing Perdita
in the *Winter's Tale,* she captivated the still teenaged Prince
of Wales. Overcome by his effusive endearments, Mary
dithered. The prince wailed his impatience. Erupting in
floods of tears, he let them stain further and pressing letters
to the lady, eventually sending a suave ambassador, Lord
Malden, to persuade her. Mrs. Robinson relented. "I will
row you across the Thames by the light of the moon,"
crooned Lord Malden. "The Prince will do the rest." He
did. But his ardor flagged when the novelty had worn off.

Insatiable for amusement, the prince quickly "grew pee-
vish," as one who knew him put it, "if there was not a
perpetual rattle for him." When the charms of Mrs. Robinson diminished, he denounced her as his father's spy, and
sought a livelier mistress in "Dally the Tall"—Grace Dal-
rymple Elliot, another noted beauty. Mary Robinson was

left so impoverished that she placed the prince's love letters to her on the market, forcing the anguished king to buy them for £5,000. To George's mounting distress, his son frequently was brought home drunk, or carried into custody by the night watch. He had learned to swear, averred an acquaintance, with the "wanton vocabulary of the brothel." Among many who were pleased to encourage his escapades for their gain or amusement was his easy-living uncle, the Duke of Cumberland, who dubbed the prince "Taffy," ran a gaming table for him in Pall Mall and introduced him to the inevitable moneylenders.

Desperately, the king sought to convert his wayward son through his own special therapeutic activity, fox hunting. On a horse in the country, the prince was safe from his dubious city associates, and at one time his father kept him hunting almost constantly. Still, he could not stop the Duke of Cumberland coming between them. "When we hunt together," the king confided to the Duke of Gloucester, "neither my son nor my brother speak to me. And lately, when the chase ended at a little village where there was but a single post-chaise to be hired, my son and brother got into it and drove to London, leaving me to go home in a cart if I could find one."

Whether at Windsor, where the king's hour of dining was three o'clock, or in London, where it was four, the prince rarely turned up for meals less than an hour late, shamelessly snubbing his father in front of the household. When the Duke of Gloucester expressed surprise that George should tolerate his son's behavior so patiently, the king replied that he had no option. If he did not bear with it, the prince would be driven further into opposition, "which would increase my distress." In fact, where his sons were concerned—especially the Prince of Wales, and the next in seniority, Frederick, Duke of York—George was consistently indulgent and almost pathetically affectionate.

By the time he was twenty-three, the Prince of Wales
was, by his own admission, £160,000 in debt, despite an
allowance of £50,000 a year and a vote of £60,000 from
Parliament to pay earlier debts. The diaries of the eminent
diplomatist, Lord Malmesbury, tell how the prince twice
sought the advice of that peer at Carlton House, bewailing
his ruin. His father hated him, the prince said—seemingly
because George had advised him to marry and set aside
£10,000 a year to repay debts. How could he do it, he
pleaded. "With the strictest economy, my expenses are twice
my income! If I stay in England, I shall disgrace myself."
The only way out, declared the prince, was to live abroad,
but the king had refused to let him leave the country. "What
am I to do? Am I to be refused the right of every individual?
Cannot I travel legally, as a private man, without the king's
consent?"

Malmesbury ventured to suggest that the prince should
indeed marry and settle for respectability, upon which
step, he suggested, a thankful Parliament might be relied
upon to settle his present debts. "It would," he said, "be
most agreeable to the king, and, I am certain, most grateful
to the nation."

Exclaimed the prince: "I never will marry! My resolution
is taken on that subject. I have settled it with Frederick.
I will never marry!"

Malmesbury looked stern. "Give me leave, sir, to say, most
respectfully, that you cannot really have come to such a
resolution. You *must* marry, sir! You owe it to the country,
to the king, to yourself."

"I owe nothing to the king!"

"Till you are married, sir, and have children, you have
no solid hold on the affections of the people. If you come
to the throne a bachelor, and his royal highness the Duke
of York is married and has sons to succeed you, your

situation, when king, will be more painful than it is at this moment."

At this, the prince flounced from the room. The thought of a marriage of convenience to some European princess of his father's approving was especially repugnant at that moment, since he had recently met the object of the most passionate love of his life, the much-admired Mrs. Fitzherbert.

Maria Anne Fitzherbert, daughter of Walter Smythe, second son of Sir John Smythe of Eske in county Durham, was a twice-widowed Catholic gentlewoman of respectable standing. Her second husband, Thomas Fitzherbert of Swinnerton, Staffordshire, had died when she was twenty-four. Now in her late twenties, and six years older than her royal admirer, she had a pleasant rather than a beautiful face, a trim figure and a mature, benign disposition which made her popular with all classes. Her Richmond home, it was said, was besieged by "half our young nobility." According to a relative, Maria was the original of a popular ballad, "The Lass of Richmond Hill":

> On Richmond Hill there lives a lass
> More bright than May day morn,
> Whose charms all other maids' surpass
> O rose without a thorn.
> This lass so neat, with smiles so sweet,
> Has won my right good will,
> I'd crowns resign to call her mine,
> Sweet lass of Richmond Hill.

The prince had first seen her at a water party on the Thames, subsequently dogging her movements so devotedly that his attentions became the most engrossing topic of the salons and coffeeshops. Declared his mother with perhaps more hope than expectation: "This passion might not be sinful. Does he not profess an unseemly devotion to the Duchess of Devonshire, which appears to be innocent, though, God knows, it is fraught with harm?" When Mrs. Fitzherbert announced her intention of departing for the Continent to escape the agitated young man, George and Charlotte felt happier again. The prince could not follow without the king's permission, which was refused.

Pronounced Maria Fitzherbert: "It must be marriage or nothing at all. Since marriage is impossible, it would be better for the prince to forget me."

But the prince's infatuation was heightened by her absence. He bombarded her with passionate, heart-rending letters. He offered her a morganatic marriage according to the laws of Hanover, which she declined. Finally, in a missive of thirty-seven pages, he made a solemn promise to marry her if she returned to England, assuring her improbably that his father would "connive at the union." Mrs. Fitzherbert relented.

Her return to Britain caused the few true friends the prince possessed much alarm. Fox went to some trouble to warn him amicably of the dangers he was running:

> I was told before I left Town yesterday that Mrs Fitzherbert was arrived; and if I had heard only this, I should have felt most unfeigned joy at an event which I knew would contribute so much to your Royal Highness' satisfaction; but I was told at the same time that from a variety of circumstances which had been observed and put together, there was reason to suppose that you were going to take the very desperate step (pardon the expression) of marrying her at this moment.
>
> If such an idea be really in your mind, and it be not now too late, for God's sake let me call your attention to

some considerations . . . In the first place, you are aware that a marriage with a Catholic throws the Prince contracting such a marriage out of the succession of the Crown . . . I have stated this danger upon the supposition that the marriage would be a real one; but your Royal Highness knows as well as I that according to the present laws of the country it cannot; and I need not point out to your good sense what a source of uneasiness it must be to you, to her, and above all to the nation, to have it a matter of dispute and discussion whether the Prince of Wales is, or is not, married.

Lied the Prince of Wales glibly: "My Dear Charles . . . Believe me the world will soon be convinced that there not only is [not], but never was, any ground for these reports which have late been so malevolently circulated."

The marriage took place with the utmost secrecy in the drawing room of Mrs. Fitzherbert's Park Lane apartment a few days after her return from the country, and the couple set out immediately through deep snow for the bride's house at Richmond. Despite rumors, the secret was remarkably well kept. Mrs. Fitzherbert's discretion was absolute, and a genuine affection for the pretty young man she had wed helped her to weather jibes at their undisguisably close connection, and the erratic behavior of her unstable husband. For a time, indeed, her maturity helped to steady the prince, who made efforts to restrict his overwhelming debts, abandoning Carlton House, his London residence, and buying a farmhouse near the sea at the Sussex fishing village of Brighton.

His good intentions were short-lived. Before long, he was building at Brighton one of the most astonishing and bizarre edifices ever seen in Britain. The prince's "Pavilion" became the jest of the country. With its gleaming oriental domes, Chinese gallery and stables modeled on the corn market of Paris, it was not only a gift to the London cartoonists, but an even greater drain on the prince's pocket than Carlton House. The Pavilion put Brighton on the social map. High society flocked to romp by the sea with the prince and his lady. When the couple went to town, the Duchess of Cumberland, always pleased to upset the king and queen, entertained them. To Mrs. Fitzherbert's alarm, her husband quickly reverted to his old habits. The faster his debts increased, the more uproarious became his behavior. He staggered into a ball given by Lady Portarlington in a state of semi-stupefaction, slobbered over the Duchess of Ancaster and threatened to knock Lord Galloway's false teeth out. Frequently, his companions had to restrain him. When Maria remonstrated, he grew maudlin and wept like a small child.

Awkward questions were now being asked in Parliament. Pitt was hinting at the secret marriage, and Fox's popularity was suffering as a result of his connections with the king's son. A cartoon by Gillray, those prints sold in London by the thousands, showed Fox giving away the bride, while Burke, clad as a Jesuit priest, conducted the service. With the prince's categorical denial of a marriage to assure him, Fox rose in the House of Commons to refute the allegations.

"In that House," he is reported to have said, "where it was known how frequent and common the falsehoods of the time were, he hoped a tale only fit to impose upon the lowest order of persons in the streets would have gained the smallest portion of credit; but when it appeared that an invention so monstrous, a report of a fact which had not the smallest degree of foundation, a report of a fact actually impossible to have happened, had been circulated with so much industry as to have made an impression on the minds of members of that House, it proved at once the uncommon pains taken by the enemies of His Royal Highness to propagate the grossest and most malignant falsehoods with a view to depreciate his character and injure him in the opinion of the country."

The same evening, at Brooks's Club, in the West End, Fox met a relative of Mrs. Fitzherbert, one Orlando Bridgeman. Taking Fox to one side, Bridgeman confided: "I see by the papers that you have denied the fact of the marriage of the Prince of Wales and Mrs Fitzherbert. You have been misinformed. I was present at that marriage." To his horror, Fox, who would not have treated his worst enemy in such a fashion, realized how deeply he had been abused by the Prince of Wales. For a year, he refused to have anything to do with him. Maria, too, was disillusioned.

"Only conceive, Maria, what Fox did yesterday," the prince told her gleefully after his friend's speech. "He went down to the House and denied that you and I were man and wife. Did you ever hear of such a thing?"

A cold silence marked the woman's disgust. Prudently, the pretty boy fled from her presence.

Of George's fifteen legitimate children, a record for a British king, nine were sons. Besides the Prince of Wales, there were Frederick, Duke of York; William, Duke of Clarence and later William IV of England; Edward, Duke of Kent; Ernest, Duke of Cumberland and later King of Hanover; Augustus, Duke of Sussex; Adolphus, Duke of Cambridge; Octavius and Alfred. The last two died in early childhood. Alfred was two when his death occurred in August 1782. In the final moments of the child's life, the king took the queen out of the sickroom and expressed a wish to read a sermon as usual, it being a Sunday evening. "He selected that of Blair on Death, which closes with the beautiful description from the Revelations of the Church triumphant," wrote Bute's daughter-in-law, Mrs. Stuart. "While reading it a slight knock was heard at the door. The King seemed to shudder but went on reading. When the description was ended he went up to the Queen, and taking her hand most affectionately said—'Such, my dearest, I humbly trust our little Alfred now is. That knock informed me he is passed from death unto life.' He then wept tenderly."

"I am sorry for Alfred," said the king afterwards, "but had it been Octavius, I should have died, too." When Octavius in fact died, aged four, next May, George was for some time inconsolable. Again, he found relief for his anguish in religion. "Many people," he declared, "would regret they ever had so sweet a child, since they were forced to part with him. That is not my case. I am thankful to God for having graciously allowed me to enjoy such a creature for four years."

In 1785, George's third son, William, serving as a naval lieutenant, had to be moved from Portsmouth, where his proximity to the daughters of the local commissioner, Sir Henry Martin, was viewed by the king as a grave moral danger to the young man. Details are lacking, but the king wrote of "a very unpleasant and unexpected event," finding it "indispensably necessary to remove him from intercourse with the Commissioner's House."

William combined the superficiality of the Prince of Wales with a fatuous self-conceit. When his mother could tolerate his behavior no longer, she denounced him as "a true trifling character, which is the most despicable of all things in the world, and the higher the rank, the more it is observed. It is surprising that with the proofs you give to the world of your offensive pride you do not feel the necessity of a proper behaviour . . . it is amazing how your indifference of behaviour is talked of both here and abroad, and the world so far is just in attributing it to your want of minding the advice of proper people, and the great opinion you have of yourself. Cease, I beseech you, to be a great-little man, which in reality is nothing at all, and return to those who are put about you in order to guide you."

The same year William was in trouble at Portsmouth, George entered Ernest, Augustus and Adolphus as students at the university at Göttingen. "They learn history, geography, moral philosophy, mathematics and experimental philosophy; so that their time is fully employed," George wrote hopefully. But his problems were not over. At twenty-two, Augustus contravened the Royal Marriage Act by marrying Lady Augusta Murray, a daughter of the Earl of Dunmore. The parties were disguised at the wedding ceremony in Hanover Square, London, and the officiating parson seems not to have recognized them. George's distress was not diminished by the fact that Lady Augusta gave birth to a son eight days after the wedding. There was, however, no prosecution, and the matter was hushed up.

Curiously enough, though George was ineffectual in restraining the habits of his wayward sons, he kept his daughters Charlotte, Augusta, Elizabeth, Mary and Amelia under close supervision at the palaces. So much so that they addressed their letters to their brothers from "the Nunnery." George regarded them with passionate devotion and termed them "all Cordelias." The death of the youngest, Amelia, still a spinster in her twenty-eighth year, was to prove a savage blow to him.

Meanwhile, in 1787, a poignant reconciliation occurred between the Prince of Wales and a distressed but forgiving father, the result of which was that George consented to settle on his son and heir an additional £10,000 a year, also authorizing an application to Parliament to discharge the young man's debts. In return, the prince promised king and Parliament to live within his income. For a while, the indulgent George was rewarded.

"I am told," reported a contemporary, "the Prince is resolved never again to quarrel with his father. Yesterday the

Drawing-room was fine, and crowded as a birthday. The Prince's household all kissed hands [with the king]. The Queen and Princesses seemed delighted, and the King was very cheerful." To add contentment to the family reunion, the Duke of York returned to the palace after soldiering in Germany. George was immensely proud and gratified to have his two eldest sons about him. Fanny Burney described him as in a constant "transport of delight."

Unfortunately, this small oasis in the king's life dissolved as abruptly as a mirage. Not only did the Prince of Wales swiftly resume his old habits, he taught his younger brother some like ones. Four months in each other's company was sufficient to transmogrify the upstanding Frederick into a drunken gambler with a mistress, the Countess of Tyrconnel, whom Mrs. Fitzherbert described as a "lady of contaminate character." Complained a friend of the Duke of York of his brother's evil influence: "We are totally guided . . . thoroughly initiated into all the extravagancies and debaucheries of this most *virtuous* metropolis. Our visits to Windsor are less frequent, and, I am afraid, will at last be totally given up." Declared another colleague: "I am sorry to say that we still go on at a most furious rate, and I cannot but lament most sincerely certain parts of our conduct which I hope we shall correct before it is too late."

Protested an indignant courtier: "The Duke of York in politics talks both ways, and, I think, will end in opposition. His conduct is as bad as possible. He plays very deep and loses; and his company is thought *mauvais ton*." Both the brothers plunged wildly at the tables. "The Prince of Wales has taken very much this year to play, and has gone so far as to win or lose £2,000 or £3,000 in a night. He is now, together with the Duke of York, forming a new club at Weltzie's; and this will probably be the scene of some of the highest gaming which has been seen in town." The king was mortified. "I am told," exclaimed a sympathizer, "that the King and Queen begin now to feel how sharper than a serpent's tooth it is to have a thankless child."

As time passed, Brighton would become synonymous with the high life implanted there by "Prinny's set." Mrs. Fitzherbert struggled unavailingly to check the worst excesses of her husband. He grew fatter, flabbier of mind, more and more futile in his amusements. His casual amours were ceaseless—the money he spent gambling and carousing, prodigious. George "Beau" Brummell appeared and transformed the prince's taste for sartorial elegance into a thoroughly ludicrous passion. Then, suddenly, a new star shone on the social scene to seduce him.

Lady Jersey was a dark-eyed climber whose distinctive physical attributes—including features of classical proportions and an opulent figure—had made her the toast of male London. Her admirers were legion. Lady Jersey had gained an entry to royal circles through a friendship with Charlotte's companion, Lady Harcourt, and soon her eyes were blazing at the Prince of Wales. The first Mrs. Fitzherbert knew of the crisis came in an unsigned note from her husband announcing that he had no intention of setting foot on her threshold again. She disdained to reply to it.

Drunkenly, the prince turned to the arms of Lady Jersey. But her caresses alone could not sustain him. With a mountain of debts towering over him, it became clear he could only escape by appeasing court and country and, at the risk of being discovered a bigamist, accepting an officially approved bride. Lady Jersey, grasping the practicalities of the matter as quickly as anyone, supported the establishment candidate, the king's niece, Princess Caroline of Brunswick, who had the merits, as she saw it, of being both simple and unbeautiful. When the prince first set eyes on his chosen bride, he screamed for a glass of brandy. Caroline was good-natured but slovenly, and not overfond of washing. She had heard, she declared, that "there was but one bath-tub in Versailles, and they grew flowers in that." Her fastidious suitor shuddered. Reported Lord Malmesbury: "The Prince is overcome by the emotions of the first interview." And, on the wedding day: "the Prince looked like death." Princess Caroline looked no better. Thanks to the subversive attentions of Lady Jersey, who had assisted in her dressing, she wore an incongruous beaver hat with an unbecoming wedding gown, and was daubed with so much rouge her face resembled a tomato.

The marriage proceeded farcically. Mrs. Fitzherbert swooned when she learned of the wedding, while Lady Jersey, extracting what amusement she could from a bridal supper that passed like a funeral feast, sprinkled Epsom salts on Caroline's plate. The prince reeled from the banquet to the bridal chamber in a drunken stupor, fell headlong into the empty fireplace and spent most of the night there. When he had sobered, he returned to Lady Jersey. Caroline subsequently gave birth to a daughter. If pregnancy surprised her—"I began to be with child, and I did not believe it,"—she was more surprised to receive a note from the prince coolly informing her that he did not ever again intend to treat her as his wife. Her first reaction was relief. "Thank God I am free," she said. But she was later discovered crying over her infant. The nation sympathized. Wrote Byron:

> *Weep, daughter of a royal line,*
> *A Sire's disgrace, a realm's decay:*
> *Ah, happy if each tear of thine*
> *Could wash a father's fault away.*

The Prince of Wales never outgrew his instability. Dropping Lady Jersey, he begged to be allowed to return to Mrs. Fitzherbert, who generously agreed to take him back.

But he became no more than "an intermittently devoted husband," and eventually left her again in finality. In due course, as George IV, he would prove as weak a king as he had a prince, his reign doing much to disgust the country with the moral turpitude he represented, and to pave the way for Victorian reaction. Much of his endeavor, in later years, was directed to trying to divorce Caroline of Brunswick. At last, he succeeded in bringing her to trial for alleged misconduct. There followed one of the most absurd court cases in English history—the king versus the queen—from which Caroline emerged the victress. "The king choked and turned purple, cursing like a madman."

Caroline died in August 1821. Nine years later, when her weary and dissipated husband expired—still chubby of cheek and curly-haired—London celebrated with open-air parties and public festivities. It was said that Mrs. Fitzherbert, who outlived them both, looked on with sadness, and that her faded admirer had worn her miniature at his death.

CHAPTER 22

Mental Derangement

On June 8, 1788, George wrote to Bishop Hurd of Worcester, one of his few close friends, that "having had rather a sharp bilious attack, which the goodness of Divine Providence is quite removed, Sir George Baker [the king's physician] has strongly recommended to me the going for a month to Cheltenham, as he thinks that water efficacious on such occasions, and that an absence from London will keep me free from certain fatigues that attend long audiences. I shall therefore go there on Saturday."

It was characterstic of this king of few intimates that he should choose as his most enduring correspondent a divine, and the author of *Letters on Chivalry and Romance.* Hurd was also a modest man, which appealed to George. In 1783 he declined the primacy, more interested in the excellent library he had built at Worcester. The monarch wrote him frequently, retailing his movements and domestic and family gossip—of the pleasure of sea bathing, the "harassing" ordeal of having to open Parliament, the sadness of bereavement, and so on. "I find myself," George confided to Hurd in one letter, "enabled to pursue one of my most agreeable occupations, that of writing to you who have never been in the most gloomy moments out of my thoughts."

At Cheltenham, the royal family borrowed Lord Faucon-
berg's lodge, a few hundred yards from the spa, to which
George repaired at daybreak each morning to swallow three
bumpers of the purgative liquid. In a letter to Baker, the
king reported frankly that "he finds a pint and a half the
proper quantity to give him two openings, these clear
him without any sinking, on the contrary he finds himself
in better spirits and has never been obliged to take the
rhubarb pills."

Apparently restored, though some thought he still looked
ill, George returned to Windsor in August. In October, he
suffered an attack of hives. One arm was so disfigured with
weals that it looked "as if it had been scourged with
cords." Shortly afterwards, he showed his equerries Budé
and Goldsworthy two large spots on his chest. According to
a contemporary diarist: "Both advised him to be careful not
to catch cold, as the consequence would probably be a
dangerous repelling of the eruption. The King as usual
rejected this advice, with some degree of ill-humour. He
rode in the Park, came home very wet; the spots disappeared, a slight fever first ensued, and, soon after, the
mental derangement."

Meanwhile, the waning powers of the Shelburne ministry,
heavily buffeted on the preliminaries for the Treaty of
Versailles, had set Westminster speculating on another
change of government. Pitt had been widely tipped for
premier, having the support of influential Whig elements
and some personal esteem in the king's eyes. But the son of
Chatham, still in his early twenties, bided his time. Fox
continued as the favorite of another Whig faction, while
North, though now lacking royal patronage, retained a
fair following. Neither Fox nor North had the strength to
govern on his own, but, as friends pointed out, a com-
bination of the two would most certainly sweep the board,

oust Shelburne, block the king and gain prizes for both sides.

The coalition of 1783 created a sensation. The two men had spent years denouncing each other, often with the utmost virulence, and the cynicism of the pact surprised even hard-bitten politicians. "If this ill-omened marriage is not already solemnized," observed Pitt, "I know a just and lawful impediment, and, in the name of public safety, I here forbid the bans." But no impediment could stop the coalition. A rich man, the Duke of Portland, was appointed first minister to reassure the Whig aristocrats; the king's friend Thurlow was kicked out, and Fox and North installed themselves as Secretaries of State. George was beside himself with shock and anger. "I am sorry it has been my lot to reign," he wrote dismally, "in the most profligate Age when unnatural coalition seems to have taken place, which can but add confusion and distraction among a too much divided Nation."

Again, he contemplated abdication. "A long experience and a serious attention to the strange Events that have successively arisen, has gradually prepared my mind," he explained, "to expect the time when I should be no longer of Utility to this Empire." He was therefore resolved, he added, "to resign my Crown and all the Dominions appertaining to it to the Prince of Wales, my Eldest Son and Lawful Successor, and to retire to the care of my Electoral Dominions the Original Patrimony of my Ancestors." Again, he stopped short of implementing his intentions. He had never been to the Continent, and the idea of leaving his beloved English countryside was one that, in the end, he could not face. Instead, he summoned his ebbing resources for another fight.

Much unpopular business faced the new government, including the introduction of further taxation, and George determined to aggravate its problems. Displaying his disapproval on all possible occasions, he stubbornly refused to create new peers, freezing the last vestiges of patronage at his disposal. By the winter, his desperation had overrun legality. Fox had introduced a bill for tightening control of the East India Company. It was much needed, but opinion among the peers on the matter was divided. The king seized his chance. Sending for Lord Temple—the second Earl—he presented him with a card which he said was to be displayed to all waverers. On it was written "That whoever voted for the India Bill was not only not his [the king's] friend, but would be considered by him as an enemy." The bill was rejected by a narrow margin. Next day, December 18, George confirmed the fate of the government. "Lord North," he wrote, "is by this requested to send Me the Seals of his Department and to acquaint Mr Fox to send those of the Foreign Department . . . I choose this method as Audience on such occasions must be unpleasant."

George had won the immediate struggle, but was not to regain his earlier authority. Through the services of Thurlow, Pitt was now induced to accept the premiership, with Thurlow as Lord Chancellor. Like his father before him, Pitt was always courteous to the king, but, like his father, was too strong to be the tool of the monarch. Throughout his long ministry, Pitt remained aloof from the court, seeking merely the formal approval of a disillusioned and ailing George.

For more than a quarter of a century, the king had battled through unremitting conflict, both outwardly and inwardly, attempting to change not only the world but his own psyche. In the name of royal duty, he had suppressed his reality—the dreamy, languid and sensuous son of his forebears—in favor of a tirelessly toiling, abstemious and businesslike super-king. It was, perhaps, the measure of his stature that he strove so strenuously to improve himself. But the strains of repression and ambition had been too much. With the whole tenor of the age against him—from the mobs in the streets to his ministers, from America to his own sons—his health had already begun to break up.

Sir George Baker would have been fascinated to know that, two centuries later, medical experts would still be arguing whether the king's illness was primarily organic (porphyria) or of the psyche. Baker, a cultured man, to whom Gray dedicated his famous *Elegy Written in a Country Churchyard*, had been in general practice for more than thirty years, and had written a book on mental disorders. He commenced his treatment with the fashionable bleedings and purges of the times, but the king's bizarre excitement soon led him to the factor of mental derangement. "The shade by which soundness of mind is to be distinguished from some degree of insanity is often faint," declared Baker, "and in many cases hardly perceptible; and nothing is more embarrassing to families as well as physicians than the condition of persons half-disordered, whom the law will not confine, though they ought not to be at liberty. Such appeared to me to have been His Majesty's case."

When George's agitation became worse, his conversation "perpetual," Baker was certain of a mental impediment— "Yet so delicate was the situation in which I was placed, that I did not dare to communicate my suspicions, or take any decisive measures in consequence of them. I hoped indeed that retirement to His Majesty's favourite place of residence [Windsor] and a total relaxation from business would in no long time have restored strength to his body and composure to his mind. In the mean time, I thought it prudent not to raise an alarm of such public importance while it could be avoided."

According to the biographer of Mrs. Siddons, the celebrated actress was the first person outside the royal family to suspect the king's mental condition. She had visited Windsor to give one of her readings, when George, "without any apparent motive placed in her hands a sheet of paper—blank with the exception of his signature—an incident which struck her as so unaccountable that she immedately carried it to the Queen, who gratefully thanked her for her discretion." Another time, in the middle of a church service, the king suddenly grasped his wife and daughters, exclaiming: "You know what it is to be nervous, but were you ever as bad as this?" During a concert of his favorite composer, Handel, "he talked continuously, making frequent and sudden transitions from one subject to another." Fanny Burney, like all the ladies of Windsor, was upset. When George buttonholed her outside the queen's room at Windsor, the hoarseness of his voice and the extravagance of his gestures startled her.

"During a conversation which lasted nearly half-an-hour the agitation of his manner, and the rapidity of his utterance, were no less painful, although in other respects he was kind and gentle to a degree that made it affecting to listen to him. Ill as he was, all his care seemed to have been to conceal his sufferings from and to allay the anxiety of others."

By the end of October 1788, Charlotte was extremely anxious and given to weeping. Nevertheless, she concealed her condition from outsiders and continued to comfort her husband. "The Queen," he said, "is my physician, and no man can have a better. She is my friend." In an attempt to kill rumors—"to stop further lies," as George himself put it, "and any fall of the Stocks"—a levee was arranged at St. James's Palace, at which the king appeared. The ploy was not successful, for the sovereign's changed manner was clear for all to see.

Events moved dramatically toward public exposure of the tragedy. On November 5, whispers filled the palace that some dire scene had taken place in the royal apartments. "Various small speeches dropped," wrote Miss Burney, "by which I found the house was all in disturbance, and the King in some strange way worse." That night, Fanny waited for news in her lonely and silent room. "Not a sound could be heard . . . Whoever was in the house kept to the other end, and not even a servant crossed the stairs or passage."

Suddenly, the secret was out. "The Prince of Wales had come to the castle, and was present when the King's malady first took a violent form. His father caught him with both hands by the collar, pushing him against the wall with some violence, and asked him who would dare say to the King of England that he should not speak out, or should prevent his whispering. The King then whispered." The prince promptly collapsed and had to be revived by the sprinkling of water on his temples and by bleeding. Charlotte had hysterics. Within hours, the prince had broken the news to the political opposition and London was a-buzz with consternation. Stocks fell. Pitt and his ministers wore grim faces. At Brooks's Club, shrine of the opposition, the prince's friends quickened with expectation. Fox, on his way to holiday in Italy with his mistress, Mrs. Armstead, was overtaken with the news at Bologna, and at once made tracks back to England. Wrote one politician: "You may naturally conceive the exultation, not wearing even the appearance of disguise, which there is in one party, and the depression of those who belong to another." It began to look as though the Prince of Wales was a new power.

He certainly thought so himself. "Nothing," wrote Miss Burney of the prince's high-handedness, "was done but by his orders, and he was applied to in every difficulty." He entered the king's study and took possession of his papers and valuables, and he snooped outside his father's bedroom "in order that he might hear his ravings at the time they were at the worst." He also brought in a Dr. Warren, noted for his loyalty to the opposition, as a spy in the palace. George was not so delirious as to miss the motive. "No man can serve two masters," he told Warren. "You are the Prince of Wales's physician—you cannot be mine." Nevertheless, when Warren suggested blistering the king's head in order to draw the poison from his brain, it was done. Chortled an opposition scribe callously:

> *If blisters to the head applied*
> *Some little sense bestow,*
> *What pity 'tis they were not tried*
> *Some twenty years ago.*

The king's condition worsened. "The veins in his face were swelled, the sound of his voice was dreadful. He often spoke until he was exhausted and, the moment he could recover his breath, began again, while the foam ran out of his mouth." Oddly enough, he had ceased to punctuate his conversations with the familiar "What? What? What?" and his language was considered by one who knew him to be "better and smarter" than at any period. It was small comfort, for not only was George a seriously ill man, but his physicians were aggravating his distress by well-intentioned but ignorant methods. Though the weather that winter was outstandingly bitter, no fire was allowed in the sickroom, which became so cold that nobody but the king stayed in it for more than thirty minutes at a time. George had no option. Not content with freezing and blistering the patient, his doctors filled him alternately with purges and sedatives, and, when he tried to escape them, ordered his pages to sit on him. This new relationship between king and servants did nothing for the monarch's equanimity.

Once, staggering wildly from his bedroom, he was stopped by Dr. Baker. Pinning the physician to a wall, the king snapped at him: "You're mistaken in my condition. It's only nervousness, and you're nothing but an old woman!" Colonel Digby, the queen's chamberlain, took the king by an arm and endeavored to lead him back to his apartment. "I will not go," exclaimed George. "Who are you?"

"I am Colonel Digby, Sir. Your Majesty has been very good to me often, and now I am going to be very good to you, for you must come to bed. It is necessary to your life."

The king allowed himself to be persuaded.

Sir George Baker came in for a rough time from his patient. One visitor to the palace found the king "swaddled in fine linen like an Egyptian mummy (Straight jackets are for the vulgar. If the sovereign be disposed to be a little outré in his deportment, he is pinioned in an envelopment of lawn). Sir George came in and unfastened his arms to feel his pulse; whereupon the royal patient gave him a blow on the forehead which laid him on the floor, and then poured over him the contents of the chamber-pot. Standing over his physician, and reciting the rules of the 'Order of Cloacina' [the goddess of privies], His Majesty exhorted Sir George to maintain its honour and dignity. He then returned to his chair and said, 'Rise, Sir George, knight of the most ancient, most puissant, and most honourable Order of Cloacina.' After which, he laughed himself to sleep."

Surrounded by Sheridan and his other cronies, the Prince of Wales was already planning his new government. Even Thurlow, convinced of the hopelessness of the king's case, had secretly offered to join them on condition that he kept his office. Fox was uneasy about developments when he returned to London, but chose to go along with them. Dutifully, Dr. Warren propounded the impossibility of the king's condition. "He will not live to be certified a lunatic," he prophesied.

Wrote an indignant supporter of the government: "The Opposition have been taking inconceivable pains to spread the idea that the disorder is incurable. Nothing can exceed Warren's indiscretion on the subject . . . So long as the Opposition considered the case as desperate, they were affecting a prodigious concern and reverence for the King's unhappy situation. Now that the people entertain hopes of his recovery, they are using the utmost industry to combat the idea—circulating all the particulars of everything which he says and does, and adding the most outrageous falsehoods."

Pitt held the fort with all his skill and eloquence. "The great object to be looked to," declared one observer, "seems to be the keeping of the Government in such a state as that, if the King's health should be restored, he might be as far as possible enabled to resume . . . I suppose there never was a situation in which any set of men ever had, at once, so many points to decide, so essentially affecting their own honour, character and future situation, their duty to their country in a most critical situation, and their duty to their unhappy master, to whom they are unquestionably bound by ties of gratitude and honour, independent of considerations of public duty towards him. I hope God, who has been pleased to afflict us with this severe and heavy trial, will enable us to go through it honestly, conscientiously, and in a manner not dishonourable to our characters."

What were the prospects? On November 22, Pitt visited Windsor. "From what he said, there is no doubt of the King's being much better: at the same time, the accounts of the physicians are gloomy." One moment George was up, the next he was down again. In his lucid periods, he spoke rationally of the delusions he had suffered, recalling the vivid impression of a great storm, and how he had seen Hanover through Herschel's telescope. The day after Pitt's visit, he "talked very rapidly on strange subjects, and sorry was I to hear," wrote an equerry, "that these were not free from indecencies."

The relaxing at last of his sexual repressions expressed itself in sallies against the ladies of the household, which frightened Fanny Burney, and even the queen, and in a violent passion for a leading beauty of the age, Lady Elizabeth Pembroke. He refused to be shaved until his beard had attained such a length that it took two hours to remove it, and he became increasingly troublesome to his attendants, who, on the twenty-eighth, could restrain him only by brute force. On the thirtieth, he "pulled one of his pages by the hair and endeavoured to kick another."

Pitt played for time. A novel mood was sweeping the country. For once in his reign, George was becoming the object of public affection. The prospect of the Prince of Wales taking the throne had made people reflect on some of the merits of his father. And, as George's stock rose, Pitt's rose with it. On December 3, the king's doctors were examined by the Privy Council. "Can the king be cured?" Burke asked bluntly. The answer was affirmative, "but it might take a long time." Warren was the most reluctant to admit the likelihood of recovery. Commented Lord Camden afterwards: "Dr Warren is a damned scoundrel."

Since some regency plan was now necessary, Pitt made it as restrictive as possible. His proposals were that the king's welfare and household appointments should be left to the queen; that the Prince of Wales should be made regent, but without right of interference in the king's property or in the granting of pensions or places, and that these proposals should be contingent upon the king's recovery. Furiously, the prince and his party opposed such restrictions. Wraxall spoke of the "agitation, violence and animosity" of the argument, which led Fox to the indiscretion of claiming in Parliament that the powers of regency were the prince's by right. Pitt exploited the error efficiently.

The Prince of Wales, he pointed out, had no more *right* to power than anyone else in the country.

"Let not the House rashly annihilate and annul the authority of Parliament, in which the existence of the Constitution is so intimately involved." The government won the debate.

Despite the advice of Thurlow that he should remain aloof and let events take their own course—"Everything, Your Royal Highness, must flow to you of its course. You will only interrupt its course by eagerness to receive it"—the prince rapidly alienated support by his crude and impatient canvassing. The Duke of York did not help. "The Princes," wrote Lord Bulkeley, "go on in their usual style, both keeping open houses, and employing every means in their power to gain proselytes . . . The Duke of York never misses a night at Brooks's, where the hawks pluck his feathers unmercifully, and have reduced him to the vowels I.O.U."

November proved a month of crisis in the palace. For the queen's safety, and because it was thought best for the king to be alone, her bed had been made in a separate room. George's efforts to get to her kept Charlotte and her ladies-in-waiting in terror. One morning, Fanny Burney heard men's voices in the queen's dressing room. "Seized with the most cruel alarm . . . I waited some time, and then the door opened, and I saw Colonel Goldsworthy and Mr Batterscombe. I was relieved from my first apprehension, yet shocked enough to see them there at this early hour. They had both sat up there all night, as well as Sandys. Every page, both of the King and ante-rooms! and O, what horror in every face I met!"

Fanny eased into the room. The queen was in bed, sitting up. She leaned her head forward and inquired softly: "Miss Burney, how are you?" Her face was pale and strained. Fanny looked at her, and burst into tears. Soon, both women were weeping copiously. At last, the queen wiped her eyes and said:

"I thank you, Miss Burney, you have made me cry. It is a great relief to me. I had not been able to cry before, all this night long."

Charlotte described what had happened. In the middle of the night, the king had burst into the her room, candle in hand, and dragged back her bed curtains. For a full half hour he had stood staring at her while she waited, terrified, for his next move. Finally, he had left as abruptly as he had entered. "The fear of such another entrance was now so strongly upon the nerves of the poor Queen that she could hardly support herself."

Refusing to let Fanny leave her, Charlotte ordered her to sit down. Trembling, Fanny obeyed her. From time to time, the queen made her go and listen outside the king's door, to learn what he was saying or doing.

"I did, and carried the best accounts I could manage, without deviating from truth, except by some omissions. Nothing could be so afflicting as this task; even now it brings fresh to my ear his poor exhausted voice. 'I am nervous. But I love you both very well; if you would tell me the truth: I love Dr Heberden best, for he has not told me a lie: Sir George has told me a lie—a white lie, he says, but I hate a white lie! If you will tell me a lie, let it be a black lie!' This is what he kept saying almost constantly, mixed in with other matter, but always returning, and in a voice that will truly never cease vibrating in my recollection."

At the end of November, matters got worse. Because it was thought that the gardens and terraces of Kew would do him good, the physicians decided to move George from Windsor. The king was violently opposed to the scheme. Of the two residences, he much preferred Windsor, and he suspected a plot to detach him from his family.

Sir Lucas Pepys, another of the doctors, saw Fanny Burney on the twenty-eighth and informed her that the household was to move to Kew the next day. The problem was how to overcome the king's resistance. If they attempted force, confided Pepys, the country would be up in arms. "He moved me to tears," related Fanny, "by telling me that none of their own lives would be safe if the King did not recover, so prodigiously high ran the tide of affection and loyalty. All the physicians received threatening letters daily, to answer for the safety of their monarch with their lives! Sir George Baker had already been stopped in his carriage by the mob, to give an account of the King; and when he said it was a bad one, they had furiously exclaimed 'The more shame for you!'"

Eventually, the demented sovereign was persuaded to make the journey on the promise that he would be allowed to be with the queen and princesses when he arrived at Kew. He looked cheerful as he rode in the coach with his aide-de-camp, General Harcourt, and two equerries. But, on reaching the new abode, he was shut in a room and permitted a mere glimpse of his daughters through a window. According to Lady Harcourt, he rushed forward to throw up the pane, only to discover that it had been nailed down. To the distress of the princesses, their father immediately threw a fit.

CHAPTER 23

The Malady Lingers

Suggested cures for George's illness, put forward by his subjects, were more plentiful than plausible. One involved soaking a napkin in hot vinegar, winding it round his temples, and feeding him on bitter almonds, primrose roots and powdered crab's claw. Proceeded another: "Boil three large handfuls of ground ivy shred small in two quarts of wine till there is but one third remaining, then strain it and add to it three ounces of the best salad oil, boil it to an ointment, shave the patient's head, warm this ointment, and chafe the head with it." The Duke of Dorset recommended dosing the king with the blood of an ass. Lord Hervey was for infecting the sovereign with the itch; while Mrs. Thrale recommended "cold water, almost to drowning point."

Of all the suggestions considered at the palace, the most sensible came from one of the queen's equerries, whose mother had been cured of a mental illness by a certain Reverend Doctor Francis Willis of Wapping. It was suggested by the equerry that Her Majesty should call Dr. Willis to the court.

The arrival of Willis, and his son Dr. John Willis, shortly after the move to Kew, marked a new era in the history of the king's malady. At seventy-three, Willis senior was a large, bald man with a bland face and a rosy, cherubic mouth. His son was extraordinarily handsome in a soulful way which much appealed to the palace ladies. With long hair, soft eyes and a dutiful manner, he had the gentle charm of an English Setter. His father was a clergyman of the Church of England who had once enjoyed a rich living in London. Holding also a medical degree from Oxford, Willis senior had established a considerable reputation in Lincolnshire, where he had a place at Gretford, for the cure of mental ailments.

To the medical profession, however, he remained an interloper, and those jealous of his activities called him "Dr. Duplicate." Willis, wrote one, "was not much better than a mountebank, and not far different from some of those who are confined in his house." The impression was heightened by his then novel application of psychotherapy. His rich patients, some of whom paid twenty-five guineas a week for treatment, were often put to work as plowmen, gardeners and in other manual labors. Such methods were readily misconstrued as cruelty. Versified Peter Pindar:

> Suppose we chaunt old Willis and his whip,
> At which the human hide revolts,
> Who bids, like grasshoppers, his pupils skip
> And breaks mad gentlemen like colts.

Others were better impressed. Declared the Archbishop of Canterbury: "Since Dr Willis has been called in, our hope has been more firm and constant, and at this moment stands very high. He has had great experience in this malady for eight and twenty years, and great success." The royal household regarded the Doctors Willis with favor. According to Colonel Digby, they were "fine, lively, natural, independent characters." Miss Burney was "extremely struck with both these physicians. Dr Willis is a man in ten thousand; open, honest, dauntless, light-hearted, innocent and high-minded. I see him impressed with the most animated reverence and affection for his royal patient, but it is wholly for his character, not a whit for his rank. Dr John, his eldest son, is extremely handsome, and inherits, in a milder degree, all the qualities of his father."

They were, she added, "most delightful people, all originality, openness and goodness."

Francis Willis appears quickly to have decided the causes of the king's malady. They were, he proclaimed, an overtaxing attention to business, excessive physical exercise, "ascetic abstemiousness" and a lack of sufficient sleep. He met George for the first time on December 5, 1788, when, it seems, there was a preliminary skirmish of wits. The king rebuked the doctor for deserting the Church for medicine. "You have quitted a profession I have always loved," said George, "and you have embraced one I most heartily detest." Willis promptly replied that Jesus had cured demoniacs. "Yes," said the king, "but he did not get seven hundred a year for it." Slyly, he suggested that Willis should take Dr. Warren into his care and remove him to Lincolnshire. Willis refused to be bullied. When George grew rough and tried to eject him from the room, the doctor showed less compunction than his colleagues in calling for a straitjacket. The sight of it seems to have quietened the moody king.

Colonel Greville, the king's favorite equerry, was "much struck with the proper manner and the imposing style of the authoritative language which Dr Willis held on this occasion. It was necessary to have this struggle. He seized the opportunity with judgement and conducted himself with wonderful management and force. As the King's voice rose, attempting mastery, Willis raised his and its tone was strong and decided. As the King softened his, that of Willis dropped to softening unison . . . This seems to have been the first solid step leading to permanent recovery."

Though Willis used the straitjacket, and other restraints, when he thought them necessary, the general liberality of his treatment alarmed the other doctors. Warren, who particularly objected to the optimism of the new physicians, was soon charging Willis with irresponsibility on three counts: allowing the king to shave himself and use a penknife, allowing him to read *King Lear,* and allowing the king to meet the queen—an action Warren described as fraught with danger.

"His Majesty," Willis replied on the first count, "had not been shaved for a long while—perhaps a fortnight or three weeks. The person that had been used to shave him could not complete the parts of his upper and lower lips; and being confident from the professions and humour of His Majesty at that moment, I suffered His Majesty to shave himself . . . he did so in a very calm manner. His nails also wanted cutting very much, and upon his assurance, and my confidence in his looks, I suffered him to cut his own nails with a penknife, while I stood by him. It is necessary for a physician, specially in such cases, to be able to judge at the moment whether he can confide in the professions of his patient; and I never was disappointed in my opinion whether the professions of the patient were to be relied on or no."

The *King Lear* incident, he said, had been an accident. The king's reading had improved, and he had asked for the works of George Colman. Willis had not realized that these included an adaption of *King Lear.* Warren subsequently weakened his case by denying that George's reading was any better since the arrival of the Willises. "I have never seen him read more than a line and a half at a time," he protested with precision. "His manner of reading is strong proof of the existence of his malady. I see no symptoms of convalescence. Sleep has produced no amendment, nor has control and coercion." As Mrs. Thrale, for one, was quick to point out: "One moment he says the King has not steadiness enough to read more than a line and a half at a time, and in the next breath laments that Willis gave him *King Lear* to amuse him, and that His Majesty's observations upon the play affected him greatly. Some of these positions must be false."

Despite Warren's protestations, the meeting with the queen was a qualified success. "At seeing the Queen, the King was much agitated: but declared it made him very happy, and he would do all he could to recover, which he was indifferent about before. He was exceedingly affectionate to the Queen." But he had a bad night afterwards and had to be in the straitjacket. In his more awkward moments, George alleged that Dr. Willis was sleeping with Charlotte, and became himself so obsessed with possessing Lady Pembroke that, on one occasion, a promised outing had to be canceled.

By the end of December, the queen was exhausted by worry for her husband, and by the ceaseless wrangles of the doctors. "The opposition physicians say everything they can to invalidate the daily testimonies of the others. It is certain that the Queen is very dissatisfied with Sir George Baker and Dr Warren, and very well satisfied with the change of treatment introduced by Dr Willis which, from the most violent and harsh, is now the most gentle possible consistent with the firmness necessary in such cases."

Meanwhile, party feeling was running at fever pitch.

"The Opposition," wrote a loyalist, "have been taking inconceivable pains to spread the idea that the disorder is incurable." Declared another: "The acrimony is beyond anything you can conceive. The ladies are, as usual, at the head of all animosity, and are distinguished by caps, ribands, and other such emblems of party." Regency caps, selling briskly from seven guineas, were described by fashion writers as "a mountain of tumbled gauze, with three large feathers in front, tied together with a knot of ribbons on which was printed in gold letters, *Honi soit qui mal y pense, de la Régence.*"

On February 12, the regency bill passed the House of Commons and was close to its third reading in the House of Lords. The opposition was delighted. Its newspapers carried details of its prospective arrangements. The Duke of Portland was to be first minister, Fox was to become Secretary of State, the Duke of York would be commander-in-chief of the Army, and Sheridan, treasurer of the Navy. A new crop of field marshals would include the Prince of Wales, the Duke of York, the Duke of Gloucester and General Conway. Many of the prince's young army friends were to be promoted to major-generals. Mrs. Fitzherbert, it was said, was to be created a duchess.

Defectors to the prince ranged from such aristocrats as the dukes of Queensbury and Northumberland—the former a lord of the king's bedchamber for almost thirty years—to the lowliest of servants in the royal household, not excluding the king's own attendants. According to one courtier, several pages were "so warped by party, or by an anxiety to pay their court to the Prince, as certainly to deserve the severest reprehension." At least four, including the king's confidential page of the backstairs, William Ramus, eventually lost their places for spying on behalf of the Prince of Wales.

Increasingly, the government and the king's loyalists pinned their hopes on the optimism of Willis; the opposition and prince's creatures on discrediting him and raising the authority of Warren. According to one peer, Warren was so clamorous in his efforts to invalidate the reports of Willis that the people were "strangely divided in their hopes and fears." The Archbishop of Canterbury deplored this. "It is a strange subject for party to exist upon, and disgraceful

to the country that it should be so," he said. Slowly, however, Willis was gaining ground. Among other treatments,
the doctor had employed warm baths for his patient with
notable success. Still, the king seesawed between progress
and setbacks. Regression lurked in seemingly normal requests.

One day, George asked to be driven to Richmond Park.
It was not until he insisted on changing into his best white
breeches that his attendants became suspicious. "Doctor,"
Greville asked Willis anxiously, "don't you see why the king
wishes to go there? Haven't you discovered the drift of
his wish?"

"Upon my word, sir, I'm not in the secret."

"The king is certainly hoping to see Lady Pembroke
there. When he comes near her house, he won't be pleased
with a refusal, and the chances are he will become turbulent."

The outing was canceled, and George, growing angry, had
to be restrained for some hours. But, by evening, he seemed
to have forgotten the incident and sang, "Hark, the bonny
Christchurch bells" with Willis and Dr. John. Later, he grew
obstreperous once more. To quiet him, he was given an
emetic and "puked very heartily."

In February 1789, Fanny Burney, who, like the other
ladies of the court, had been closely guarded against the
king's advances, underwent a revealing experience. That
morning, she had asked John Willis where it would be safe
for her to take her daily walk. He had told her in Kew
Gardens, since the king would be in Richmond. Accordingly,
when she could spare a few moments, Fanny strolled among
the lawns and flowering shrubs of the palace grounds. She
had completed half a circuit of the garden "when I suddenly
perceived, through some trees, two or three figures. Relying
on the instructions of Dr John, I concluded them to be work-

men and gardeners; yet tried to look sharp, and in so doing, as they became less shaded, I thought I saw the person of his Majesty!"

Much alarmed, she did not wait to see more. Turning on her heels and hitching up her long skirts, Fanny ran for cover. For a moment, it seemed that she had escaped. Then, to her horror, she heard footsteps behind her.

"Miss Burney! Miss Burney!" It was the king's voice.

Fanny Burney was ready, she recalled later, to die. She dared not imagine in what state her pursuer might be at the time. All she knew was that the orders to avoid the king were emphatic, and that her mistress, the queen, would herself have been appalled by an encounter. Furthermore, in the king's present excited state, her running away would very possibly strain him beyond reason. Nevertheless, she sped on, too terrified to slow her pace, searching desperately for a dark passage among the labyrinths of the garden through which to escape. The faster she ran, the heavier grew the pounding of the steps behind her. She could hear the more distant footsteps of the king's attendants, trying to catch and restrain the patient.

From the distance came the voices of Dr. Willis and his son, loudly exhorting the sovereign not to overheat himself. "Heavens, how I ran . . . My feet were not sensible that they even touched the ground . . . I knew not to what I might be exposed, should the malady be then high."

At last, a calmer voice reached her: "Doctor Willis begs you to stop."

"I can't! I can't!"

She flew on in panic.

"You must, ma'am. It hurts the king to run."

The words pulled her together, and she drew to a breathless halt. Turning round, she saw that the doctors were holding the king between them, while three attendants hovered nearby. Asking one of them to stand close to her, she tried to control herself.

"Why did you run away?" asked George in a hoarse voice.

There was no discreet answer. Instead, she forced herself forward to meet him. It was, she recalled later, "the greatest effort of courage I ever made." Suddenly, the king was free of the Willises and shambling toward her, arms reaching forward. Fanny stood pertrified. Then she felt a gentle arm round her shoulder, a soft kiss on her cheek. Looking into his eyes, she saw "something still of wildness," but mostly tenderness and kindness. George was talking of his pleasure at seeing her after so long, leading her away from the Willises. He was, he assured her, as well now as he had ever been in his life. He asked how she was, and how she was coping with a doughty colleague of the household, Madame Schwellenberg.

"Never mind her," he said. "Don't be oppressed. I am your friend. Don't let her cast you down. I know you have a hard time of it, but don't mind her."

She curtsied, but said nothing.

Continued the king: "Stick to your father; your own family; let them be your objects. I will protect you, I promise you that. Depend upon me." Refusing to be parted by the doctors, who considered he had said enough, George next touched upon the disloyalty of some of his pages, asked some awkward questions about his illness, which Miss Burney tried to fob off, and eventually got around to his favorite theme of Handel. "When I was a youth, Handel said of me, 'While that boy lives, my music will never want a protector.'" The quotation delighted him, and he began to sing a number of the composer's oratorios, "but so dreadfully hoarse that the sound was terrible." Again, Willis attempted to separate the couple.

"Come, Sir, now do you come in and let the lady go on

her walk. Come now, you have talked a long while, so we'll go in, if your Majesty pleases."

"No! No! I want to ask her a few questions. I have lived so long out of the world, I know nothing."

Growing irritable, George confided to Fanny that he had been very dissatisfied with the behavior of a number of his state officers during his illness, and meant to form an entirely new establishment. He took a piece of paper from a pocketbook and showed her a list of names. He said that her father, the author of a history of music, should have had the post of master of the band. "But Lord Salisbury used your father very ill in that business, and so he did me! However, I have dashed out his name, and I shall put your father's in—as soon as I can get loose again . . . As to Lord Salisbury, he is out already, as this memorandum will show you, and so are many more. I shall be much better served. When once I get away, I shall rule with a rod of iron."

At last, the Willises prevailed upon the king to let Fanny go. Grasping her shoulders and imparting a farewell kiss, George exclaimed earnestly: "Depend upon me! I will be your friend as long as I live. I here pledge myself to be your friend." Observed Fanny upon recovering: "What a scene! how variously was I affected by it! but, on the whole, how inexpressibly thankful to see him so nearly himself—so little removed from recovery!"

Shortly afterward, George visited the royal observatory and chatted normally with its keeper on astronomical subjects. He also talked intelligently of horticulture and discussed his sheep. He had begun to shave himself regularly, and was allowed to use a knife and fork. By mid-February, Willis considered it safe to let the king escort Charlotte upstairs to her bedroom at night. Greville saw "his readiness in coming down" as a measure of his returned sense, "from which real good may arise." The king and queen could now be seen walking arm in arm in Richmond

Gardens, and Fanny Burney described the delight which prevailed in the household. On the seventeenth, George was officially pronounced to have advanced into convalescence. Fox, it seems, still looked forward to the accomplishment of the regency, but the king's improvement had rendered his colleagues pessimistic. "If it were possible," wrote Fox, "to do anything to cure that habitual despondency and fear that characterizes the Whig party, it would be a good thing; but I suppose that is impossible."

The Prince of Wales and the Duke of York were shattered at the fading of their fondest hopes. "I have not heard yet," declared one peer, "but conclude they were both rioting and drunk at the masquerade, as they were at one a week ago. The truth is that they are quite desperate, and endeavour to drown their cares, disappointments and internal chagrin in wine and dissipation."

On February 20, the Chancellor was allowed to regale George with some of the political developments which had occurred since his illness. According to one report: "The Chancellor was yesterday with his Majesty, and for the first time talked to him upon business, and opened to him in part the measures which had been taken during his confinement. I understand that His Majesty was by no means the worse for the conversation. Dr Willis, who attends him, says that, were he a private man, he would advise his following now his usual occupation, as the mode of living most likely to restore him. But, God knows! His Majesty will have a severe trial when he is informed of all that has passed during the unhappy interval. Every possible care will no doubt be taken to prepare him. You will hear from other hands, probably, that the Prince of Wales has got complete possession of the Duke of York, and that they had meditated such changes in the State and Army as would have grieved him exceedingly. No scruple has been made of declaring that a general sweep of all places would be made if the Regency were to last only a day."

On the twenty-third, the brothers visited their father to check on his progress for themselves. George, as yet ignorant of the worst of their behavior, received them fondly, but Charlotte was frigid. The queen refused to leave them alone with her husband. Declared Lord Bulkeley: "Lord Wichelsea, who was at Kew at the time, told me that the Prince and the Duke of York, though appointed at one, did not arrive till half-past three; and that when they came out, they told Colonel Digby that they were delighted with the King's being so well, and remarked that two things, in the half-hour's conference they had with him, had struck them very forcibly—that he had observed to them how much better he played at piquet than Mr Charles Hawkins, and that since he had been ill he had rubbed up all his Latin. And these facts, which *are* facts, I expect to hear magnified by the Carlton House runners into instances of insanity."

Bulkeley was not far wrong. On the evidence of another observer, the prince and the duke drove straight from the palace to Mrs. Armstead's house in Park Street "in hopes of finding Fox there, to give him an account of what had passed. He not being in town, they amused themselves yesterday evening with spreading about a report that the King was still out of his mind, and in quoting phrases of his, to which they gave that turn. It is certainly a decent and becoming thing that, when all the King's physicians, all his attendants, and his two principal Ministers, agree in pronouncing him well, his two sons should deny it!" Even Warren admitted that the monarch was better. Joked George when next he met his friend Miss Burney: "I'm quite well now. I was nearly so when I saw you before, but I could overtake you better now!"

By the end of the month, Dr. John Willis could observe that the king was "quite right except a hint or two at Lady

Pembroke," and, on March 10, the physicians finally left Kew Palace. That night, London showed its appreciation in a spontaneous display of illuminations and happiness. In all the years George had ruled from strength, the ordinary people had viewed him with reserve, even distaste. But the old capital could not resist a sick dog, and, during his illness, compassion had welled up. The Archbishop of Canterbury, who watched the scene from the windows of Lambeth Palace, described the festivities as universal, and the streets as being as crowded and noisy as at midday.

"London," wrote Wraxall, "displayed a blaze of light from one extremity to another; the illuminations extending, without any metaphor, from Hampstead to Highgate and Clapham, and even as far as Tooting; while the vast distance between Greenwich and Kensington presented the same dazzling appearance. The poorest mechanics contributed their proportion, and instances were exhibited of cobblers' stalls decorated with one or two farthing candles."

Charlotte, leaving her youngest daughter, Amelia, in the king's care, took the older princesses to see the sights. George and Amelia enjoyed a private display of lights in the palace courtyard. During the evening, the princess proudly handed her father a book of congratulatory verses by Miss Burney, specially commissioned for the occasion by Charlotte. "The little bearer begs a kiss," ran the postscript, "from dear papa for bringing this." Exclaimed the authoress later: "The little bearer begged not in vain. The King was extremely pleased. He came into the room in which we had a party to look at the illuminations, and there he stayed above an hour, cheerful, composed and gracious."

The queen and the other princesses did not arrive home until after one o'clock. "When the coach stopped, the Queen took notice of a fine gentleman who came to the coach-door without a hat. This was the King, who came to hand her out. She scolded him for being up so late; but he gallantly replied he could not possibly go to bed and sleep till he knew she was safe."

But, for all the delight and thanksgiving of the moment, George was now well enough to realize that any hope of his resuming his old power had been dashed. His limitations had been spelled out, and, in a letter to Pitt, he admitted them:

"I feel the warmest gratitude for the support and anxiety shown by the nation at large during my tedious illness," the king wrote, "which I should ill requite if I did not wish to prevent any further delay in those public measures which it may be necessary to bring forward this year; though I must decline entering into a pressure of business, and, indeed, for the rest of my life, shall expect others to fulfil the duties of their employments, and only keep a superintending eye which can be effected without labour or fatigue."

CHAPTER 24

Fresh Dangers

Between the cure of his first major breakdown and his death in 1820, George suffered a series of similar episodes, and his mental variations were such that it was often hard to evaluate his capacity to know just what was happening about him. On the whole, his illness had left him with a greater tolerance of the limitations surrounding the monarchy in an age of changing political values, and a greater readiness to leave things to others, than before. In a period of reform, development and "new enlightenment" his insistence on reaction—"I will have no innovation in my time"—had both battered and mellowed him. The loss of America and the trend toward popular government continued to cause him lamentation.

His memory, he told a friend, George Rose, was a good one, and what he did not forget he could not forgive. Nevertheless, he added, he tried hard to remember the good qualities of people, and to forget the bad ones. He said that in his dealings with men, "it had been an invariable rule with him not to suppose them bad till he found them so; that there had been instances of men becoming good, or at least considerably improving, by letting them understand they were considered as better than they were."

For some events, George could muster no tolerance. The onset of the French Revolution, which Fox, and even Pitt, saw fit to praise, filled the king with dread and horror, not only for the threat he saw in it to the British Crown, but for the vistas of atheism and infidelity it suggested to him. "I have lived," exulted Fox, "to see thirty millions of people indignantly and resolutely spurning at slavery, and demanding liberty with an irresistible voice . . . methinks I see the ardour of liberty catching and spreading, and a general amendment beginning in human affairs; the dominion of kings changed for the dominion of laws, and the dominion of priests giving way to the dominion of reason and conscience." Not so George. The sight of his own image burned in effigy, of pamphlets ridiculing his "divine authority" and other protests engaged by English partisans of the "people's cause" roused all his old fury and stubbornness. He responded with his own proclamation:

"Whereas divers wicked and seditious writings have been printed, published, and industriously dispersed, tending to excite tumult and disorder by endeavouring to raise groundless jealousies and discontents in the minds of our faithful and loving subjects . . . whereas we have also reason to believe that correspondences have been entered into with sundry persons in foreign parts . . . and whereas the wealth, happiness and prosperity of this kingdom do, under Divine Providence, chiefly depend upon a due submission to the laws . . . We therefore issue this our royal proclamation, solemnly warning all our loving subjects, as they tender their own happiness, and that of their posterity, to guard against all such attempts which aim at the subversion of all regular government within this kingdom, and which are inconsistent with the peace and order of society."

It was a period of considerable personal risk to the king, and he faced the physical dangers philosophically. Already, an army lietuenant named John Frith had made an unsuccessful attack on his coach near Carlton House. Frith had been consigned to Bedlam for his trouble. Warned of the peril of exposing himself incautiously to the public, George replied shortly, in a statement of perhaps inadvertent prophecy: "Sir, I must differ from you there. If there be any man so desperate to devote his own life to the chance of taking away the life of another, no precaution is sufficient to prevent him altogether from making the attempt. A system of constant precaution against such dangers . . . converts the life of a person so guarded into a scene of perpetual restraint, anxiety and apprehension. No, sir, the best security that a man can have against such dangers is to act openly and boldly like a man. If an attack is made upon him, his best chance of escaping is to meet it like a man; but if he should fall under it, why, sir, he will fall like a man!"

George had several lucky escapes from assassination. Once, at the theater, a man fired a horse pistol at him as he stood at the front of the royal box. Fortunately for the king, another member of the audience knocked the marksman off aim at the vital moment, and the bullet flew over the head of its target. "The King, on hearing the report of the pistol," wrote a witness, "retired a pace or two, stopped, and stood firm for an instant, then came forward to the front of the box, put his opera-glass to his eye, and looked round the house without the smallest appearance of alarm or discomposure."

Later, a colonel named Despard planned to kill the king with a cannon stationed at the north side of St. James's Park. The plot was discovered. There were also numerous letters threatening the king's life. "I very well know," George declared with resignation, "that any man who chooses to sacrifice his own life may, whenever he pleases, take away mine, riding out, as I do continually, with a single equerry and a footman. I only hope that whoever may attempt it will not do it in a barbarous or brutal manner."

As the excesses of the French Revolution became known in England, the mood of the country as a whole swung behind the king and constitution. Moderate opinion was appalled by the tales of horror from Paris, and all parties, with the exception of the most radical of Whigs, joined ranks against any such happenings in Britain. Many Whigs accepted posts in Pitt's government, leaving Fox deserted, his popularity broken. One commentator wrote: "Fox is a very clever and highly gifted man, but he has never discovered the great secret, that John Bull is a Tory by nature." Suddenly, the upper classes and the bourgeoisie were united—"God Save the King" became the most fashionable tune in the country. In this atmosphere there passed, little noticed, the deaths of North and Barré, within a fortnight of each other. Both had ended their lives blind, and it was said that North, droll to the last, had once greeted his old opponent in Tunbridge Wells with the observation: "Well, Colonel, whatever may have been our former animosities, I am persuaded there are no two men who would now be more glad to see each other than you and I!"

The loyalty of the lower classes, however, still caused apprehension. In a speech to Parliament at the end of 1792, George opined that "the industry employed to excite discontent on various pretexts, and in different parts of the kingdom, appeared to proceed from a design to attempt the destruction of our happy constitution and the subversion of all order and government, and that this design had evidently been pursued in concert with persons in foreign countries." In the circumstances, he thought it his duty to call up a section of the militia in the interests of internal tranquility and general peace. Neither George nor Pitt was anxious for another war, but the invasion of Holland by the forces of the French Convention, and the execution of Louis

XVI, which staggered Europe's courts, made hostilities inevitable.

"My natural sentiments," the king told the premier, "are strong for peace," but, "duty, as well as interest, calls us to join against the most savage as well as unprincipled nation."

An unsuccessful campaign in the Netherlands under the Duke of York further lowered the stock of George's male progeny and caused the king more personal misery. Popular outcry against the duke became so clamorous that Pitt was obliged to ask the king for the recall of his second son. George did not decline, but his reply was couched in terms of touching paternal loyalty:

"Mr Pitt cannot be surprised at my being very hurt at the contents of his letter. Indeed, he seems to expect it, but I am certain that nothing but the thinking it his duty could have instigated him to give so severe a blow. I am neither in a situation of mind, nor from inclination, inclined to enter more minutely into every part of his letter; but I am fully ready to answer the material part . . . every failure is easily to be accounted for without laying blame on him who deserved a better fate. I shall certainly now not think it safe for him to continue in the command on the Continent, when everyone seems to conspire to render his situation hazardous by either propagating unfounded complaints against him, or giving credit to them . . . even a son of mine cannot withstand the torrent of abuse."

War brought a rising price for provisions, and many people in London went hungry. By October 1793, the popularity George had enjoyed since his illness no longer applied among the lower classes of the capital, and, on the twenty-ninth, his coach was mobbed on its way to Parliament. The people wanted food and peace, and they made their wishes known vociferously. Halfway between St. James's Palace and Carlton House, the crowd surged so thickly round the carriage that they separated the king, and the peers with him, from their military escort. "Bread! Bread!" the pedestrians shouted, peering with hungry faces at the well-fed occupants of the vehicle. Witnesses feared that the king would be pulled out.

"Sit still," George ordered one of his fellow passengers who was showing alarm, "we must not betray fear whatever happens." To the well-to-do, the protests of the impoverished were traitorous. "Everything seemed French about them; their cries, their gestures, their principles, and their actions, all plainly indicated the polluted source whence they sprung, and proved that they were not of British growth or origin." According to one lordly observer, he had never seen "such an assemblage of ill-looking, desperate wretches as were collected together on the present occasion. And as far as the designs of men can be inferred from their looks, their language and their gestures, the designs of this rabble, who so basely dishonoured the name and character of Englishmen, were most treasonable and murderous."

As the coach reached Whitehall, one of its windows was shattered by a bullet fired from a house by the wayside. The prospect of the return journey threw George's courtiers into dire agitation. He silenced them with an impatient flourish. "My Lords, one person is proposing this, and another is supposing that, forgetting there is One above us who disposes everything, and on whom alone we can depend." His trust was well founded. Though the crowd roared insults, and at one time dragged on the carriage wheels, the royal party returned to the palace in safety. Considering the distress of their families and the prevalence of famine, the people of the city were commendably restrained.

All the same, the government was shaken. Soon afterward, a bill was carried through Parliament decreeing that if anyone should threaten the well-being of the king, or "depose him, waylay in order by force to compel him to

change his measures or counsels, or to overawe either
House of Parliament, or to incite an invasion of any of his
Majesty's dominions, and shall express and declare such
intentions by writing, printing, or any overt act, he shall
suffer death as a traitor." Later, when a stone was hurled at
George and Charlotte during a coach outing, a reward of
£1,000 was offered for the arrest of the offender. Nobody
claimed it. In a fit of depression, George moaned that he
would probably be the last King of England.

In view of his conservative nature, there was some surprise when George backed William Wilberforce in his anti-
slavery proposals. Wilberforce, who had been at Cambridge with Pitt, and had maintained the friendship struck
at that early stage, had the support of the premier in his
campaign to abolish the slave trade, and the ideal appealed
to the ordinary Briton. But among the property-owning
classes, there was opposition. Many otherwise respectable
Englishmen considered the slaves better off under white
domination than in their native habitat. Had they not
been introduced to "civilization"? Were they not happy
in their new tasks? If England withdrew from slave
trading, would not France and Spain capture her markets,
and would not the slaves then be worse off? For some time,
George wavered. It was put to him that abolitionism was
linked with revolutionary tendencies. He pondered. But
Wilberforce was persuasive. Morever, to his credit in the
king's sight, he was a rich man of social distinction who
could hardly be classed as a dangerous radical. At last,
George gave his assent to the abolition of the slave trade. It
was a significant decision, for without royal support the
measure would probably have proved too contentious to
carry Parliament.

Ironically enough, had George not lost America, slavery
would not have persisted in that land of "liberty" until

1865. The British Government abolished slavery altogether throughout its domains in 1833. On the smoldering problem of Catholicism, George was more negative. In July 1800, the legal union of Great Britain and Ireland once more raised the issue of religious equality. Pitt favored a law of emancipation which would enable Irish Roman Catholics to sit in Parliament and hold offices of state. The majority of British people was against it. George was not ahead of his time. True, he was no bigot. He had friends among Quakers and Methodists, and doctrinal differences among Christians were of no great concern to him. But he was a man of his word, and he had sworn at his crowning to uphold the Protestant religion and the rights and privileges of its clergy. "I could give my crown and retire from power," said George. "I could quit my palace and live in a cottage; I could lay my head on a block and lose my life, but I cannot break my coronation oath."

Pitt was incapable of changing the king's mind. Wrote George to his premier: "A sense of religious as well as political duty has made me, from the moment I mounted the throne, consider the oath that the wisdom of our forefathers has enjoined the kings of this realm to take at their coronation. . . . as a binding religious obligation on me to maintain the fundamental maxims on which our constitution is placed: namely, that the Church of England is the established Church; that those who hold employment in the State must be members of it, and consequently not only obliged to take oaths against Popery, but to receive the Holy Communion agreeably to the rites of the Church of England." His view was backed by the Protestant hierarchy of both England and Ireland.

The first major clash between Pitt and the sovereign was imminent. The premier's determination to introduce a bill of emancipation aroused the king's anger. It would be, he declared, "a most mischievous measure," and he

asked the Speaker of the House, Henry Addington, to try
to divert Pitt from his purpose. "I should be taking up the
Speaker's time very uselessly if I said more, as I know we
think alike on this great subject. I wish he would, from himself, open Mr Pitt's eyes on the danger arising from the
agitating this improper question, which may prevent his
ever speaking to me on a subject on which I can scarcely
keep my temper." As usual, when his conscience was aroused
and his will obstructed, George grew obsessive and distressed. Assembling his family, he read them the coronation
oath. "If I violate it," he exclaimed, "I am no longer legal
sovereign of this country!" To one of his equerries, General
Garth, he cried passionately: "I had rather beg my bread
from door to door throughout Europe than consent to any
such measure."

Faced with the king's inflexibility, Pitt resigned. George
summoned Addington, a close friend of the departing
premier, to take his place. Reluctantly, Addington accepted,
regarding himself as a "sort of *locum tenens*." George was
growing distracted. "An unfortunate resolution implanted in
the mind of Mr Pitt by persons in no way friends to our
happy Church and State establishment," he wrote Bishop
Hurd, "has made me reluctantly permit him to retire from my
service . . . I have persuaded Mr Addington to succeed
Mr Pitt, and can assure you his attachment to the Church
is as sincere as mine, and you may depend on his equal
attachment to our happy civil constitution, and his being
no admirer of any reforms or supposed improvements."

A fortnight later, the king developed a severe cold and
could scarcely speak. Within a week, he had a high fever
and his familiar ramblings about the loss of America, Lady
Pembroke, and even Sarah Lennox, were manifest. Dr.
John Willis was called to the palace. He proclaimed that dis-
agreement with Pitt had brought on the illness. Pitt, deeply
concerned, asked whether his assurance never to raise the

matter of Catholic emancipation again would help improve the king's health. "Certainly," replied Willis, "and to the recovery of his life, also."

Pitt thereupon authorized the doctor to assure his patient on the subject. "I told him," Willis later wrote the former premier, "what you wished; and after saying the kindest things of you, he exclaimed, 'Now my mind will be at ease.' Upon the Queen coming in, the first thing he told her was your message, and he made the same observation of it."

The king had become ill in February 1801. By March, he was sufficiently recovered to observe that he had "presumed a great deal more than I ought on my constitution. Be assured I shall be more careful in future." In May, George appeared to be better, though Addington, for one, was not entirely happy. "During a quiet conversation of an hour and a half with the King, there was not a sentiment, a word, a look, or a gesture I could have wished different from what it was. And yet my apprehensions, I must own to you, predominate." Addington's intuition was right. In June there was a relapse, and the elder Dr. Willis was consulted. In his opinion, the king rode too much, spending five or six hours a day on horseback. "He has a great thirst upon him, and his family are in a great fear. His Majesty still talks much of his prudence, but he shows none. His body, mind and tongue are on the stretch every minute."

George showed scant gratitude toward the Willises. "No person," he wrote, "that has ever had a nervous fever can bear to continue the physician employed on the occasion." And, as soon as he felt recovered, he ignored their advice. He continued to ride in all weathers. Of a weekend with the king on the edge of the New Forest, a friend wrote: "A heavy shower fell while his Majesty was on the road about a mile and a half short of this place. No entreaties could prevail with him to put on a greatcoat, and he was wet through before he reached the Town Hall, where he remained about three-quarters of an hour speaking to the Mayor and several gentlemen. He then went to Sir Harry Neale's, and dined without changing his clothes; then rode back here and was again wet . . . The exercise must have been, I fear, too much after the disuse of riding for some time. His Majesty intends going to Southampton—ten miles —on horseback today and returning to dinner."

The king considered such activities relaxing. "I am forced to be very careful," he told Hurd, "but feel I am gradually gaining ground. The next week will be rather harassing, as I must open the session of Parliament, and attend the ceremonies in consequence; but I shall return every day to Kew, that I may be more quiet." Kew, with its gardens, the river and the pleasant run to Richmond, was to be George's delight in the later years of his life, when his summers were spent there in increasing privacy. According to one of his sons, the style of life he led from 1801 to 1810 "was the most recluse that ever man lived, for he lived as regular as clockwork. He resided constantly at Kew from May till November, and literally never saw a living soul there but the equerry-in-waiting, who came down every morning from London to accompany him on horseback, and then instantly returned to town, so that he had not a single gentleman near him."

Toward the end of 1799, a coup d'etat in France put that country in the hands of Napoleon Bonaparte, the shrewd Corsican of prodigious and ruthless ambition who, in the service of the French Government, had already overrun Italy and invaded Egypt. George was not inclined to be impressed by such an upstart. "I know you are no great lover of political subjects," he wrote Hurd on New Year's Day, 1800, "yet the impudent overthrow of the monstrous French Republic by a Corsican adventurer, and his creating himself to be lawgiver and executor of his own decrees, must have astonished you. Without more foresight than common-sense dictates, one may allege that his impious pre-eminence cannot be of long duration."

It was not the first time George had been betrayed by common sense. By the time Napoleon was standing on the French coast examining England through his eyeglass, the king was making plans for the safety of his wife and the princesses. Again, to the bishop: "We are here in daily expectation that Bonaparte will attempt his threatened invasion, but the chances against his success seem so many that is it wonderful he persists in it. I own I place that thorough dependence on the protection of Divine Providence, that I cannot help thinking the usurper is encouraged to make the trial that his ill-success may put an end to his wicked purposes. Should his troops effect a landing, I shall certainly put myself at the head of mine, and my other armed subjects to repel them; but as it is impossible to forsee the events of such a conflict, should the enemy approach too near Windsor I shall think it right the Queen and my daughters should cross the Severn, and shall send them to your Episcopal Palace at Worcester . . . Should such an event arise, I certainly would rather that what I value most in life should remain during the conflict in your diocese and under your roof, than in any other place in the island."

Plans to meet an invasion were drawn up by the king's hand:

> Lord Cornwallis to take command of the central army, being the real reserve of the Volunteers and all the producible force of the kingdom, in case the French made any impression in the coast.
>
> The King to move to Chelmsford if the landing was in Essex, or to Dartford if in Kent, taking with him Mr Addington and Mr Yorke of the Cabinet.

The Queen, etc., to remove to the Palace at Worcester.

The Bank books to be removed to the Tower, and duplicate books and treasure to the cathedral at Worcester in thirty wagons under Sir Brook Watson's management, escorted from county to county by the Volunteers.

The merchants to shut up the Stock Exchange.

The artillery and stores from Woolwich to be transported inland by the Grand Junction Canal.

The Press to be prohibited from publishing any account of the King's troops, or of the enemy, but by authority from the Secretary of State, to be communicated officially twice a day to all news-writers indiscriminately who may apply for it, else their presses to be seized and their printers imprisoned.

The Privy Council to be sitting in London, to issue all acts of Government.

By February 1804, it was commonplace in parliamentary circles that the strain of the crisis had overtaxed the king, and that he had had another return of ill health. What would happen, the opposition demanded, if the French landed while the king was indisposed? The country should be informed of the king's precise condition in order that the necessary security measures could be taken. But Addington maintained that a statement on such matters would be "not only inexpedient but highly indecent," assuring Parliament that if an invasion did take place, countermeasures would not be obstructed by royal incapacity.

In May, when Addington gave way to Pitt's second administration, George was well enough to veto Pitt's desire to bring Fox into the government. Yet he was by no means his true self. His temper was short, he was excessively voluble, and there were signs of paranoia. He distrusted the most loyal of his servants, dismissed the queen's favorite coachman and ordered hitherto acceptable lords from the palace. Noted Lord Malmesbury in his diary: "Lady Uxbridge very anxious about the King. Said his family were quite unhappy; that his temper was altered. He had just dismissed his faithful and favourite page, Braun, who had served him during his illness with the greatest attention.

"Quiet and repose were the only chance."

CHAPTER 25

The Twilight Years

Early on the morning of June 18, 1815, Napoleon Bonaparte mounted his horse to reconnoiter Wellington's position at Waterloo. Wellington had many of his men hidden behind high ground, and Napoleon was delighted to see so few troops. Someone suggested that the British general would be joined by Blücher and his Prussians, but Napoleon dismissed the idea. "Blücher," he said, "is defeated. He cannot rally for three days. I have seventy-five thousand men; the English, only fifty thousand. The town of Brussels awaits me with open arms." General Foy, who had experienced English tactics in Spain interposed: "Wellington never shows his troops; but if he is out there, I must warn your majesty that the English infantry, in close fighting, is the very devil." Napoleon ignored him. He was still looking at the British lines. "I have them at last, these English!" He was jubilant.

Within twenty-four hours, seventy thousand Frenchmen, Prussians, Britons, Germans, Nassauers and Brunswickers lay dead at Waterloo. The flower of Europe's soldiery had fallen. "The thunder of 500 cannon, the roll of musketry, the shock of mail-clad horsemen, the Highland slogan, the Irish huzza, were heard no more; and the moon gleamed coldly on a field of death whose silence was only broken by the groans of the wounded as they lay in helpless wretchedness beside their dead companions." Next day, holes were dug in the stained soil, and thirty to forty "fine young fellows, stripped nude," were tumbled into each one. So haphazardly were they covered that hands and feet stuck out from the loose mold.

Wrote a visitor to the field shortly afterwards: "In some spots they lay thick in clusters and long ranks; in others, one would present itself alone; betwixt these, a black-scathed circle told that fire had been employed to consume as worthless refuse what parents cherished, friends esteemed, and women loved. The summer wind, that shook the branches of the trees, and moved the clover and the gaudy heads of thistles, brought with it a foul stench, still more hideous to the mind than to the offended sense. The foot that startled the small bird from its nest among the grass disturbed at the same time some poor remnant of a human being—either in the showy habiliments in which he took pride, or of the warlike accoutrements which were his glory, or of the framework of the body itself, which he felt as comeliness and strength the instant before it became a mass of senseless matter."

The fighting was over. Seventy thousand had perished, and Napoleon was beaten.

In the land of the ailing George, the gossiping, drink-swilling, scandalmongering London of Dr. Johnson was moving into the new century with a blossoming awareness of social injustices. Men of talent and capacity were no longer inevitably cocooned in self-interest. The phenomenon called democracy was awakening, and with it came people such as William Cobbett and Francis Place, fighting for political readjustment; John Howard and Mrs. Fry, transforming the prisons; Robert Owen and the factory reformers, striving to improve working conditions; Bentham and Romilly wiping the grime from the criminal laws.

It was the age that gave birth to Dickens, a social reformer of inestimable worth—an age which had turned its back on the brittle, diamond-hard wits of George's accession and was spawning writers with softer feelings and warmer hearts. On Wednesday evenings, at the Inner Temple, Charles Lamb played host to Wordsworth, Coleridge, Hazlitt and De Quincey. Oblivious to the rumblings of the Napoleonic struggle, the son of a livery stable keeper named Keats was scratching his claim to immortality at Hampstead, or wandering across the meadows with Leigh Hunt and Shelley to Belsize Park.

For George, life was now a mist of sensations through which the greatest of events could not penetrate with clarity. Emaciated and hollow-cheeked, the once powerful king had grown a thick white beard, wore a velvet cap on his cropped poll, and pottered about the corridors of Windsor at all hours in a violet coat. Gone were his great minister, Pitt, and his lively opponent, Fox. Pitt had lived to have his elation over the battle of Trafalgar dashed by Napoleon's victory at Austerlitz. He never got over it. "Poor Pitt, I almost believe, died of a broken heart," wrote a friend after his demise in January 1806, "for it is only due to him to declare that the love of his country burned in him with as ardent a flame as ever warmed the human bosom, and the accounts from the armies struck a death's blow within . . . he was the highest in power and estimation in the whole kingdom; the favourite, I believe, on the whole, of King and people." Added Sir Walter Farquhar: "At the age of forty-six, he died of old age as much as if he had been ninety."

So affected was George by the death of Pitt that he could not bear to mention it for two days, and refused to receive his ministers.

Pitt's death was followed swiftly by that of Thurlow. The same summer, Fox became seriously ill with dropsy. When Fox died in September, at Chiswick House, the home of his celebrated friend the Duchess of Devonshire, the brightest lights of eighteenth-century English politics had been extinguished. "The giant race is extinct," wrote a contemporary, "and we are left in the hands of the little ones." Even George, who had disliked Fox perhaps more than he had disliked any man, was touched. "Little did I think," he mumbled, "that I should ever live to regret Mr Fox's death." The burial of Fox's remains at Westminster Abbey, within eighteen inches of those of his illustrious rival, appealed to the sentiments of the nation. Sir Walter Scott wrote an epitaph:

> Drop upon Fox's grave the tear,
> 'Twill trickle to his rival's bier.
> O'er Pitt's the mournful requiem sound,
> And Fox's shall the notes rebound.
> The solemn echo seems to cry—
> "Here let their discord with them die.
> Speak not for those a separate doom
> Whom fate made brothers in the tomb;
> But search the land of living men,
> Where wilt thou find their like again?"

From about 1811, George had been blind and largely irrational, the pathetic creature of his own imagination. The harpsichord and flute, on which he still played his favorite Handel, provided tenuous links with past reality. In February of that year, the inevitable Regency Bill was laid solemnly before him. He signed it with vacuous pleasantry. The next day, the Prince of Wales, supported by his six brothers, took the oath of regent at Carlton House. His first act in office was to keep the ninety-two members of the Privy Council waiting almost an hour and a half before making his appearance in the council chamber. With the Crown glittering alluringly before him, the prince quickly repaid his old friends by deserting them. They were no longer grand enough. When the faithful Mrs. Fitzherbert asked him what her place was now, he told her rudely: "Madam, you have none."

George plunged deeper into his fantasies. He had grown too old to terrorize the women of the household, though he had a disconcerting habit of exposing his genitals. In September 1811 he was reported to believe that George I and George II were still alive, and that he had powers of life-giving and rejuvenation. He had signed, he said, the death warrants of his own sons. In October, he proposed to escape to Denmark from a great calamity which he supposed to be sweeping the country. He had only one son left, he said, and, according to the physicians, periodically "stamped with both feet by Order of God Almighty." During November and December, he insisted on giving a concert for a number of people who were long dead, sang hunting songs, gave his daughter Amelia (who had died the year before) a detailed account of her own funeral, laughed and cried by turn, professed the power to condemn his subjects to hell, and babbled a great deal in German.

"His conversation in extravagance is like the detail of a dream," wrote one doctor. The most persistent of the king's delusions were that he was the Elector of Hanover, and that he was married to Lady Pembroke. "Is it not strange," he asked the Duke of Sussex, "that they still refuse to let me go to Lady Pembroke, although everyone knows I am married to her?" Much of the time, the monarch was quite cheerful. He held long make-believe conversations with angels, deceased statesmen and admiring ladies. In such moods, he was capable of relating accurate anecdotes of himself and his reign, elaborating them with character sketches of the remarkable men of the period. He still laughed when he talked of John, Earl of Sandwich, now dead a quarter of a century, referring to the peer by his nickname "Jemmy Twitcher."

But there was no hope of George's recovery. In 1812, the evidence of the royal physicians, given before committees of both Houses of Parliament, left little doubt that George's mind was permanently unbalanced. Deafness, impinging on what remained of his senses, rendered communication with the old king nearly impossible. At the end of each day, his chair was tilted by the attendants to signify bedtime. "When removed, he would offer up his prayers, after which it was his custom never to speak till he had again made his supplications in the morning. When his irritability was so violent that he could not pacify himself, he would cram his pocket-handkerchief into his mouth till it was bitten through and through. He then generally fell asleep like an infant."

Wrote his daughter Elizabeth: "If anything can make us more easy under the calamity which it has pleased Heaven to inflict on us, it is the apparent happiness that my revered father seems to feel. He considers himself no longer the inhabitant of this world; and often, when he has played one of his favourite tunes, observes that he was very fond of it when he was in this world. He speaks of the Queen and all his family, and hopes they are doing well now, for he loved them very much when he was with them." To these testing times, Charlotte responded with singular courage and good sense. Despite the jibes of her detractors, she had made George a good wife—a woman behind whose apparent simplicity and homeliness lay a deceptive astuteness and intellectual liveliness.

Trained to be thrifty by her husband, she took a strong

objection to his misfortune being exploited by the doctors, whose efforts now seemed purposeless. Medical expenses had reached the exorbitant figure of thirty-four thousand guineas a year—the Willises alone claiming about twenty thousand —and she backed her advisers in making economies. In other fields, she presided over social obligations with dignity and graciousness. Indeed, to some extent she blossomed in adversity. She entertained at St. James's, gave fêtes in the country and attended the races at Ascot. "There was a benignity in her manner," it was written of her in her seventies, "which, in union with her age and rank, was both attractive and touching."

Richard Rush, the United States ambassador, described her at the wedding of Princess Elizabeth in 1817: "The conduct of the Queen was remarkable. This venerable personage—the female head of a great empire—in the seventy-sixth year of her age [in fact, she was seventy-three], went the rounds of the company, speaking to all. There was a kindliness in her manner from which time had struck away useless forms. No one did she omit. Around her neck hung a miniature portrait of the King . . . a token superior to a Crown. It bespoke the natural glory of wife and mother, eclipsing the artificial glory of Queen. For more than fifty years this royal pair had lived together in affection. The scene would have been one of interest anywhere."

Charlotte survived the wedding only a short while. In November 1818, she died peacefully in her arm-chair after an illness. The loss of the queen, predicted her secretary, Sir Herbert Taylor, would be deeply felt by the whole nation, "which cannot fail to do justice to her Majesty's virtuous conduct during so long a period passed under manifold trials." He was right. The woman who so often had been lampooned in her lifetime was now, as her companion, Madame D'Arblay, put it, "set up as an example even by those who only after death know, or at least *acknowledge,* her virtues." But her funeral struck no chord in the king's world. The college magazine of Eton carried a verse for him:

Unconscious art thou, as thy ne'er had been,
Of regal troubles and the cares of State.
Unmarked, beneath thee passed this funeral scene,
The shroud of her, thine own long-cherished mate;
Thou only didst not sigh, when England wept of late.

Once or twice after the queen's death, a glimmer of reason appeared in the king's face, and his physicians attempted to make rational contact. One night in January 1819, George sat alone, dressed in his customary finery for dinner, playing host to imaginary guests, when "by direction of the Council, immediately after the King's meal, Sir Henry Halford addressed His Majesty by asking respectfully how he did, and mentioning his own name. The King appeared to collect himself, lifted up his eyes and hands and immediately began striking rapidly on the Keys of the Harpsichord." It was no use. "In some minutes, a second attempt was made, which was treated in the same manner; but the keys of the instrument were struck with greater violence."

The beginning of 1820 saw a marked deterioration in George's bodily health, which, throughout the previous decade, had been reasonably good. The king was eighty-one. He had reigned for sixty years, longer than any English monarch before him. Now his strength became weaker, his body colder, he lost his appetite. On Thursday, January 27, the doctors decided that his life was in imminent danger. On Friday afternoon, it became apparent that death was not far off. By Saturday morning, members of the family had been summoned to the apartment, and all the physicians were present. Perhaps happily, no return of reason visited the dying king. He remained oblivious of the circumstances to the end. It came at thirty-five minutes after eight o'clock that evening.

According to an official pronouncement: "His Majesty did not suffer any pain, and died at last without a struggle, but for many hours he was oppressed with difficulty in breathing and great restlessness."

Outside, the bells tolled mournfully. Princess Elizabeth sighed with relief: "The change is a blessed one."

George's death made little impact on a nation for which, virtually, he had ceased to exist for almost ten years, and his posthumous career proved a clouded one. In Britain, he was blamed for losing America; in America, for trying to hold on to the colonies. Few judged him on the merits of his character. George had crippled both his strength and reputation trying to swim against the tides of the moment. His choice of destinations could be faulted. But in his time he was a man of rare integrity not only among kings, but among commoners. Truthfully, it could be said that he had spent a lifetime trying to do what he believed to be right. His inferior sons were suitably awed by their father's death. The Duke of York fled to his older brother for comfort. The new king, George IV, was with the Archbishop of Canterbury, praying for strength. One hundred and ten times, it was said, the guilt-ridden prince repeated the Lord's Prayer. The Lord, as far as history would bear witness, turned a deaf ear.

SELECTED BIBLIOGRAPHY

SELECTED BIBLIOGRAPHY

This book is an attempt to portray a king and man of remarkable character, along with something of his times, for the general reader. It does not pretend to be a study for scholars, though the author is greatly indebted to the work of many scholars, past and present, who have made it possible. Nor does it attempt to be a history of a reign. There are a number of such histories dealing with the times of George III, among which the author has been particularly guided by Steven Watson's admirably comprehensive *The Reign of George III*. Of the earlier biographies of George III, it is perhaps worth recommending one of the longer variety—J. H. Jesse's multi-volume *Memoirs of the Life and Reign of King George the Third*, which still makes vivid reading—and, among the shorter, and more recent, J. C. Long's *George III*, which is concise, urbane and knowledgeable. Technical debate on the causes of George's mental illness has been avoided, since, at the time of writing, the issue did not seem conclusive. The subject of the king's malady warrants (and has been accorded) volumes in its own right. The best of these, from the psychiatric viewpoint, is Dr. Manfred S. G. Guttmacher's excellent *America's Last King: An Interpretation of the Madness of George III*, while Charles Chevenix Trench's *The Royal Malady* provides another fascinating insight. For the social aspect of the period the author is particularly indebted to, among others, Rosamond Bayne-Powell's delightful trilogy on life in eighteenth-century England—*English Country Life in the Eighteenth Century; Travellers in Eighteenth-Century England; Housekeeping in the Eighteenth Century;* and Elizabeth Burton's *The Georgians at Home, 1714–1830*.

Aspinall, A. *The Later Correspondence of George III.* London: Cambridge University Press, 1962.

Barnes, Donald Grove. *George III and William Pitt, 1783–1806.* California: Stanford University Press, 1939.

Bayne-Powell, Rosamond. *Travellers in Eighteenth-Century England.* London: John Murray, 1951.

——. *English Country Life in the Eighteenth Century.* London: John Murray, 1935.

——. *Housekeeping in the Eighteenth Century.* London: John Murray, 1956.

Belsham, William. *Memoirs of the Reign of George III.* 2 vols. London: Hurst, Robinson and Co., 1824.

Boswell, James. *Boswell's London Journal.* London: Heinemann, 1950.

——. *Life of Samuel Johnson.* Oxford: Clarendon Press, 1934–50.

Boustead, Guy M. *The Lone Monarch.* London: Bodley Head, 1940.

Brougham, Henry. *Statesmen in the Times of George III.* London: Charles Knight, 1839.

Buckingham and Chandos, Duke of. *Memoirs of the Court and Cabinets of George the Third.* 2 vols. London: Hurst and Blackett, 1853.

Burton, Elizabeth. *The Georgians at Home, 1714–1830.* London: Longmans, 1967.

Butterfield, H. *George III, Lord North and the People.* London: Bell and Sons, 1949.

——. *George III and the Historians.* London: Collins, 1957.

Campbell, T. *Annals of Great Britain.* 3 vols. Edinburgh: Mundell, Doig and Stevenson, 1807.

Chancellor, E. Beresford. *The Private Palaces of London Past and Present.* London: Kegan Paul, 1908.

Chevenix Trench, Charles. *The Royal Malady.* London: Longmans, 1964.

Compton-Rickett, Arthur. *The London Life of Yesterday.* London: Constable, 1909.

Cunningham, George H. *London.* London: Dent, 1927.

Curtis, Edith Roelker. *Lady Sarah Lennox.* New York: Putnam's Sons, 1946.

Davies, A. Mervyn. *George III and the Constitution.* Oxford: Oxford University Press, 1921.

Davies, J. D. Griffith. *George the Third.* London: Nicholson and Watson, 1936.

de Castro, J. Paul. *The Gordon Riots.* London: Oxford University Press, 1926.

Donne, W. Bodham. *George III, Correspondence with Lord North.* London: John Murray, 1867.

Fitzgerald, Percy. *Life and Times of John Wilkes, M.P.* 2 vols. London: Ward and Downey, 1888.
Fortescue, Sir John. *Correspondence of King George the Third.* 6 vols. London: Macmillan, 1927–28.

Green, John Richard. *A Short History of the English People.* London: Macmillan, 1907.
Green, William. *Annals of George the Third.* London: S. Tipper, 1808.
Guttmacher, Manfred S. G. *America's Last King: An Interpretation of the Madness of George III.* New York: Scribner's Sons, 1941.

Hamilton, Lady Anne. *Secret History of the Court of England.* 2 vols. Boston: Page and Company, 1901.
Hervey, Lord John. *Memoirs of the Reign of George II.* Edited by Romney Sedgwick. London: Eyre and Spottiswoode, 1931.
Hobhouse, Christopher. *Fox.* London: Constable, 1934.

Ilchester, Earl of. *Lord Hervey and His Friends.* London: John Murray, 1950.

Jesse, J. H. *Memoirs of the Life and Reign of King George the Third.* 3 vols. London: Tinsley Brothers, 1867.

Keyes, N. B. *Ben Franklin.* Kingswood: World's Work, 1956.
Knollenberg, Bernhard. *Origin of the American Revolution, 1759–1766.* New York: Macmillan, 1960.

Landor, W. S. *Charles James Fox.* London: John Murray, 1907.
Long, J. C. *Mr Pitt.* New York: A. Stokes Company, 1940.
———. *George III.* London: Macdonald, 1962.
Lloyd, Christopher. *The Diary of Fanny Burney.* London: Roger Ingram, 1948.

Macaulay, Thomas Babington. *Two Essays on William Pitt, Earl of Chatham.* Cambridge: Cambridge University Press, 1900.
Macfarlan, R. *History of the Reign of George the Third.* London: T. Evans, 1847.
Malone, Dumas. *The Story of the Declaration of Independence.* New York: Oxford University Press, 1954.
Massey, William. *A History of England in the Reign of George the Third.* 4 vols. London: John Parker and Sons, 1855.

Melville, L. *Farmer George*. 2 vols. London: Pitman and Sons, 1907.
Miller, John C. *Triumph of Freedom*. Boston: Little, Brown and Company, 1948.
Mumby, Frank Arthur. *George III and the American Revolution*. London: Constable, 1923.

Namier, Sir Lewis. *England in the Age of the American Revolution*. London: Macmillan, 1930.
——. *The Structure of Politics at the Accession of George III*. 2 vols. London: Macmillan, 1957.
Nobbe, George. *The North Briton*. New York: Columbia University Press, 1939.

Palmer, R. R. *The Age of the Democratic Revolution: A Political History of Europe and America, 1760–1800*. Princeton: Princeton University Press, 1959.
Pares, Richard. *King George and the Politicians*. London: Oxford University Press, 1953.
Park, Joseph Henderson. *British Prime Ministers of the 19th Century*. New York: York University Press, 1950.
Phillimore, J. G. *Reign of George the Third*. 2 vols. London: Virtue Brothers, 1863.
Plumb, J. H. *The First Four Georges*. London: Batsford, 1957.

Rose, George. *Diaries and Correspondence*. London: Richard Bentley, 1860.
Rosebery, Lord. *Chatham, Early Life and Connections*. London: Arthur Humphreys, 1910.

Scudder, Evarts. *Benjamin Franklin*. London: Collins, 1959.
Sedgwick, Romney. *George III, Letters to Lord Bute*. London: Macmillan, 1939.

Taylor, J. *Relics of Royalty*. London: Newman and Company, 1820.
Thompson, Grace E. *The First Gentleman*. London: Jonathan Cape, 1931.
Thoms, William J. *The Book of the Court*. London: Henry Bohn, 1844.
——. *Hannah Lightfoot*. London: W. G. Smith, 1867.
Tunstall, Brian. *William Pitt, Earl of Chatham*. London: Hodder and Stoughton, 1938.

Vulliamy, C. E. *Royal George*. New York: Appleton-Century, 1937.

Walford, Edward. *Old and New London*. Vols. III & IV. London: Cassell, Peter and Galper, 1872–78.

Walpole, Horace. *Memoirs of the Reign of King George the Second.* 3 vols. London: Henry Colburn, 1847.
———. *Memoirs of the Reign of King George the Third.* 4 vols. London: Laurance and Bullen, 1894.
Watson, John Selby. *Biographies of John Wilkes.* London and Edinburgh: Blackwood, 1870.
Watson, J. Steven. *The Reign of George III, 1760–1815.* London: Oxford University Press, 1964.
Wraxall, Sir N. W. *Historical and Posthumous Memoirs.* Edited by H. B. Wheatley. New York: Scribner's Sons, 1884.

Index